# *THE HEART OF THE LION*
## *COEUR DE LION BOOK III*

# The Heart of the Lion

## Coeur de Lion Book III

# Pamela Todd-Hunter

*A Breach in Time*
*Coeur de Lion Book I*
*The Making of a King*
*Coeur de Lion Book II*

## ~ *Acknowledgements* ~

*For my parents, Robert and Cable, who always supported me.*
*I'd also like to thank Kay C., Karen P., Kahina N., and Preye I. for all their*
*help.*

# ~ *Chapter 1* ~

HEAVY IS THE HEAD THAT wears the crown.

Those haunting words would never prove to be more true, but for now, Richard's first Christmas court since his coronation was a veritable success. Numerous conversations, interspersed with bursts of laughter from noblemen, their wives, knights, and squires, filled the great hall.

Although every fiber in Alix's body longed to join him at court in Normandy, France, she'd planned to remain behind in Poitiers to be prudent. Her presence would create gossip that, as a newly crowned, unmarried king, he didn't need. Richard had remained silent on the subject of her accompanying him. She'd assumed she would not, until he'd ordered his page to pack her clothes.

After several days, the guests' initial whispers and curious looks eventually stopped. The tension that had coiled her stomach into knots dissipated and now she could relax and enjoy the royal celebration.

Richard had left in search of wine, but even with hundreds of people filling the hall, it was impossible to overlook him. He was one of the tallest, most physically imposing men in the room, and his distinctive red-gold hair shone in the candlelight. He stood with his cousin André and with Rob, two of his trusted household knights, laughing at something one of them said. Although he was king, the camaraderie he shared with his men hadn't changed.

Alix fingered the gold brooch pinned to her dress. The piece depicted a knight mounted on a steed, a replica of Richard's personal seal. She'd purchased it from a shop at Nottingham Faire near Austin, but after pricking her finger, she'd been transported from the 21$^{st}$ century to the year 1183. On a dirt road near the town of Poitiers, she'd encountered Richard when he was the Duke of Aquitaine. To survive, she'd joined his household until she could figure out a way to return to her own time. She hadn't expected to fall in love, but now couldn't imagine a life without him.

His piercing blue-gray gaze locked upon hers and his lips curved upward. Alix's pulse quickened and she returned the smile, her heart filled with love for this man. Richard was more reticent around her in public since his actions were scrutinized, but he always managed to show his attentiveness. A jab hit her heart and her breath hitched. One day she would need to return to her own time and her own life and leave him in the past.

She walked toward where the men stood until a young woman stepped in front of her, halting her progress.

"I can't tell you how happy I am to see you, Alix. It's been years, but you haven't changed at all."

Alix smiled, pleased to see Richenza, Richard's niece by his sister, Matilda. She gave her a sisterly kiss. "How are you faring? I was saddened to hear of your mother's death. Matilda was always very kind to me, and I looked upon her as a true friend."

Although Richenza resembled her mother, she'd inherited her dark hair and eyes from her father instead of the red-gold hair and light eyes that characterized Queen Eleanor's children.

"She spoke highly of you as well." Richenza looked around the great hall in awe. "Uncle Richard's Christ's Mass court is so lavish, it outshines Grandfather's. I remember visiting his court in Caen as a child and thinking nothing could rival it. I stand corrected." She arched her brow. "I see your hand in much of this."

Since Richard was still unmarried, Alix had offered to help with the festivities. She wanted his first Christ's Mass court to be a success.

Alix laughed. "I had no idea how much work goes into planning such an occasion, but Richard wanted a celebration that no one would soon forget. Queen Eleanor's ladies and the servants here were of great help. Left to his own devices, Richard would have ordered barrels of wine, proving that Aquitaine has the best in France, a minimal amount of food, excellent minstrels, and left it at that."

She tucked a wayward lock of auburn hair behind her ear and surveyed her handiwork with a critical eye. The long wooden trestle tables were laden with meat, vegetable dishes, and flagons filled with spiced wine. One sweet confection, designed as a life-sized swan, complete with sugary feathers, stood on a separate table.

Highly polished lanterns hung from the wooden rafters. Sconces flickered on the walls and provided additional light for the attending noblemen and their families. A hot fire roared in the immense fireplace, but with the amount of body heat in the hall, it was almost unnecessary. Fresh cut evergreens adorned the window frames. The spicy scent of pine mingled with the fragrant wood smoke. Small tables were placed near the walls, so guests could gamble, play chess, and socialize.

Servants hovered in the background, emerging long enough to clear used dishes and pour more wine before melting back into the shadows. A lilting tune echoed through the hall and couples caused a brief commotion as they carved out enough space to perform a circle dance.

Pleased with the finished results, a small smile curved Alix's lips, then faded. Alys, King Philippe's sister, stood across the crowded hall. Nearing thirty, she was no closer to marriage or becoming queen, despite her betrothal to Richard when they were young children.

Richenza glanced in the same direction. "I feel for Alys. Is it true that Richard wishes to wait until he returns from the Holy Land to marry her?"

Although they were still formally betrothed, only a few people knew Richard was planning to marry another woman, Princess Berenguela of Spain. He wanted to wait to make the announcement until he and Philippe reached the Holy Land. Richard couldn't afford for Philippe to hear the news and refuse to travel.

Alix's mouth dried and her throat tightened as cold chills snaked through her body. She'd accidentally changed history, and in order to correct it, she had to create a reason for Richard to abrogate his marriage. She prayed Richenza hadn't heard the rumors of an illicit romance between Alys and Henry, Richenza's grandfather.

"Yes. Richard thought it best to wait since it might be years before his return. He didn't want to leave his new queen the daunting task of maintaining control of his kingdom."

To maintain the appearance that he still meant to make her his wife, Alys had been invited to tonight's celebration, but for her, dreams of marriage and a crown would never come to pass.

Richenza nodded. "I can understand that. Philippe has been a constant thorn in my family's side. Richard's nobles might not be willing to pay allegiance to her."

"I must admit, I'm surprised to see Constance in attendance. I thought she would have stayed far away from here, considering her husband, um . . . Geoffrey, allied with Philippe against Richard." Alix focused on a crack in one of the floor stones. How else could one describe Richard's duplicitous brother, Geoffrey?

Richenza's eyes narrowed. "I am sure it's not to celebrate Richard's ascension to the throne." Her lip curled. "I've no doubt the primary reason she's here is to ensure protection of her lands."

Richenza was more right than she knew. With Richard leaving on crusade without an heir, he needed to name his successor in case the worst happened. Alix was certain that Constance was here to ask for her son Arthur to be named.

"One can't blame her. After Geoffrey's death, she ruled Brittany, but then Henry forced her to marry Ranulf de Blondeville, and all know how that union is faring."

"The Bretons have never accepted Ranulf as their duke like they did Geoffrey, and they never will," Richenza returned. "Besides, he spends more time in England than in his own marriage bed."

"That's a terrible thing to say!" Alix exclaimed, but laughed as she said it, not having a particular liking for the Breton countess. She'd met her once before in Caen and the meeting had been decidedly icy.

Richenza added, "I wonder how much of their animosity was caused by Constance. As much as I dislike her, I believe she loved Uncle Geoffrey and never got over his death. Being forced to marry another must have been painful and galling to her pride." Her eyes widened. "Speaking of which, she's coming this way."

"Alixandra, Richenza, this is quite the occasion, is it not?" Grudging admiration laced Constance's tone. "Richard has obviously spared no expense. Although I would have thought he'd use his vast coffers to aid his crusade instead of spending it on wine and song."

Richenza's eyes hardened at her words. "My uncle deserves to enjoy his first of many Christ's Mass courts. You should consider it an honor he thought enough of you to invite you after what you tried to do to him," she retorted, her voice shaking with anger. She nodded to Alix, then stalked away.

"*Gast*," Constance muttered in Breton under her breath as Richenza left.

Alix bit her lip to hide her displeasure. She was unfamiliar with the word, but sensed it wasn't flattering. "Your Grace, did you wish to have a word with me? I'm sure you're not here to discuss the festivities."

"You still have Richard's trust, do you not? With his crusade approaching, I wonder if he has yet named an heir. I'm aware that my son Arthur has been mentioned, but I would like assurance that Richard will consider him."

"Richard has given careful thought to whom he will name, but as of now, he has said nothing. He will announce it in good time."

Constance grasped Alix's arm impulsively. "You must sway him. He owes me. He owes Geoffrey. If Richard were to die in the Holy Land, by right, the crown would have gone to Geoffrey as the next in line. Arthur deserves to be his heir in his stead. I've lost so much. Please talk to him. Make him see that my son should be named."

"I'm truly sorry for what you have been through. Richard is considering his decision, and it's one he doesn't take lightly." Constance released her grip and nodded, but Alix couldn't ignore the despondent look on her face. "I'll speak with him."

Constance glanced up, hope flaring in her eyes.

"However, if he has already decided on his course of action, I won't be able to change his mind."

Constance nodded. "Thank you, Alixandra. You don't know how much that would mean to me." She turned away, then faced her again. "Being of noble birth and a woman, I've never been able to make my own decisions concerning my life. King Henry invaded Brittany and forced my father to accept my betrothal to his son, Geoffrey. After my husband's death, Henry gave me to another man to wed." Anger and hatred burned in her eyes. "For a brief moment I was the sole ruler of Brittany. I must ensure that my son receives his birthright."

Alix stared after Constance's retreating figure, compassion for her plight welling inside. Highborn women had few to no rights concerning whom they married or how they lived their life. She'd experienced firsthand the restrictions women faced in this time. After joining Richard's household as a servant, she'd chafed at the rules and regulations forced upon her. With her knowledge of herbs and healing, she became the palace healer, which allowed her more independence. Her modern ideals still opposed the limitations society forced upon her, but now she accepted her position.

A deep baritone voice spoke softly in her ear and her heart pounded as it always did at his closeness.

"By the look on your face, I imagine that hellcat desired to speak to you of my intentions regarding an heir." Richard handed her a goblet of wine.

Alix laughed. "You must know my mind well to assume that, but yes, you're correct. I told her I would mention it to you, but you've already made your decision," she stated as she looked up at him.

Richard put his hand on her shoulder. "I have, although I fear it could be to my detriment. Fortunately, Mother and my chancellor will keep John in line. I'd hoped John's young wife would work her wiles in the bedchamber and keep him occupied, but it seems he's confined her to one of his castles and conveniently forgotten where that was." Amusement dripped from his voice.

John, Richard's younger brother flirted with one of the serving girls. Alix raised her brow. "That appears to be his predilection. I've only seen Isabella once since they married, poor child. The thought of marriage to that man makes my blood curdle. It might be a blessing in disguise for her to be abandoned." She glared at the short, dark-haired man, who pulled the simpering girl onto his lap and whispered in her ear. "You'd better treat your future bride with more courtesy." Tendrils of dread twined through her. Once he married, their relationship would have to end.

"Of course I will. Besides, I warrant you'll remind me lest I forget." Richard smiled cockily at her.

*~*~*

Eleanor scanned the crowded hall. The vast number of noblemen who were in attendance was in clear contrast to Henry's last Christ's Mass court. Her lip twisted in recognition of some of the men who had joined Hal and Geoffrey's rebellion against Richard. Time would tell if their intent was merely to get into the good graces of the new king. She wished he would remain in France to oversee his kingdom, but he was so set upon going to the Holy Land.

Footsteps rang out behind her. A hand patted her shoulder, and John flashed a disarming smile. "*Mamà*, I trust you are enjoying the festivities."

"Yes, I am. Very much."

"Do you mind?" He gestured to the empty seat next to her. "There are some . . . matters we need to discuss."

Eleanor took a deep drink of wine, not looking forward to the conversation she'd been expecting. In truth, she hadn't been surprised that her younger son had waited so long to broach the subject. John was savvy and knew when to hold his tongue. For months he and Richard had been at odds, but each passing day brought Richard's journey closer. Decisions concerning the realm and what role he'd play, if any, must weigh on his mind.

"I'm sure Richard and you have discussed in detail in what manner his kingdom will be guarded while he's in the Holy Land." John's tone was even, but tension emanated from him in waves. He beckoned to a servant who was carrying flagons of wine.

Eleanor gave him a steady look. "Yes, we have. He'll make his wishes known soon."

"I hope he's put his mistaken assumptions concerning me aside and realizes that I'm the only realistic heir he could choose."

"Richard has every reason to be suspicious of your motives." She raised her hand to stop his outburst. "Henry hadn't even drawn his last breath before you abandoned his side to rush to Richard's, no doubt trying to show your renewed allegiance to him. That doesn't strike me as someone who is loyal."

John frowned. "That was a failure in judgement, and I've been trying to make amends. I swear to you, Richard has my full support and my fealty. If asked, I'd willingly protect his kingdom in his absence."

He lifted the goblet to his lips, then gestured toward Richard.

"Mother, what if your precious son doesn't come back from the Holy Land? We both know this crusade is more for his personal glory than defending the True Faith. I've heard rumors he's considering Arthur as his heir. Naming Geoffrey's son, a mere child, is inviting every man who has taken umbrage against him to overthrow his realm should he die. And that list grows longer each day. Richard may be many things, but foolhardy is not one of them. He'd never put his kingdom at risk, even to thwart me."

Eleanor's heart clenched with fear that his words might come true. Richard was a formidable commander and skilled soldier. Tales of his exploits and his almost careless disregard of his own safety on the battlefield were regaled after his many victories. However, Jerusalem and the other Christian states that made up Outremer were harsh lands and if men didn't die in battle, sickness was another adversary they faced. She'd buried two sons already and could not bear to lose another.

"Richard will meet with us in the coming days and let you know his decision. Until then, John, I suggest you don't antagonize him."

# ~ *Chapter 2* ~

RICHARD STRETCHED HIS LEGS OUT toward the hearth as he dangled a wine cup from his hand, but his relaxed position belied the tension that knotted his muscles. The crackling fire warmed Eleanor's rooms, but did little to dispel the chill that existed between him and his brother. His mother's watchful gaze shifted between them, ready to summon a servant should they come to blows.

"I gave you a wealthy bride, and I'm allowing you to retain the revenue of the counties that have been gifted you. In return, you will stay out of England for three years. If I were you, I'd think very carefully about what I am offering," Richard said.

John stared out the window, his jaw clenched. He took deep, measured breaths, then faced his brother.

"You made our half brother Geoff, archbishop of York. That must have been a coup for you, but how did you manage it? All know he'd rather hunt and drink than pray and be pious."

Richard's eyes narrowed at the change in topic. It had been a necessary move on his part. Ordaining Geoff removed a potential rival for the throne. "I gave him no recourse. I ordered the canons to accept him, but I have no doubt he protested up until the last minute he was made a priest." Richard smiled and winked at his mother, who shook her head, frowning slightly. But humor flashed in her eyes.

"An illegitimate son given so much power, while the true son of a king is to be slighted." John took a few steps toward his brother. "Granted, my lands will bring me wealth, but why am I not ruling Anjou, or Normandy, or even your precious Aquitaine in your stead? You've stripped me of any real power. What would happen to your kingdom should you not return from the Holy Land?" A vein throbbed in his neck.

"Arthur is to be named heir for the time being, and I've appointed Bishop Hugh de Puiset, Justiciar, and William Longchamps as Chancellor. Mother, of course, will oversee the affairs of my kingdom as well while I am away."

"A child of two as your heir?" John whirled toward his mother. "Surely, he must be jesting!"

"If you find my terms not to your liking, I can always renegotiate. Of course, any new decision might leave you with very little in way of land and revenue." Richard leapt to his feet. He stomped toward John and towered over him. His brother's face turned crimson.

John looked again at his mother, but resoluteness reflected in her eyes. "I see you're of the same mindset, Mother. It's no secret that you've preferred Richard to all your other sons, and even now I'm made to feel unequal."

"You haven't given us much reason to trust you, John. And until you can prove your loyalty, I agree with Richard's decisions," Eleanor stated. "If you uphold your part of the terms, we'd be open to future discussions."

John's jaw tightened, and blood suffused his face. He turned toward Richard, hatred burning in his eyes. "I accept the terms. I swear to you that I will give you no reason to doubt my loyalty."

"Make sure that you do not, little brother. I don't want to hear of any treachery."

John nodded stiffly to him, then to their mother, and left the room.

"That went well, don't you think?" Richard asked wryly, refilling his cup, then offering the flagon to Eleanor.

"Keeping him out of England and limiting the amount of power he has is a wise decision. I only pray that you haven't made a new enemy. I don't trust him."

Richard's brows drew together. He couldn't forget how John had switched his allegiance to him while their father lay on his deathbed. He had no doubt that John would do it again if the opportunity to gain more power arose.

"Neither do I, Mother. But if we can keep him on a short leash, I won't have to worry about his scheming while I'm in Outremer. I hope that dangling Arthur as my heir keeps him honest, but even John must know that leaving my kingdom to a child is comparable to inviting the devil to invade my realm."

As a skilled battle commander, Richard had been trained to look for and exploit any weakness in an opposing army. No doubt his enemies would seek out the same during his absence. He'd spent months choosing trusted men to manage his affairs and protect his kingdom.

"It sounds as if you have your kingdom in order, but aren't you forgetting one important person?" Eleanor asked.

He frowned, and then his face cleared. "I'll escort you to Poitiers before I depart in the spring to confer with that French snake, Philippe, if that's what you're referring to."

"I do not speak of myself." Eleanor laid her hand on his arm. "I've never pried into any of my children's private lives. You in particular are reticent about romantic affairs, but what will you do about Alixandra? It's obvious to everyone she has your heart."

Richard took a deep drink from his cup. When Alix had told him she loved him, he'd been surprised and speechless for possibly the first time in his life. His response had been heartfelt. Admitting the depths of their feelings had strengthened their relationship. He'd lost her once before and the void that had filled his soul had almost consumed him. He didn't want to live a life without her.

"She'll travel to Outremer with us."

"You wish for her to join you? Richard, you can't be serious. I assume you haven't forgotten I'm escorting your fiancée to Sicily?"

"As I said, she's coming with me."

The glacial-blue light of winter illuminated the room enough for Alix to attempt to mend a small tear in one of Richard's shirts, but now, the garment lay forgotten beside her. Richard was meeting with his mother and John to discuss the measures he'd taken to safeguard his kingdom. Another reminder that each passing day brought them closer to his departure and upcoming marriage. The familiar ache crept through her chest and settled in her heart.

She'd become immersed in his world and was confident of her place in his life and heart, but this wasn't her time. Their paths were quite different. She missed her family and friends back home, and she had goals and plans. After completing her history dissertation, she wanted to explore all the opportunities she had and create her own life.

Richard was traveling to the Holy Land and, en route, would marry. Their relationship would end since she refused to become a married man's mistress. The only option left to her was to use the brooch, return to her own time, and lose him forever.

"Your Grace, is there anything you require?" Jacques asked as the door opened.

Alix jumped and pushed her dark thoughts away.

"No, not at the moment, lad," Richard said as he marched in and tossed his mantle over a chair. He poured a cup of wine and joined Alix on the settee.

"Jacques is proving to be very loyal to you, considering he was in your father's household."

Richard glanced at the boy and nodded. "I knew he was trustworthy when he had the courage to tell me the truth about what my father had done to you."

Jacques had been King Henry's squire and was present at Angers when Henry had forced her to convince Richard to pay homage to his eldest brother, Hal. Richard believed she'd betrayed him and abandoned her.

In a panic, trying to make her own escape from Angers, she'd dropped her pouch, spilling its contents across the floor. Grabbing the brooch, she'd pricked her hand and was transported in time back to Austin. At home she discovered Richard's history had changed because of her actions. She'd spent months attempting to return and right it. When she did succeed, three years had passed in Richard's time.

Richard picked up his shirt to examine the unmended tear and cocked his brow. "Should I even ask how long you've attempted this task?"

Alix shrugged. "It's the thought that counts."

"True, but if I leave it to you, I fear it will never get mended." He chuckled, then beckoned to Jacques, who took the shirt and left.

"How did John take the news?"

"Blood wasn't drawn, but Mother will have her hands full making sure he's not up to his neck in treachery. He swore his loyalty, but somehow his words continue to ring false." Richard paused to sip some wine. "I had no idea safeguarding my kingdom would be such a balancing act," he admitted, a rueful smile crossing his lips.

"I think you've made some shrewd decisions. The men you've chosen to oversee your realm seem to be extremely trustworthy. Arthur is another matter. Do you think it a wise idea to name a two-year-old boy the next king of England, if—God forbid—something should happen in Outremer? Too many nobles would be more than willing to use him for their own devices."

Alix took the cup from his hand and took a sip, Constance's plea echoing in her ears. "Would Constance be named regent since Arthur is a child? I know she ruled Brittany for some time, but many people feel that a woman's place is not in politics."

As a historian, Alix knew almost every detail about Richard's history, but kept her secrets, lest questions about her background arise. She also had to fight to keep from divulging information that could change history. She'd unintentionally changed the past once, and after managing to right it, couldn't make another catastrophic mistake.

He shrugged. "Her new husband is disliked, I'm not certain if she would be able to maintain the loyalty of her subjects. She's not as strong as my mother, who ruled Aquitaine for many years and excelled politically."

"Of course not, but your mother is an exceptional woman." He nodded in agreement, and Alix continued. "Unless, of course, naming Arthur is a strategy to keep John in line, then when he proves himself . . ."

He chuckled. "Exactly, Love." The casual endearment warmed her. "We leave for Poitiers in a fortnight," he continued.

"It will be nice to head home. I've missed Maud and Sybilla and am looking forward to seeing them." The knights' wives were pleasant, but Richenza was the only woman at Richard's court whom Alix considered a true friend.

They sat in silence, watching the flames dance in the fireplace until they died down to smoldering, burnt-orange embers. Richard went to add another log and crouched down to stoke the fire. He moved back from the burst of flame but remained standing.

"What's troubling you, Richard?"

"I'm certain that the arrangements I've put in place will protect my kingdom, but I have my doubts about . . ."

"John?"

"Yes. I know my brother all too well. Although he has lands and a wealthy wife, John isn't content. He's always coveted more. In my absence, who knows what mischief he might devise?" Richard returned to the settee and pulled her close. "All of my other plans are falling into place."

Alix wanted to ask how or if she fit into his plans, but the thought of hearing the logical answer sent icy numbness coiling through her veins. After all they'd gone through to be together, he'd expect her to stay. She took a shaky breath and focused on the fire. Even though her heart would break, his departure would provide the perfect cover for her to leave the man she loved in the past.

## ~ *Chapter 3* ~

ALIX RECLINED ON THE SUN-DRENCHED window seat in Richard's chambers in Poitiers, a small smile on her lips. Richard muttered to himself, walked to the table, scrawled notes on a piece of parchment, then resumed his pacing.

"Stop, Richard, before you wear a hole in the floor and fall through!" Alix laughed. She stood and took the parchment and quill from him. "You pace, I'll write."

She returned to her seat, crossed her legs, and studied what he had written. Her knowledge of written archaic French was limited, but Richard's notes were short and to the point.

"So, you will bring between six thousand and seven thousand soldiers to Outremer, and you will have what, one hundred ships?" She looked at him in shock. "How much will that cost?"

"More than I have at my immediate disposal. I've raised a large amount from England to supplement it. The tax tithe brought in a good amount of money, but I also fired all the sheriffs who were in the employ of my father and forced them to re-purchase their positions if they wished to retain them."

Alix raised her brow. "I think it very magnanimous of you to allow people who were swayed by religious fervor, and then recovered their wits, to buy out of their oaths."

"Who could doubt that I'm a fair king?"

She threw her hands up. "You're basically selling everything to pay for your war. Lands, titles, and positions."

Richard glared at her. "I need money to fund my campaign and those that can afford it are willing to pay. God's bones, Alix! If I could sell London, I would!"

"I have no doubt of that, considering your love for ... how did you describe it? Oh yes, that miserable, cold, rainy, accursed island." She waved her hand toward him. "Continue. Let's begin with your army. Men can't live on wine alone and they need to eat, so what provisions will you bring? Once in Outremer, you can purchase food, so this is to be for traveling to and from Marseille on your ships?"

He planted his hands on his hips. "Write this down. I'll need beans, grain, salt, and dried meat. Also, barrels of wine and water. We'll bring horses, and they must be fed, so fodder, as well as blankets and horseshoes, must be purchased. Nobles and knights will have their own armor and weapons, but foot soldiers will need supplies. The ships will be outfitted with war supplies in ports and sailed to Marseille, where they will be provisioned."

He walked to her and took the parchment, then knit his brow.

She yanked the paper back and rechecked it. "What's wrong? I wrote down everything you said . . . oh, sorry. You were speaking so quickly that I wrote in English since it was easier. I'll rewrite it for you. If you like, I could help you with English," she offered. "Many of the words are Norman in origin."

To protect herself and anyone who was associated with her, she'd given herself a new storyline. The lie that her family was originally from England but moved to France became easier to tell with time. But she remained vigilant so as not to slip and reveal the truth.

His lips thinned and he turned away. Richard was educated, speaking Latin and several of the French dialects, but was unfamiliar with the English tongue. The silence stretched out as she wrestled to think of something to say to mitigate his discomfort.

Richard clasped his hands behind his back and exhaled. "I think that might be quite useful." He pivoted to face her. "However, it will have to wait until I return victorious."

*~*~*

The beautiful, cool spring days had given way to an unexpected early summer heat wave that held the realm of Aquitaine in its tight grasp. Although Richard provided everything she needed, she continued in her capacity as the palace healer. She enjoyed the position and the sense of independence it gave her. By the time Alix had reached her small medicinal and culinary herb plot, she was damp with sweat. A layer of gray dust coated the bottom of her skirt.

Drops of perspiration trickled down her back, and she pulled the dress fabric away from her skin. She tucked a lock of auburn hair behind her ear, then picked up a bundle of cut feverfew and tied a red string around the stems. After learning the hard way that dried herbs tend to look alike, she used assorted colors to tell them apart. The bunches of sage, mint, and feverfew would dry in a couple of weeks and then would be used to treat winter illnesses.

She sat back on her knees and assessed how many plants remained to be harvested.

"Great." Alix swiped her brow with her sleeve. Richard was leaving for Outremer in a little over a month and with her own departure not far behind, she wouldn't have time to harvest the herbs. Melisende oversaw the servants and Alix didn't want to put more responsibility on her shoulders, but she had little choice.

Alix's exhale mixed with the hot breeze that rustled the leaves on the trees. She closed her eyes and raised her face to the sun. Her time with Richard was ending. She'd never met anyone like him. He was unpredictable and passionate. He challenged her and made her rethink her values as they applied to his time. As much as she loved him, they'd never had a future together. She'd lock each day they had left away in her memories and heart forever.

With the bunches of herbs gathered, she walked back to the palace. To avoid seeing anyone, she took the backstairs that led to the servants' room.

The room was empty, as was the hallway. She went to the study to hang the cuttings on the hearth above the fireplace. Melisende rarely used the room and Alix had appropriated it for drying and storing the herbs. Once the herbs were hung, she continued to Richard's chambers to dress for dinner.

The sun's rays traversed across the stone floor as the hours passed. By the time she'd bathed and was in clean clothes, the setting sun had tinged the gauzy clouds pink and orange. She dragged a brush through her tangled coppery hair. Her bangs were longer, and her highlights were still visible. She continued to get odd looks from people for her hairstyle, but it was a comforting reminder of home. Before she left the room, she went to the fire and stoked it so there'd be light when she returned.

A cacophony of voices echoed from the huge dining hall. With longer summer days, the palace inhabitants took their meals a bit later. Knights, clergy, and servants milled about. Alix entered, curtsied to Queen Eleanor, and went to the servants' table. Richard had traveled to Bayonne to meet with

Princess Berenguela's father to solidify the marriage details. In his absence, she felt uncomfortable sitting with the queen.

She sank down on the long bench next to Sybilla, one of her closest friends, and nodded toward the empty space across from them. "Where's Maud? I hope she's not feeling poorly."

"She received some unfortunate news. Her father had been unwell for some time and died a fortnight ago."

Heaviness twined through Alix's heart. "She must be devastated. Does she have any other family? I know her mother passed when she was young."

Sybilla shook her head. "She's all alone now. Melisende's with her, trying to offer some comfort."

"Alix, might I have a word?" Melisende placed her hand on Alix's shoulder.

Alix stood and followed the older woman to a quiet corner of the hall.

"I assume you heard the news concerning Maud's father."

Alix nodded.

Melisende wrung her hands. "She's inconsolable, and I don't know what else I can do for her. Would you please go and talk to her?"

"Certainly. I hope I can offer some comfort."

Alix opened the door to the servants' chambers. She'd never lost a close family member and was unsure of what to say. The last thing she wanted to do was upset Maud more than she already was. She found her curled up in a ball on her pallet, her blond head buried in her pillow.

"Maud?" She sat on the bed.

The girl jolted upright, her eyes red and puffy from hours of weeping, and threw herself into Alix's arms.

"What am I to do, Alix? The queen is sending me away!" Her iron grip around Alix's neck tightened.

"What? This is your home!"

"Not anymore. I'm to be married to a man of her choosing." Maud sat back and swiped her cheeks. "My family had some financial difficulties, and with Father's death, any dowry that had been set aside will now go to pay off debts."

Maud's mother had been one of Queen Eleanor's favorite ladies-in-waiting, and upon her death, Maud had entered Eleanor's service as a young girl of twelve. Now, at eighteen, she was somewhat past the marriageable age, but with no dowry, she had no prospects.

"I'm sure she will arrange a good marriage for you."

"I wish to stay here. Please help me, Alix. Don't let her send me away!"

Alix looked into Maud's red-rimmed blue eyes. "I thought you wanted to marry. Maintain your own household for your husband and have children."

Maud drew a shaky breath. "I do, but what if this man is cruel and heartless? I can't live with a husband whom I fear and loathe. What am I to do?"

Alix brushed the younger girl's long, curly blond hair off her tear-streaked face and tried to think positively. But Maud had every right to be afraid.

"Let's see what Queen Eleanor decides. Perhaps she will choose one of Richard's knights. If so, there's the chance that you would spend much of your time here. And if he's not to your liking, he'll be in Outremer for quite a while."

Maud's eyes widened. Then she gave a weak laugh and nodded. "I hope that's true. The thought of leaving fills me with dread."

Alix reached out, gripped the girl's hand, and forced a smile. Her chest tightened. What would happen to her? When Richard returned from Bayonne, she would speak with him. If she knew that Maud was taken care of, perhaps fear for her well-being wouldn't haunt her forever.

# ~ *Chapter 4* ~

THE ROOM WAVERED, THEN CAME back into focus. Alix stared at Queen Eleanor as her world careened around her. This wasn't what she wanted or had expected to hear. She needed to return to her own time and Richard's departure presented the opportunity.

She shook her head. "No, please, I can't do this . . ."

Eleanor stood and fixed her steely emerald gaze upon the younger woman. "You *will* go to Sicily and then to Outremer. It has been decided."

Her attendants huddled in a darkened corner, quiet as church mice. The queen rarely showed her temper, but when it was raised, even the most stalwart quailed.

"Your Grace, I don't understand why my presence is required."

"Correspondence arrived from Sicily concerning my daughter, Joanna," Eleanor stated. "Her husband, William, died last year, but the news didn't arrive until months later." She turned and walked to the window, her hands gripped. "I fear for Joanna's safety. Her country is politically unstable since she's a queen without an heir." Eleanor whirled to face Alix. "I've heard nothing from my daughter."

"Maybe her letters were lost or detained . . ." Alix offered.

"William's illegitimate cousin Tancred has taken control of Sicily, and I believe that he's imprisoned Joanna."

"Joanna is the queen. Surely Tancred is treating her with courtesy, as befits her position."

Eleanor's face tensed. "I have no way of knowing if she's been . . . mistreated."

Alix's pulse jumped when she understood what Eleanor was inferring. "Your Grace, I can't imagine that he would allow any of his men to . . .

dishonor her virtue. With Richard, the king of England, as her brother, none would want to raise his ire, especially since he's traveling to Sicily with a vast army."

"Alix, don't be naïve!" Eleanor straightened her back and hardened her gaze. "You've experienced men's cruelty. You can't be unaware of what happens to women when towns are captured by their enemies. My daughter might have need of a confidant."

Alix knit her brow. Richard must have told his mother about Alix's attack back home in Austin, but an attempted mugging paled in comparison to the suffocating terror of being raped. Alix wanted to alleviate Eleanor's fear, but any words she uttered would be hollow consolation.

"If Joanna was violated, I'm not sure my presence would help or would be welcomed. I'm a stranger to her. Not to mention Sicily is the last place I want to be since Richard has plans to marry." Alix said the last sentence without thinking, and heat crept up her cheeks.

Eleanor frowned, then her brow cleared, and she ordered her ladies to leave them. When the heavy door clicked behind them, she took a seat at the table, poured a cup of wine, and motioned for Alix to join her.

"I apologize for my words, Your Grace, but Richard's marriage is the reason why I can't travel with him. Once he's married, our relationship is over. I love him and it would be too painful to see him with someone else."

Eleanor took a sip of wine, then gazed into the dark burgundy liquid. "I do understand your reluctance. Henry had his faults, more than I wished for in a husband, but I loved him. He was one of the most intelligent men I'd ever met, and we shared the same dreams for our realms." She gave Alix a half smile. "I knew Henry strayed, but I accepted it as long as he kept his dalliances private. He did. Then he met Rosamund."

Her knuckles whitened on the goblet, as if the mere name of the woman still brought an ache to her heart.

"In the beginning, I'm sure he was charmed by her simply because she was the opposite of me in every way. Henry and I were having a difference of opinion, and she was a means of escape." Eleanor shrugged. "When she was brought to my notice, I didn't concern myself with her. She was another flighty girl whom he had to bed."

Alix choked on her wine, and Eleanor laughed. "I'm not as conventional as I seem, dear."

"I never thought you were." Alix smiled.

"Henry became smitten with her. I thought he'd tire of her and find someone new. He never did. I had to turn a blind eye to his infidelity and accept it. I'm sure Berenguela knows this and expects it. Richard cares deeply for you and it's obvious you care for him. His upcoming marriage should have no bearing on that."

Of course royalty often strayed, but Alix's morals railed against that idea. Richard had been unfaithful to her in the beginning. She'd been hurt and disillusioned to learn of his infidelity, but with time she was able to move past it and their relationship had grown stronger. Berenguela likely would accept his dalliances, but Alix didn't want to be the cause of any potential pain.

The sun's last golden rays stretched out across the floor as dusk fell. With Eleanor's attendants gone, Alix rose to light the lanterns on the small table. A warm glow suffused the room.

"Alixandra, my concern lies with my daughter," Eleanor said as she walked to Alix. "I've been to Outremer, and I know the hardships that both Joanna and Richard's wife will face. You're independent and have shown great courage in the past. There's a strength in you not found in many women. My mind would be greatly eased if you were there."

"It would?"

Eleanor placed her hands on Alix's shoulders. "You're loyal to my son, and I know he respects your judgment. Although he will never reveal it, he depends upon you. You'll be an asset to my children in Outremer."

Alix steadied her breath. As a commoner, she couldn't very well openly refuse the queen's order. "I'd be pleased to go to the Holy Land, but Richard hasn't mentioned his wishes concerning me. I'm sure he has no desire for me to travel with him."

"That's where you're mistaken. This is his decision." A smile crossed her lips. "I have a feeling he feared you might have protested if it came from him."

Numb, Alix walked back to Richard's rooms, her feelings in turmoil. Her heart was thrilled that he wanted her with him, but her rational mind rejected it. Richard's infidelity had been painful, but they'd just begun their relationship. She'd had no claim on him. Her father had been unfaithful to her mother, and she'd witnessed the pain and anguish it had caused. Although she wasn't religious, she believed in the sanctity of marriage. Adultery was an ethical line she wouldn't cross.

The dry rushes crackled under her footsteps as she entered the large chamber. The room was dim, and smoke curled upward from the dying fire that provided the only source of light now that night had fallen. She stoked the embers and used a rushlight to light the lanterns.

Alix slumped into a chair and stared at the crackling flames. She could use the brooch and return home to her own life like she'd planned, but Eleanor's announcement tempted her like the forbidden fruit.

Her dissertation was in the final editing stage, but what if she could imbue it with firsthand accounts of events? Traveling to Outremer afforded her further opportunity to bear witness to Richard's greatest triumphs and shortcomings, one being the atrocity he'd committed in Acre. Since being thrust into Richard's time, she'd been present during many of the pivotal events that had brought him his crown.

His crusade was legendary. How could she give up the chance to experience it with him?

*~*~*

Built upon a rocky promontory, Chinon Castle was visible for miles. This was the first time Richard had been to the site of his father's death. A brief pang of guilt over his treachery against his father had assaulted him when he entered the bailey, but that feeling had long since faded. If his father hadn't pitted himself and his brothers against each other, the outcome would've been different.

The rooms were austere, containing a table and some chairs, but lacked wall hangings or a comfortable settee, indicative of Henry's spartan taste. Richard had never cared for the castle and, since he rarely visited, saw no reason to change it.

"It's about time you arrived." Eleanor swept into Richard's chambers. "I've been waiting for three days."

"I apologize. It took longer to return than I anticipated."

He motioned to the servant to pour the wine, then requested privacy. His own carefully placed spies occupied positions in some of the most important castles in his realm, and he was leery of falling victim to the same scheme. Once alone, Eleanor raised her brow as she sat down on a chair next to the fireplace.

"Tell me, was your meeting with Sancho successful? Am I still to escort your betrothed to Sicily?"

"Yes, although in the beginning I began to doubt there would be a marriage. Sancho is understandably protective of his only daughter, and the idea of her traveling to Outremer unnerved him, to say the least. It took quite a bit of convincing, but the proposition of a crown helped immensely, as did the offer of you as a chaperone." Richard's lips twisted. "I thought keeping my kingdom safe was an endeavor, but I never imagined a marriage proposal from the King of England himself would prove more challenging."

"Has the dowry been agreed upon to your satisfaction?"

Richard shrugged. "Sancho has offered two castles, but the protection of my southern borders is more important to me politically. This marriage is a coup, for certes."

Eleanor took a sip of wine. "The Count of Toulouse has a long history of contention with you, and I have no doubt that once you are away from France, Raymond will attempt to overrun your lands. It would behoove Sancho to safeguard your kingdom, if not for you, then for his daughter."

"My thoughts exactly." Richard laughed, then became solemn. "Philippe and I will convene at Vezelay. Many details still need to be agreed upon before we leave France."

"The sooner you leave, the better. I can't stop thinking of Joanna, and I worry about her safety. I can only hope that receiving no news from Sicily simply means she is denied correspondence. If the worst had happened, we would have heard something . . ." Eleanor's voice trailed off.

Richard's jaw clenched. He prayed that Tancred saw Joanna as a valued asset and not a hindrance to his goal of claiming Sicily for himself. If it were him, he'd keep his highborn prisoner alive for a ransom or to demand the crown, but he knew nothing of Tancred's mind.

"I, too, worry about her," Richard responded softly.

"Are you still set on Alixandra accompanying you? I thought that you were going to let her decide. She was none too happy when I told her."

Richard's brows drew together. For weeks he'd vacillated on the wisdom of Alix traveling with him. He had his counsel, but he valued Alix's astuteness when it came to political decisions. She was adept at seeing both sides of the issue, although her choices didn't always align with his. Alix was his confidant, and he trusted her advice. He wanted her by his side when he reclaimed the Holy Land.

"I want her with me, although I believe she made negotiations of her own?"

Eleanor laughed. "Yes, she did. Honestly, Richard, couldn't you have found someone meeker and more pliant? That woman could drive a priest to curse God's holy name. However, I agreed to them, considering what you're asking of her."

His upcoming marriage was nothing more than an alliance. His heart belonged only to Alix. Continuing guilt for putting her in this position gnawed at him, but he'd become proficient at pushing it away. He'd lost her once and couldn't bear to lose her again.

# ~ *Chapter 5* ~

ALIX FANNED HER FACE AND wished for a breath of cool air. The leaden, rain-swollen clouds that had been their constant companion since their departure several days ago slowly drifted south. The sun occasionally pierced the dark clouds with pale beams, promising drier days ahead, but the air was thick with humidity. Swarms of gnats and mosquitos gave the travelers no respite from their stinging bites.

Heavy rain had halted their journey from Chinon, but Richard refused to allow the severe weather to delay him any longer and ordered his army to begin their lengthy march to Vezelay.

The long line of men and horses spread out as far as the eye could see. An endless train of carts carried much-needed provisions for them, since living off the land was limited, and townspeople were unwilling to give what little food they had to a passing army. Polished armor flashed in the sun and the sound of hoofbeats, jingling metal, creaking wagons, and men's voices morphed into a garbled tone, the different dialects and vernaculars streaming together.

Richard's army counted well into the many hundreds. More men, some nobles but mostly peasants yearning for adventure and the opportunity to retake the Holy Land, joined as they traveled east.

The small horse-drawn cart Alix and Maud rode in pitched as it hit a deep rut carved into the muddy, rain-soaked ground by numerous wooden tires. Maud cried out as she was tossed from her seat onto the trunks that occupied much of the space while Alix grabbed the top of the edge to avoid falling off the narrow strip of wood that served as a bench. As they regained their seats, the wagon behind them hit a rut and lurched to a stop. The foot soldiers that accompanied them rained curses upon the dismal conditions.

"At this rate, by the time we reach Vezelay, the French king will have left and arrived in the Holy Land," grumbled one of the soldiers. He motioned to the other men, and they went to help.

About a half-dozen women from Chinon, employed as laundresses for Richard's household knights, clambered out of the cart, their feet sinking into the thick, earthy-scented mud. They slogged through the depths of the sticky quagmire to drier ground.

The roles of laundress encompassed other tasks, too, such as cooking and sewing. As the army passed through small towns and villages, women eager to offer their skills joined. Many of them were older and took this as an opportunity to escape an unwelcome marriage or poverty if they were widows. For some of the younger women, this position presented a way out of prostitution or as a way to give their families one less mouth to feed in an already destitute household.

"I know you dread meeting the king's betrothed, but for me, this is an incredible opportunity." Maud's eyes shone with anticipation. "I can't believe I was allowed to travel with you. How did you manage to convince Queen Eleanor?"

Her journey with Richard inevitable, she'd met with Eleanor and asked if Maud might be allowed to accompany her, a request which Eleanor granted. Alix was still concerned about Maud's future, but for now, any impending marriages were put on hold. She'd also begged to return to France with Eleanor after she'd delivered Richard's fiancée. Sympathy had flashed in Eleanor's eyes, but she'd remained silent on that topic.

The sun burst out from behind a bank of clouds, and Alix squinted. "Having already been on a crusade, the queen knows the amount of work that's involved in keeping a camp of thousands in order. Although doctors will travel with the army, I brought a supply of herbs in case any of Richard's knights or household members fall ill. I asked if she would allow you to help me in that capacity."

Several foot soldiers rocked the stranded cart back and forth while another held the horses' reins to keep them from bolting. After much slipping and sinking into the mud, the wheels dislodged from the thick muck with a sucking sound, and the horses leapt forward.

"Ladies, back in the cart. Hurry!" the man in charge called out.

Alix shaded her eyes and gazed at the long, snaking army of men marching ahead. She couldn't see Richard, but imagined he was riding up and down the line, laughing and joking with his soldiers, barely able to contain his excitement that the crusade had begun.

"How long do you think it will take to reach our destination?" Maud asked once they began moving.

"I'd say at least a month, if the weather improves and the roads dry."

Maud glanced around and leaned closer to Alix. "I haven't seen the king since we left Chinon. I'm surprised he hasn't come to see how you are faring."

Alix shrugged. "I'm not. In truth, I haven't seen much of him since he returned from Bayonne. He's been occupied with final details concerning the safeguarding of his kingdom and his crusade. We haven't been forgotten." Alix nodded toward the handsome dark-haired boy of about sixteen who rode ahead of the cart.

"Oh yes, Jacques. I noticed him several days ago." Maud's cheeks reddened and she fidgeted in her seat.

Alix bit her lip to hide her smile. "I'm sure he's reporting back to Richard on our well-being."

"I still can't believe the king's not to marry Alys. I feel sorry for her. She's waited so long. What will become of her?"

"I feel for her, as well, but I support Richard marrying the Spanish princess. She's a much better match politically." Alix glanced around and lowered her voice. "Maud, remember, no one is to know of Richard's betrothed journeying to Sicily. I told you because I don't want you to be shocked when she arrives with Queen Eleanor. We need to keep this to ourselves."

Maud smiled and whispered, "I won't say a word. What do you think his bride will be like? I wonder if she's quiet and meek or spirited like you. Will she be kind and a good queen? Do you think they'll have a happy marriage?"

Historical accounts reported Richard's marriage to Berenguela would be the opposite. "One never knows with arranged marriages, but I hope they find happiness, or at least have a satisfying union."

*~*~*

The sun was high as they approached Vezelay. The flat expanse of green plains ahead of them graded into the hilltop upon which the town was built. Alix gasped at the sight that unfolded before them. In the distance, a huge conical pavilion had been erected, its banners snapping in the breeze. Philippe had arrived, and a veritable tent city had sprung up on the grounds outside the city gates.

The foot soldiers led the horse-drawn cart to where Richard's squires were raising his own huge tent.

"Miss, you and your friend will stay over here."

Alix turned to see Jacques standing behind them, carrying a neatly folded pile of cloth and long tent poles. He motioned with his head for them to follow as he walked, his feet scuffing the lush grass. As they passed Richard's lodging, Alix peeked in. The tent was spacious enough to contain a strategic planning area that accommodated more than a dozen men, as well as sleeping quarters for the king.

"Aren't you going to stay with the king?" Maud murmured as they trailed Jacques.

"No, we've already discussed it. Philippe believes that Richard will honor the plight troth and marry Alys. We must maintain the deception, and I don't want my appearance to cast any doubt upon it. Richard desires to keep the peace. He needs Philippe's army if he wants to claim victory against the Saracens."

Alix also feared Philippe's anger toward her concerning the rumors of Alys's involvement with Richard's father. As far as Philippe knew, she was the only person who could expose the truth—that Philippe had been more than willing to use the rumor to foster an alliance with Richard. The French princess's reputation was marred, but she was still technically betrothed to Richard. Once he discovered Richard had no plans to marry her, would he hold Alix responsible or refuse to fight alongside Richard?

Jacques stopped at the edge of the small clearing not too far from Richard's tent. The women from Chinon were setting up their living spaces, but stopped and stared as they approached. The women's voices echoed behind Alix as she walked past. They knew who she was. She'd heard the not-so-quiet whispers as they left Chinon. No doubt they were curious as to why she wasn't staying with Richard.

Alix turned her attention to a large, thick, cotton cloth that was spread out on the ground. Jacques walked the perimeter of the neat square and staked poles into the ground near the corners. He then draped the cloth across the poles and fashioned a crude opening that faced Richard's campsite. His task completed, he bobbed his head to Alix and hurried off.

Alix cocked her brow as she pulled the cotton fabric aside and peered in.

"This tent is roomier than it looks. We can put our trunks on the far side and still have space to sleep."

Maud entered the structure. "At least it's high enough to stand in. If we raise the side opposite the door, we'll get some air. At night, it should be cooler." Maud assessed the tent once more, her lips pursed. "However, if I were you, I would reconsider. Richard's tent is far more luxurious . . ." She squealed, ducking out of the tent and out of range of Alix's playful swat.

*~*~*

Later in the afternoon, squires brought their trunks and belongings. Alix and Maud removed their clothes from their trunks, shook out the wrinkles as best they could, refolded them, and stowed them neatly. Wiping the perspiration off her forehead with the back of her hand, Alix exited the stuffy tent. Muted laughter and voices floated from Richard's camp, where she assumed nobles mingled with Richard's household knights.

"Hopefully, you'll be able to see him soon." Sympathy echoed in Maud's soft voice.

"I'm sure I will. I know he's busy strategizing, and that takes precedence."

A breeze wafted through the campsite, carrying the aroma of cooked meat. Alix's stomach clenched and growled, reminding her that lunch had been hours ago. She beckoned to Maud, and they walked to a sizeable tent where men lined up.

Alix approached a harried-looking middle-aged woman whose graying brown hair was tied in a messy bun. "Can we help in any way?"

The woman narrowed her eyes, then shrugged and handed her a ladle. "If you two don't mind getting dirty, you can serve the vegetables and your friend can help me with the cooking."

Alix spooned dried pork, boiled vegetables, and legumes onto crudely carved wooden plates. A woman next to her handed the men hard crusty bread and cups of ale or water. When the last man had left, Alix fixed a plate and joined Maud and the other ladies around the nearby campfire. Alix took a bite of pork, wrinkled her nose at the rancid taste, but chewed and swallowed it. It wouldn't be long before the meat became inedible. She hoped they could purchase much-needed provisions in Vezelay or the surrounding towns.

One of the many hungry dogs that wandered through camp stopped and stared at her. She finished the last of her limp, boiled vegetables and tossed the dog a piece of bread. She laughed as he nosed the fare and ran off in search of something more appetizing.

A discreet cough captured her attention. She turned to see Jacques. The ladies' conversation came to a standstill. Jacques wore Richard's coat of arms, two lions on a red background. No one could doubt upon whose orders he'd been sent.

"Miss, a word, please?" The young squire drew nearer and continued, "The king requests your presence."

Alix glanced down and grimaced at her travel- and now food-stained dress. A film of fine dust and grime caked her bare skin, and her hair was in an untidy braid. The army had traveled east, following the Vienne River to take advantage of an available water source. Since the river's abrupt turn to the south, she hadn't been able to bathe or do laundry in days. The water they'd collected was used only for cooking and drinking.

"You must go, Alix. It's been weeks since you've seen him," Maud urged.

"I don't feel right leaving you here."

"He's the king. You can't refuse." Maud's dimples showed through the smudges of dirt that streaked her pink cheeks.

"I'm not to return without you," Jacques announced.

"In that case, of course, I will meet with him." *Although once he sees me, he'll likely change his mind and send me away.*

Jacques smiled his endearing, crooked smile, and bid Maud good night, his eyes lingering a bit longer than necessary. Alix stood and tried to ignore the titters and glares, but they bothered her more than she wanted to admit.

She went to pack a clean dress and undergarments in a small bag, then followed the boy. Adrenaline sparked through her body at the thought of finally being able to see Richard. Rob materialized out of the gloom as they approached the tent.

"Alix, how are you and Maud managing?"

"We're fine, although I long for a bath. Men are content to go for weeks without bathing. Women aren't."

"Point taken." Rob laughed.

Alix peered around him into the tent, careful not to be seen. Fabric tossed over cords partitioned areas for sleeping or bathing. Lanterns stood on the table and hung from wooden stands to light the interior. A thin layer of smoke hovered near the top of the tent, which had small openings in the cloth to allow it to escape. Clergy and nobles surrounded Richard as he leaned over a table, studying a map. Richard glanced up as he spoke to one of the men, his face drawn with weariness that weighed on him like armor. The crusade was in its infancy, but was already taking its toll.

Rob pointed out a few of the more illustrious men crowded into the tent. "Those men with Richard are Archbishop Baldwin of Canterbury and Hubert Walter, the bishop of Salisbury. The older man next to André is Hugh de Lusignan, one of Richard's Aquitaine barons. Richard plans to meet with Philippe soon and wants his men to know what his decisions are concerning the journey."

Alix hid her frown. Philippe would have different ideas. Rob took Alix's arm and led her around the side of the tent. A fabric door flapped in the breeze, and Rob held it open for Alix to enter. She walked past him into a small room cordoned off from the larger one, where Richard and his men convened and clasped her hands to her chest.

Richard had forgotten nothing. Warm water filled the tub, the steam spiraling into the air. A block of soap was in a wooden holder attached to the side. On a small table stood a flagon that had to be filled with wine if Richard had requested it, along with plates of meat and fresh vegetables. Upon the cot was a folded towel.

"Richard will probably be occupied for a bit longer, but he'll join you as soon as he can."

"I'm sure I can find some way to amuse myself."

Rob left, and she wasted no time undressing, relieved to be out of her soiled garment, and sighed as she sank into the tub. Alix took her time scouring her skin clean with the bar of soap and lathered her hair multiple times to remove layers of dirt. All too soon, the water cooled. Reluctantly, she got out, dried herself, and got dressed.

Her stomach growled as she inhaled the aroma of cooked meat. She put boiled chicken and legumes on her plate, using the dark crusty bread to sop up the thick gravy.

Richard walked in as she poured a second cup of spiced wine. "I hope I didn't forget anything?" He pulled out a chair and sat at the table.

"No, you always know exactly what I need." She glanced at the tub. "I appreciate your foresight."

He took a sip from her cup, then stifled a yawn with his hand.

"Richard, you're exhausted. Get some sleep while you can. I know you plan to meet with Philippe, and that can be quite a challenge, especially trying to keep your temper in check."

"You're absolutely right on that account." He closed his eyes and rubbed his temples.

Alix walked over, drew him to his feet, and led him to the cot. He sat, pulled his shirt off, and handed it to her before he removed his boots. It was clean, indicating that he'd bathed and changed before meeting with the archbishop.

She folded it and placed it on top of a trunk in the corner of the room. When she turned around, he was lying down, his arm flung over his eyes. She covered him with a light blanket and brushed his hair from his brow, surreptitiously testing his temperature.

"I'm not feverish, Alix, just tired."

"Sorry. I know the quartan fever manifests when you overexert yourself. How many hours have you slept since departing Chinon?"

"Not nearly enough. I had plans for tonight, but I must postpone them, lest I disappoint you."

"You never disappoint me." Alix bent to kiss his lips.

The voices of the squires and pages in the other room grew lower and the thin fabric wall that separated them swayed in the stirred air as the men settled down for the night. She extinguished the candles, and he drew her close as she lay next to him on the narrow cot. Soon his regular breaths indicated sleep.

Alix nestled nearer, relishing his comforting warmth and his familiar scent of leather and horses, content to be with him. A wave of homesickness washed over her. In France, she could see him almost daily, but here she had to be careful. Traveling with him as his personal healer wouldn't raise suspicion, but she couldn't risk a careless remark reaching the wrong person.

# ~ *Chapter 6* ~

"WHAT DO YOU MEAN HE refuses to meet with me?" Richard's angry tones rang throughout the tent amid the grumblings of his men as he stared in disbelief at the messenger.

"Your Grace," the squire squeaked as he stepped back. "He still wishes to meet, but rather he wants for you to come to him."

"God's bones! How can a meeting place have any bearing on our discussions? Is he fearful of leaving the safe confines of his tent?" Richard glared at the quaking squire. "Evidently so. Very well." A thin smile crossed his lips. "Tell Philippe that I will meet him at a site of his choice."

The squire nodded, bowed, and practically ran from the tent.

André chided his cousin. "Is it wise to antagonize Philippe so early in our travels? We haven't even left France."

"Probably not, but he vexes me to no end."

The two kings met in the spring to swear that they'd protect the lands of the crusaders as well as each other's. Their barons had sworn to keep their fidelity and peace while Philippe and Richard were in Outremer. Their decision to depart in June was delayed following Queen Isabella's unexpected death.

"By now we'd be on our way to Sicily since we were making headway at our meeting in Nonancourt." Richard rubbed his brow. "The death of his queen was unfortunate."

"The birth of a child can be a great gift or a great loss. It is one event where God has the final decision," the Archbishop of Canterbury remarked solemnly as he crossed himself.

Richard's eyes narrowed at the words, but they were true. Many women died giving birth, and crowns had been warred over and lost when there were no heirs. He nodded and walked to the table to pour some wine.

"This meeting will be our final one. I have no more time to waste on petty differences concerning our agreement. I'm concerned about the political upheaval in Sicily, not to mention the well-being of my sister. I pray we have no more delays." He took a deep drink of the sweet, spiced wine.

"What of your mother escorting your fiancée to Sicily?" André asked in a low tone. "Their arrival will only serve to increase the existing animosity between you two. I also don't agree with your decision to bring Alix with us."

Richard's lips thinned and high color rose in his angular cheekbones.

"I know Alix invented the scandalous rumors concerning Alys and your father in order for Philippe to gain an alliance with you against him. But Jesu, Richard, no one could predict the consequences. Now, there are rumors of an illegitimate child. We know them to be false, but they will blacken the unfortunate woman's reputation." André paused as a servant offered more wine, then continued.

"Once Philippe discovers you mean to abrogate the betrothal, his wrath will be limitless. He will be saddled with a sister whom no man will be eager to marry, even if she is a French princess. I fear for Alix's safety should their paths cross. You're aware he'd hold her accountable for his family's shame. He'll never admit to his own guilt in this sordid affair."

"God's bones, there's no need to caution me. I can and will protect Alix!" Richard's eyes glittered in the gloom of his tent. He'd wanted her to travel with him and was prepared to do everything in his power to keep her safe. If anything happened to her, he'd never forgive himself. "Should Philippe dare to threaten her, he'll answer to me. Death by the hand of a Saracen will be much preferable to what I can dole out."

*~*~*

The sounds of strident voices, one unmistakable baritone being Richard's, woke Alix from a deep slumber. After the fog of sleep lifted, she dressed, then finger-combed her hair, as angry words referring to the French king drifted to her. Aware that Richard would be occupied, she crept out the back entrance and hurried back to her camp. Guilt weighed on her that she'd slept in a soft cot next to the man she loved while Maud had to make do with blankets on the hard ground.

She reached her tent and found the girl absent. Assuming that Maud had offered to help the women serve food, Alix made her way to the cooking tent. Some women smiled. Others threw her hateful looks.

As she passed, one muttered under her breath, "Although she shared the king's bed last night, she shouldn't get used to it. He's probably like his father and has a wandering eye. He'll tire of her soon enough."

Alix clenched her teeth to bite back the venomous retort that threatened to burst from her lips and instead gave her a cold smile. She joined a couple of ladies serving food and took the spoon handed to her. If she was seen pulling her own weight, maybe the snide remarks would stop.

The sun glared down and, combined with the warmth from the cooking fire, the tent was sweltering. Perspiration trickled down Alix's back, and she wiped beads of sweat from her brow. She bent over a deep iron pot and stirred the thin liquid flavored with the last of the dried meat and wilted vegetables.

"Don't mind them. They're jealous," Maud murmured as she joined Alix. "What will happen to us once we reach Sicily? Will we stay with the king or return to France?"

Alix shrugged. "I don't know, but let's not worry about that now."

Excitement flashed in Maud's eyes. "I hope we can stay with him and travel to the Holy Land. Visiting the birthplace of the true religion is a dream that I never would have believed possible. I'd love to see it."

Alix was familiar with what Jerusalem had become in her time, but what was it like in the twelfth century?

She understood Maud's desire. The chance to experience the Holy Land firsthand burned within her as well, but there were too many reasons not to. "We'll have to see what happens, but first we have hungry mouths to feed."

Men lined up, and Alix ladled broth into wooden bowls alongside the woman with whom she had spoken with the day before.

"I didn't introduce myself yesterday. I'm Alix."

"I'm Elisabetta." The older woman added more vegetables to the broth, then fixed Alix with a quizzical look. "I'm sure there are other places you'd rather be. Why are you helping us?"

Alix focused on stirring the broth, her stomach churned along with the circular motion of the spoon. "What do you mean?"

"There's no shame in being the king's chosen woman. There are more than enough girls who are willing to take your place. He's a very handsome man. If I were prettier, I'd offer my services." Her smile crept up until her crooked teeth showed.

Smallpox scars marred her pleasant, though heavy, features, and Alix took her to be about ten years older than her own twenty-five years.

The woman chuckled. "I'm certain you never noticed me, but I was a servant at Chinon. You were always by the king's side, and seeing you here, he obviously doesn't want to let you go. More's the pity for his betrothed."

A hot flush crept up Alix's face, and warmth flooded through her body. She changed the subject. "If I may ask, why did you decide to join his crusade if you had a position at the castle?"

Elisabetta's hearty laugh rang out. "Look at me, girl!" She gestured down at her plump figure. "I'm not as young as I'd like to be, and I was never a great beauty." She winked at the next man as she poured soup into his bowl. A shocked look crossed his face and she chuckled. "My husband passed several years ago, God assoil his soul. The king pays well, and truth be told, I'm not looking for another man. I was very happy with my William. He was good and gentle, and I might not be so fortunate again. If I were you, I wouldn't think twice about staying with the king."

She waved her hand in the direction of the multitude of tents behind her. "You and your young friend aren't used to these men. They take what they want. When and wherever they want it."

Alix studied the rough, hardened men in line, and guilt washed over her. As Maud poured ale and water into their cups, she seemed delicate and out of place compared to the other women. She'd promised Maud she'd be safe, but instead, the girl was in danger of being mistaken for a camp prostitute. An oversight Alix needed to correct.

Her stomach in knots, she could only manage to eat a chunk of bread dipped in broth for her lunch.

"For your sake, I hope the king asks you to join him again or you'll waste away to nothing." Elisabetta laughed as she poured the rest of the soup into her bowl.

The meager meal finished, they lugged the pot out of the tent to wash it before preparing dinner. The sun's rays blistered down from a cloudless sky, and soon Alix was drenched with sweat and caked with dust. Once the pot was clean, they returned to the tent, where they began to prepare vegetables and soak dried beans for supper.

Hours later, with smoky tallow candles to light the interior of the darkening tent, the last man was fed.

Elisabetta's words continued to churn in Alix's mind. In order to keep

Maud safe, perhaps she could stay with Richard and convince him to allow Maud to as well.

Twinges, sharp as daggers, ripped through Alix's lower back from hours of bending over the cooking vessel. She kneaded her fingers into her tight muscles and exited the tent. The air was hazy and redolent with the fragrant scent of smoke from the thousands of fires that glowed on the flat plain. She trudged to the women's campfire. Her discomfort was made more bearable when she spied the person she'd hoped to see.

Jacques lounged on the ground near the crackling fire. Several younger ladies sent him flirtatious looks, but his focus was on Maud. At Alix's approach, he bounded to his feet and swiped the dust from his chausses or leggings.

"Miss, I was looking for you. His Grace requests your presence tonight."

"Is he going to send you every night to ask me to join him?" She grinned.

A breeze rustled his dark, curly hair, and he laughed as he brushed it out of his eyes. "I expect so, miss. He won't accept a refusal."

"I wasn't going to refuse, but I insist Maud join me," she said as she shifted uncomfortably in her still-damp dress.

His eyes lit up. "I'm sure that will be acceptable."

Alix bent down to Maud and whispered in her ear. Maud's eyes widened and she jumped up and hurried off.

Elisabetta smiled widely at Alix as she walked toward her. "I see you took my advice."

"When we began this journey, I told her she'd be safe, but I can't truly protect her. If something were to happen, I'd never forgive myself."

Maud rejoined them with a bulging sack, which Jacques took from her.

"Will I see you tomorrow, then?" Elisabetta asked.

"Of course! There's only so much talk of war a woman can take."

Elisabetta laughed, then winked at her. "Have a good night. I'll see you in the morning."

*~*~*

Alix and Maud entered the main room of Richard's tent, having both taken advantage of the luxury of a bath. Now dressed in clean garments, they were looking forward to the hearty meal of vegetables and dried meat that had been served to the king and his men.

André and Rob sat at the table with Richard. A couple of pageboys filled cups with wine, then withdrew to a corner to take their own meals.

"How was your meeting with Philippe?" Alix sat next to Rob.

"It was very productive." Richard tore a chunk of bread in half. "The earlier agreement we made concerning the protection of our nobles' lands will stand. It has been decided that all new conquests of land and plunder will be shared equally between us."

André paused as he lifted his cup to lips. "I wager Philippe will profit more from this agreement than you."

Richard finished chewing and nodded. "I had to agree to the terms or put off our departure yet again. I was reminded anew of how shrewd Philippe is. Not to mention, he has excellent counsel. I only hope he keeps his word."

"I fear keeping the peace between you two will be more difficult than defeating the Saracens." Rob picked up a cup and poured some wine.

"Too true!" Richard laughed and nodded to Jacques to refill his cup. "I've never trusted Philippe. I detest having him as an ally, but we will be victorious in Outremer. I swear it, even if I have to defeat the infidels myself." He raised his cup to the heavens and drank.

Rob leaned close to Alix. "Richard is always eager for a fight, but never have I seen him this intense."

"He's getting more restless as the days go by, and I, for one, will be glad to start this journey."

"Truly?" Rob asked.

Alix knit her brow, then deducing what he was referring to, gave him a rueful smile. Rob was part of Richard's inner circle. Of course, he was privy to the upcoming marriage.

"No." She sighed. "It wasn't my decision to come, but now that I have, I'd like to see Sicily. However, once Queen Eleanor arrives, everything will change."

The woman who'd destroy their relationship loomed over her like the sword of Damocles.

Sympathy flashed in Rob's eyes. "I understand if you choose to return to France. I worry about Sybilla and the children. It would ease my mind greatly if you were in Poitiers. However, I wager Richard won't like your decision."

Alix took a sip of wine and watched Richard gesturing as he spoke to André.

"Between planning battles and the marriage bed, he won't have time to spare a thought for me."

Rob eyes widened. "Alix!"

"What?" She laughed at his shocked expression. "He's to be married. Besides getting to know his wife, I'm sure siring an heir will be on his mind."

While researching her dissertation she'd often wondered why Richard had chosen to marry Berenguela in Sicily instead of waiting until his return from the Holy Land. Her first thought was that he wanted an heir in case something should happen to him, but another idea had taken hold.

Marriage to the Spanish Princess ensured that her father, Sancho, had a reason to help protect France's southern borders. If they were just betrothed and Richard's lands were attacked in his absence, would Sancho feel obligated to lend his aid?

Rob drained his cup. "He does need to secure his legacy." He stood and joined André and Richard near the opening of the tent.

Maud had been conversing with Jacques, but after Rob left, she hurried over to Alix. "Are we returning to our camp?"

"I'll speak with Richard, but I don't see why he wouldn't let us stay the night."

"I hope he does. It would be nice to sleep in a spacious tent."

"I agree."

The short amount of time Alix had spent in their tent had been uncomfortable. During the day they opened the tent flap and rolled the sides up but the little air that flowed in did nothing to cool it. Since the incessant buzzing of mosquitos made sleep impossible, at night the tent was sealed and it became stifling.

Once the men had left, Richard walked to the table, took Alix's hand, pulled her up, and led her toward his room. Maud shuffled her feet, her eyes downcast.

"Wait." She stopped him before he lifted the thin curtain that partitioned the rooms. "Can Maud stay as well?"

Richard cocked his brow. "I doubt she will want to share our room," he murmured in her ear. His warm breath sent shivers down her spine.

Jacques approached, holding a lantern.

"Jacques, find some blankets for Maud in the main room and make sure she's comfortable."

"Yes, Your Grace." He placed the lantern in Richard's sleeping quarters, set fire to the wick, and hastened to prepare a sleeping area.

Alix nodded good night to Maud. Before the curtain fell into place behind them, Richard had wrapped his arms around her. She nipped his lower lip, then teased his mouth open with her tongue. He gasped and she inhaled spiced wine. Her tongue tangled with his as he deepened the kiss. Need coursed through her and she pressed against him, her heart pounding in rhythm with his. Richard tore his lips from hers and caressed her cheek with his sword-roughened hand. She shivered, imagining his hands traveling down her body.

Desire darkened his gray-blue eyes. "You have no idea how much I need you, Love."

Taking her hands, he walked her backward until they reached the cot. Richard wasted no time in loosening the laces on her dress. Seconds later, it was bunched around her waist. "God's bones, why is there so much material?"

Alix laughed. "My thoughts exactly. Men's clothing is so much easier to manage."

He shoved the garment past her hips to fall in a pile around her feet. A small gasp escaped her throat as he lifted her and placed her on the cot. By the time she'd moved to one side and pulled the blankets up, his clothes were scattered on the floor. The flickering light from the lanterns accentuated his muscles as he settled next to her.

She shivered as he trailed hot kisses along her throat to her shoulder. Heat flooded her veins as his hand inched upward, caressing her inner thigh. One of the pageboys coughed and rustled his blankets on the other side of the thin fabric partition. She froze.

"Wait, we can't do this. Not now," she hissed.

"Then I suggest we be very quiet."

"Please, Richard, not tonight," Alix murmured as her desire faded.

She'd never gotten used to the pages and squires sleeping in his chambers, but in Poitiers and other cities they'd visited, the bedchamber was usually separated by a wall, which gave them some semblance of privacy. Here, with only thin cotton separating them, she felt exposed and vulnerable.

Richard brushed her coppery hair from her face, his gaze locked upon hers. A tender smile crossed his lips. "I understand your reluctance, and when we next make camp, I'll make certain the sleeping arrangement will be different. Jesu, Love, having you near and not being able to be with you is torture. I've never wanted any woman as much as I want you."

Warmth flooded her heart. Even though she knew he loved her, it still amazed her that this legendary man had chosen her. "I feel the same. I don't want to be with anyone else."

Alix let out a surprised laugh when he rolled to his back and pulled her on top. She leaned down to kiss him, and he held her close. The summer night air chilled her skin and Alix shifted to get under the covers.

She lay her cheek on his chest. "I've missed being with you."

He tightened his arm around her. "I'll have Jacques move your belongings here. Maud's as well."

"I don't wish to cause trouble for you."

"Then don't question the king's orders."

## ~ *Chapter 7* ~

ALIX STRETCHED AND REACHED FOR Richard, only to find a cold, vacant space. She sat up and rubbed her eyes.

"You're awake."

Alix jumped, believing herself to be alone in the room. Maud sat at the table with a trencher of bread and cheese in front of her.

"What time is it?"

"It's midmorning, but the king has been up for hours. He sent me in here to wait for you."

"I'm sorry I'm still abed. We went to sleep late."

Alix's cheeks heated as she realized what she'd inferred. She was about to get up when she remembered her nakedness. She pulled the blanket up higher. "Um, can you hand me my dress, please?"

Maud hid a smile as she brought her clothes to her. "I've separated our soiled garments to be laundered." She turned away.

Alix dressed, walked to the table, and picked up a knife to cut a chunk of the dark, crusty bread. She sniffed the contents of the flagon on the table and smiled at the gesture. Richard always remembered she didn't care for wine at breakfast. She and Maud ate in silence, listening to low voices tumbling over each other in the outer room.

The curtain shifted as Jacques pushed an edge open. "If you ladies are ready, please join us."

Alix moved the curtain aside, expecting to see Richard's men, but his household servants were the only ones present. Jacques smiled at Maud before turning to Alix.

"The king is busy preparing for our departure tomorrow, but he bade me tell you that he'd like me to escort you to gather your belongings."

The upside of being mobile was one never unpacked, so it didn't take long to sort their clothes. Alix took her pouch out of her coffer, opened it to double-check the brooch was still inside, then tied the small cloth pouch around her waist. The brooch was the only thing that anchored her to her life in Austin. If she should lose it, she could never return.

The afternoon sun glared down from a cloudless sky. Alix waited by the cart that Jacques had brought to transport their trunks and fanned her face.

Elisabetta joined Alix. "I assume you'll spend your nights elsewhere."

"You were right about protecting Maud. If anything should happen to her, I'd never forgive myself. Being under the king's protection will help ensure her safety."

"While Jacques is busy, come and get some food for you three. We have more than enough, and I don't want it to go to waste." Elisabetta took Alix's arm.

Maud stayed with Jacques while Alix went to fill their plates. When she and Elisabetta returned, the tent had been taken down and stowed along with their trunks in the cart. Maud and Jacques sat on the ground, chatting and laughing, lost in their own world.

Elisabetta sighed. "I hope she doesn't break that poor boy's heart. He's completely smitten with her."

"I'm sure she harbors no true romantic feelings for him. She's likely flattered by his attention. Besides, he aspires to be a soldier, and that life is fraught with danger. Being a soldier's wife isn't easy."

"The king leads that life, and you seem willing to accept it."

"That's different."

"How is it so different?" Elisabetta crossed her arms. "He puts his life in peril each time he sets foot on the battlefield."

Alix frowned at her own hypocrisy. She knew the outcome of Richard's life, but so many who traveled with him weren't included in history. Although her time with Richard would end, she didn't want Maud to experience the grief of giving her heart to a man she might lose.

"My own William had no money and no prospects, but I loved him. You can't help who you fall in love with."

"The heart wants what it wants." Alix gave her a half smile. "I know that all too well."

They finished their meal and continued to chat until dusk fell. Jacques bounded to his feet to make a final check on their belongings.

Alix turned to Elisabetta. "I hope to see you when we make our next camp."

"I'm sure you will, dearie." A smile creased the older woman's face.

The campsites bustled with men preparing for travel, but there'd be last-minute things to attend to in the early morning. They threaded their way through the camp and passed dogs nosing about the fires in the hope of finding forgotten scraps.

They arrived at Richard's tent, entered, and stared. The table and chairs were gone, presumably stowed in a cart. The only items in the room were blankets piled high in a corner and lanterns hanging from wooden stands.

Richard emerged from his sleeping quarters, his longish hair darkened and damp from a bath. A hot flush crept up Maud's face and she stared at the ground as he ordered the squires to prepare his room for travel.

"Would you care for food or wine? I'm sure something can be found."

"We've eaten, but wine would be nice," Alix replied.

Maud remained mute and continued to focus on the ground. Richard's eyes lit upon her, and he tried to hide a smile at her obvious embarrassment.

"Go outside. The benches are still there. I'll join you soon."

Maud spun around and rushed to the opening of the tent, followed by Alix. By the time Richard and Jacques exited the tent holding cups of wine, Maud's coloring was almost back to normal. Jacques handed Maud a cup, then went back inside while Richard sat next to Alix. She leaned into him as he put his arm around her shoulders and drew her close.

"Your crusade begins tomorrow. At last, you will finally be on your way." Alix looked up at him.

"After months of meetings and preparations, I believe I've covered all potential crises. I have complete faith in Mother and my chancellor that my kingdom will be closely guarded. I doubt it will be an easy matter to keep John in line. If Philippe abides by our agreement, that will be one less thing to worry about."

Alix studied the fire. The orange and red flames danced and twisted in the light breeze that swept across the plains. She wanted to warn him of Philippe's and John's duplicity. That their oaths were not to be trusted, but was unable to explain how she knew this.

"I still don't understand why you didn't leave me behind. I can't imagine Joanna would welcome any support, should she need it, from a stranger."

"I quite enjoy sharing my bed with you. Not to mention our activities leading up to sleep." He grinned.

Her heart tightened. Eleanor was going to escort Richard's fiancée to Sicily. Once they arrived everything would change.

"Alix, you know my feelings for you, and as I've told you before, your counsel and opinions are important to me. You're the only person I know who has pitted two kings against each other and emerged unscathed. Mother opposed Father and ended up his prisoner for sixteen years."

"I know." The idea that any man could do such a thing to his wife and the mother of his children was reprehensible.

His eyes hardened at the memory. "Knowing that Philippe desired an alliance with me and convincing him to suggest my father had swived my betrothed was a brilliant, yet dangerous, move. You should count yourself fortunate that you weren't imprisoned, or worse."

"Alys has always been a pawn, used like a chess piece to hold at bay whichever king, French or English, would profit from her. How did she react when she was told that her betrothal to you has been abrogated?" She glanced at him, the fire illuminating his face in the darkness.

Richard lifted his cup to his lips to avoid her eyes.

"She has no idea? I hope someone tells her before you marry Berenguela."

"Philippe can't know my mother is bringing my fiancée until we're well on our way to Outremer and he has no recourse. Otherwise, he might take his army and return to Paris in a rage. I need well-trained soldiers, and many of them, to defeat the infidels."

A burning log popped and she leaned back to avoid the embers that drifted toward her. "He'll be furious when he is told of your deception. Watch him carefully, Richard. You don't want to make him more of an enemy than he already is."

He laughed. "There is no need to warn me. I trust few people implicitly. You know I value your loyalty."

"You have it and you always will." She reached up to caress his cheek.

He caught her hand and pressed it to his lips. "You have mine as well. It's getting late, and we have an early start tomorrow. I'll be in shortly."

Alix stood, concerned as to where Maud and Jacques had disappeared to, but when she entered the tent Maud was already asleep on blankets in the corner. She took a lantern, pushed the curtain aside and entered Richard's room where she undressed and put on a shift.

Her pouch lay on the cot. She picked it up, sat down cross-legged, and untied it. The items that had been with her when she was transported to

Richard's time—the vial of perfume, pot of lip gloss, and compact—were still there, although the lip gloss was long since used up. She wished she'd brought more, but she hadn't expected to stay this long.

She'd replaced her perfume with some purchased in Poitiers, but she was running low. The spicy, warm scent of sandalwood was Richard's favorite and she hoped to find more on their journey.

A smile curved her lips. The ruby pendant with the letters *A* and *R* entwined was wrapped in soft cotton to protect it from damage. It was a gift from Richard. Although she rarely wore it, in case anyone should be curious as to who the letters referred to, it meant everything to her.

The brooch lay at the bottom. Alix reached into the bag and pulled it out, careful not to prick herself on the pin. She ran her finger over the engraved depiction that Richard used as his seal, then replaced the jewelry in the pouch. A hollow ache filled her soul at the thought of leaving Richard. It would only grow worse once it became reality. She'd suffered through it once before, but her life wasn't here. One day she'd have to return to her own time.

She was no closer to determining when she'd make that decision, but tomorrow Richard's crusade began. Her heart pounded with excitement and trepidation. Watching history being written was an experience she couldn't turn down, but she had to be careful. As much as she might want to, history couldn't be changed again.

## ~ *Chapter 8* ~

THE TRAIN OF MEN, CARTS, and horses wound its way through the countryside, skirting dense green forests and flat desolate plains to avoid fording rivers. They circumvented the towns, but the townspeople flocked outside and cheered the thousands of men streaming by on their way south.

At night, small tents dotted the fields, but most men chose to sleep on blankets tossed upon the ground, their campfires keeping away unwanted insects and curious animals. Richard refused to use his large tent, since it was time consuming to raise and pack it again, and he slept on the ground as well, but insisted Alix and Maud sleep in a nearby small tent for privacy.

The thick forest that bordered the plains thinned until sparse trees littered the landscape amidst neatly plowed fields. The soldiers made better time over the hard-baked roads. Several weeks later, a large hill on the horizon came into view. Below it, the city of Lyons lay on the banks of two converging rivers, the Rhône and the Seine—two arteries that provided merchant ships easy access to sell and buy goods.

"Are we staying here for a while?" Maud stood and stretched after the cart rocked to a halt.

"I hope so. We need to replenish our food supplies. I'm also in desperate need of a bath and clean clothes," Alix replied as she shook out her rumpled linen dress. So much ingrained dirt was smeared on it, she doubted it would ever come clean.

"Miss, allow me." Jacques hurried to the cart, his eyes focused on Maud. He held out his hand and she took it and climbed out.

Alix arched a brow as she recalled Elisabetta's words concerning Jacques's potential feelings for Maud. He then offered his hand to Alix.

"His Grace has asked me to escort you to his tent."

Once she was on the ground, he jumped back up on the cart and retrieved their bags. Richard's tent had been raised, an indication that they were staying for at least a day or two. Jacques swept aside the fabric door to allow them entrance.

Alix paused, then walked in, dreading to see a crowd of men, but Richard sat alone at the table in the middle of the room. His pages rushed around, hanging fabric to cordon off rooms and servants filled plates with food from the serving dishes upon the table.

He smiled at their entrance. "Knowing you, I imagine you would like to bathe before dining."

She nodded. "I'm filthy, and I daresay Maud would like to take advantage of cleaning up as well."

Richard motioned to Jacques, and the boy nodded and hurried off to do as he was bid. He returned with a bucket of steaming water and soap and placed them behind the curtain. Alix quickly scrubbed her skin clean, aware that Maud was waiting. Once clothed in a clean linen dress, she left Maud to her privacy and joined Richard in the large room.

The cloth door was tied open to allow in the welcome breeze that blew across the plains and the lantern flames flickered, casting amorphous shadows upon the tent walls. Birds called to each other as dusk fell.

Richard gestured for her to sit. A pageboy placed a plate and trencher in front of her. Alix took a bite of dried beef from the trencher and noted that the dishes contained mostly vegetables. "I hope we will have a chance to replenish our stores."

"We must before continuing the journey. I met with Philippe earlier today, and although the land provides fresh game and drinkable water, it's apparent there isn't enough to sustain two large armies with the necessary provisions. We've decided to separate until we reconvene in Messina. Philippe will travel by way of Genoa over the Alps, and we're sailing from Marseille. I imagine you are looking forward to returning home and seeing your mother, are you not?" He rested his hands on either side of his trencher. "I would like to meet her myself."

Alix's chest tightened as icy fingers of dread swept over her. Years ago, forced to fabricate how she had come to be in France, she'd told him she and her mother were originally from England and now resided in Marseille. At the time, he appeared to have accepted her story. She couldn't bear it if he learned of her deception. He'd never trust her again. Not to mention, she couldn't tell him the truth, of course, that she was from the future. She felt the weight of his gaze and gulped some wine, trying to think of something to say.

Maud pushed back the curtain, providing a much-needed distraction. Her long blond hair was beginning to dry into ringlets, and her skin was pink from scrubbing it clean. Jacques pulled a chair out for her, and she curtsied to Richard before she sat down.

"Thank you, Your Grace, for allowing me to join you this evening." Her voice was soft and quivered a bit, no doubt in awe of sitting at the king's table.

Richard nodded to her. "You are most welcome."

"How long are we staying in Lyons?" Alix switched to a safer topic. For now, the subject of Marseille was dropped, but with Richard, nothing was ever forgotten.

"A couple of days," Richard responded as he refilled his cup before his servant could make a move. "God knows I'm exhausted, and I'm sure the men could use the rest. I'd imagined traveling with Philippe would be taxing, to say the least, but the man is insufferable. I need his army to help defeat the infidels, but this is my crusade. I warrant most of the spoils of victory will come by way of my army while he will garner half by sitting in his tent, enjoying his wine."

"It's true that he had no great desire to join you, but he's a seasoned soldier. You'll be glad to have his sword by your side."

A melodic laugh interrupted her, and she glanced over to see Maud dimpling at Jacques and the other pages. Weeks of travel with little to do except watch the scenery stream by had given Alix time to dwell on her situation. For Maud, this was a new experience far from Poitiers.

For Alix, it was an ending. She missed her family and friends in Austin and wanted to be with them again, but she'd also miss this life just as much. She toyed with her fork, drawing circular trails in the thick gravy that had congealed on her plate. By now Eleanor was either preparing to travel to Navarre, or already was on her way to meet Berenguela.

"What's troubling you, Alix?" Richard asked.

All the misgivings she had eddied like a whirlpool inside her. "Once again, I'm doubting the wisdom of traveling with you. I'd like to meet your sister, Joanna, but even if you introduce me as a healer, would she believe that's all I am?"

Richard leaned back in his chair, stretched out his long legs, and crossed his arms. "I seem to recall having a similar conversation not too long ago."

Irritation colored his tone. "I've told you I want you with me. You have been by my side through the important moments in my life, and I daresay my victory in Outremer will count as one." He raised his brow at her, then stood and held out his hand.

She rose and walked around the table to take it, annoyed with herself that she had put herself in this position. Granted, the king had issued an order that she couldn't have refused, but she'd had other options. She just couldn't bring herself to take them.

"I want to see this through with you, Richard, but when Berenguela arrives, what then? I will have no place with you."

The desire to travel to the Holy Land still consumed her thoughts, but each day brought his fiancée and the end of their time together closer.

"I can't be with you once you're married. You must know that."

A troubled look crossed his face, as if the thought of her leaving him had never entered his mind.

"It would be best if I return to France with your mother." Once she was in France, it would be much easier to simply disappear and return to her own time.

"God's bones, best for whom?" he growled. His hands tightened painfully on her shoulders, and she winced. He relaxed his grip and cupped her face, his eyes burning into hers. "You are the most vexing, intriguing, and captivating woman I've ever met." He leaned closer, his lips hovering above hers. "I never expected this, but you have my heart."

Alix's own heart soared at his admission, her fears erased for the moment. "I love you."

He ran his thumb over her lower lip and kissed her. His warm, wine-scented breath caressed her cheek. His kiss deepened until her head swam. He pulled back, and she glanced around the room, her cheeks heating at what Maud and the pageboys must think, but they were alone.

Desire burned in his eyes. Richard walked her into his room, then claimed her lips again. He removed her dress, teasing and caressing her with his mouth and hands. Rational thought fled and aching need consumed her.

For now, he'd won the argument.

# ~ *Chapter 9* ~

THE SUN RETURNED FROM ITS nocturnal journey and broke over the horizon, spreading beams that washed the sky in hues of orange and pink. A stream of men, carts, and animals began to traverse the wooden bridge across the Rhône River. Richard and his household, including Alix and Maud, were some of the first to cross. With time on her hands while they waited for the rest of the knights and foot soldiers to plod over the rickety structure, Alix took advantage of the available water source to do laundry.

"There you are, dearie!" a voice called out.

Alix raised her hand in greeting as she and Maud picked their way through the tall grass and rushes that layered the steep banks of the river to where the laundresses were busy washing travel-stained clothes.

"Elisabetta, how have you been?"

"I'm fine, but whatever are you doing here? Doesn't the king have his own servants to do his clothes?" She raised her eyebrows as she looked at the overflowing basket Alix carried.

Alix chuckled. "I offered to do it. To tell the truth, I've heard so much talk of war, it's nice to take a respite from it."

She put down the heavy basket piled high with dresses, shirts, and pants and swiped her arm across her forehead, already sweating in the midday heat.

"If I were you, I would take advantage of being the king's woman." Elisabetta winked at Alix, and then glanced at Maud. "What about you, girl? Your young man can't keep his eyes off you. Have you finally decided to give him a chance?"

A red stain crept up Maud's cheeks, contrasting with her blond curls. "I haven't . . . I wouldn't . . . he's just a boy."

"A handsome one with a man's appetite. You should claim him soon or someone else will."

Maud gaped at her, and Elisabetta smiled at her embarrassment. "Don't worry. You're the only woman he has eyes for. Now, come. There's a nice shallow area down here to wash your clothes."

She led them down a crushed path through the reeds and the tall, thick grass. The harmonious singing of insects quietened as they pushed their way through, displacing them. At the bottom a small crescent of land jutted into the wide river. Alix dumped the basket, took a dress, and handed one to Maud to soak in the cold, dark water. The river was lower here, but the swift water churned, and even in the shallows, the current's pull was strong.

Several hundred yards upstream, was the high wooden bridge which men crossed. Horses pulled heavy carts and a multitude of soldiers accompanied them. The support beams trembled and creaked as the immense burden rolled over them.

"Is what Elisabetta said true? Do you think Jacques has any interest in me?" Maud plunged one of the pageboy's shirts into the water, then scoured it with a bar of strong-smelling lye soap.

"He appears to be quite taken with you, and you seem to get along. There's plenty of time to get to know each other." Alix didn't want to discourage Maud from spending time with Jacques, but she also didn't want her to fall in love and be crushed if nothing came of it.

Hope flashed in the girl's eyes. "He's very kind and his stories make me laugh, but I'm being foolish. It's too much to hope that I could choose the man I marry. Once we return to France, Queen Eleanor will arrange a marriage for me. I shouldn't expect anything else." Her earlier excitement faded. "I consider myself fortunate that she will look out for me now that my parents are gone." She crossed herself.

Frustration that Maud was in this situation grated on Alix, but women had little independence in the Middle Ages. Richard was more progressive than she'd thought and allowed her more freedom than most women had, but in other ways, he was very much a man of his time.

Maud handed the shirt to Alix to beat clean against the rocks, then picked up a dress to soak in the water. "My heart aches for you, though. I wish Richard were a commoner instead of the king."

"As do I, Maud, but he isn't. I've always known that our time together was limited, but I wouldn't change anything . . ."

Alix broke off as distant rumbling caught her attention and glanced around for the source. Loud cracking sounds accompanied by terrified screams of men and horses rent the air.

"Jesu! The bridge is collapsing!" a laundress shrieked.

The wooden bridge pitched, and support beams fractured, plunging the men and horses into the cold, dark swirling water below. Dragged down by the weight of their armor, the men fought to keep their heads above the water. Soldiers on both sides of the bank rushed down to the water's edge and waded in to help those lucky enough to be within reach.

Alix stared into the frothing river, her chest constricting as the panicked screams of men and animals filled the air. A man struggled to reach the small tongue of land, but his movements grew sluggish as exhaustion from fighting the current began to take hold. His head bobbed below the surface.

"Ladies, help me!" Alix yelled.

She waded into the river, pinwheeling her arms to keep her balance as the swift current swept past. Numbness inched up her body as the cold, rushing water entangled her skirts about her legs. She struggled to move one foot in front of the other, keeping her eyes on the man. He reappeared and threw out his hand. She lunged forward to grab it, losing her precarious footing in the process, but Elisabetta's strong arms grabbed her about her waist, and she managed to steady herself. Alix clutched the soldier's hand in hers and dragged him to the shallows until his feet hit the soft mud below. He crawled out of the river, then collapsed onto the ground.

"Alix, are you alright?"

She nodded at Elisabetta and Maud, her teeth chattering too much to speak. Other men in the river were slowly making their way out of the water and the women rushed forward to help them. Exhausted, the rescued men collapsed on the riverbank.

A scream captured her attention and Alix shaded her eyes from the bright sun as she searched for the source. A small, thin youth was trying to make his way to shore, but his head kept sinking below the surface.

"Alix, that poor boy will drown!" Maud grasped Alix's arm.

Alix's heart stopped. Her gaze scoured the river, but no one seemed to notice the boy. Several feet behind her, a skeletal tree balanced on the edge of the bank. She lunged for a low-hanging limb and twisted until it snapped, then waded knee-deep into the river and held out the limb in the hope he'd grab it. His hand brushed it, but the current swept him out of reach. His head submerged again.

She had to try to save him. With no further thought, Alix plunged into the water.

Coldness sank into her bones, but she forced herself to keep swimming to the last place she'd seen him. She stopped to search, turning and treading water as the river threatened to pull her downstream. A piece of fabric floated several yards ahead of her and she swam toward it. The boy's feeble movements were barely keeping him afloat. She grabbed his wrist and began the arduous process of reaching the shore, but her heavy, waterlogged clothes combined with the boy's weight to drag her below the surface.

She kicked as hard as she could, her skirt heavy around her legs, impeding any real progress. Alix churned her arms and managed to reach the surface. She took a gulp of fresh, sweet air and sank back down. The blue sky above shimmered and vanished as black water enveloped her in its frigid embrace. The current tossed her about until she was unsure which direction she was facing. Her lungs were on fire and her limbs were dead weight pulling her down into the icy depths. She was running out of air.

Her grip upon the youth loosened as fear of death paralyzed her. Murky darkness claimed her as she sank deeper. Images of loved ones flashed before her—her parents, Cara, Thomas, and Richard. She'd never see Richard again.

*No! I refuse to die this way.*

She tightened her numb fingers on the boy's shirt, summoned the last of her energy, and kicked hard, propelling herself and the boy to the surface.

Screams and shouts filled her ears as hands grabbed her arms and pulled them to shore. She lay exhausted on the bank, coughing and gasping for air, as Maud and some other women hovered over her. White clouds drifted by in the azure sky. Tears pricked her eyes at how close she'd come to never seeing the simple beauty of nature again. Waves of relief mixed with fear washed over her. Then she remembered.

"Is the boy . . .?"

Men surrounded him while the women wept and covered their eyes.

"Please move back," she said as she walked unsteadily toward him and sank to her knees beside him.

She leaned down and placed her ear near his mouth. No warm air whispered against her skin. Pressing her cold fingers against his wrist, she felt for a pulse. She choked back a cry as she found none. Numbness seeped through her.

Alix centered her hands on his bony chest and started compressions, praying she wouldn't crack his ribs. She counted to thirty, then tilted his head back, pinched his nose shut, and gave him two breaths. Muttering erupted about her, but she focused only on the boy and kept repeating the steps. She continued to try to revive him for what seemed like hours.

"Dearie, it's no use. He's gone to God," Elisabetta murmured.

"No, he's not going to die."

Alix continued her ministrations. *Please don't let him die.* The boy's body jerked, and his chest rose of its own accord. He coughed and water spewed from his lungs, followed by vomit. Alix turned him on his side until his breathing evened. She slumped on the ground, her body trembling with exhaustion and relief, and looked at the boy she had rescued.

"You brought him back from the dead," a woman exclaimed as she crossed herself and looked suspiciously at Alix. "He wasn't breathing. What witchcraft is this?"

"He wasn't dead," Alix said sharply, aware that if labeled a witch, meeting Richard's fiancée would be the least of her problems. "If a person nearly drowns, performing this procedure can help them begin to breathe again. He needs to see a physician and continue to be monitored. Maud, can you go find one?"

Maud nodded and rushed up the bank. Accepting her explanation, the soldiers muttered amongst themselves, but Alix sensed their continued wariness.

"I've brought the doctor, Alix," Maud called out.

A middle-aged, paunchy man picked his way carefully down the bank. He knelt by the patient and listened to his breathing, then took the boy's wrist in his hand and felt his pulse.

The doctor glanced up at Alix. "I was told this boy was dead and you resurrected him? Somehow, I doubt you have that power." Although his demeanor was austere and professional, humor flashed in his brown eyes. "How did you know what to do?"

"I'm the palace healer in Poitiers. When I realized the boy had stopped breathing, I used a procedure to resuscitate him. It's a method where you force air into a person's lungs until they can breathe on their own. He needs to be observed for the next day or two since I don't know how long he went without air," Alix explained.

The doctor regarded her. "From your accent, you're not French."

"No. Originally, I'm from England." Alix held her breath, hoping he believed her lie.

"I'd be very interested in learning about the medical techniques that are in use in your country. You have some background in healing and could prove to be quite valuable on our travels."

Alix nodded, unwilling to announce that her travel plans didn't include the Holy Land. "I wish to learn from you as well. I pray the boy will make a full recovery."

"I believe your quick actions saved his life, but I'll watch him through the night. I would examine you as well, but it looks as if no harm was done."

She waved him away. "I'm fine. Please keep me apprised of the boy's status."

The doctor nodded, and Alix returned to where Maud stood with Elisabetta.

"You terrified me when you leapt in the river, then when you vanished . . . I thought you were dead." Maud's hands trembled.

The same fear had occurred to Alix. She knew better than to try a hands-on rescue, but there'd been no time and no other option. "Luckily, that didn't happen."

Elisabetta patted her on the shoulder, her eyes filled with concern. "Go and see to yourself. There's nothing more you can do here."

Maud nodded. "She's right, Alix. You look a mess. The king will be worried if he sees you."

"What about the laundry?"

"I'll finish it and bring it up when it's done," Elisabetta offered. "Maud does have the right of it. I doubt the king will be pleased by your actions today, although you saved the boy's life."

A twinge of apprehension gave her pause, but she shook it off. Richard would be upset, but the boy's life was more important. Maud and Alix wound their way through men who conversed in groups or unloaded carts.

For now, their journey was halted since the bridge lay in pieces at the bottom of the river and more than half the army hadn't made it across. Tents on both sides of the river had been set up and the smoky smell of campfires hovered in the air.

The sun was low in the sky, casting a blueish tint over the land. Alix's dress clung to her body and the stench of the river enveloped her. A light breeze swept across the Rhône, and she shivered as the earlier sweltering heat of the day dissipated.

"Hopefully, Richard will be occupied and I can change without being seen."

"Alix, I don't think that's possible." Maud laid her hand on Alix's arm as Rob approached them, a warning look in his eyes.

## ~ *Chapter 10* ~

RICHARD'S REACTIONS WERE QUICK AS lightning. When the bridge collapsed, he raced down to the river's edge and ordered his men to help the victims. He plunged into the icy water himself and dragged floundering men and horses from the swift current. These men were under his protection, and he refused to give up until each one had been accounted for. He continued to prowl the bank, searching for any forgotten victims.

"Rob, are there any more in the water?"

"I can't see . . . wait." Rob shaded his eyes and scanned the river for survivors. "There looks to be one downstream."

Richard jogged to where Rob stood and stared as the distant figure struggled, then sank below the surface.

"You and I could never reach him in time. God help him."

Hope bubbled in his chest as someone swam out and reached the victim. They began their arduous task to reach the riverbank, then both disappeared. His jaw tightened, powerless to prevent their almost-certain demise. One of the figures broke the surface and began swimming to shore. More men waded into the water to pull them both to safety.

"I thought they were dead, for certes." A smile of relief crossed Richard's lips, then he squinted in the bright sun. "God's legs!" he roared as one of the near victims struck a chord of recognition. Icy fingers of fear clutched his heart. "Rob, go get Alix and bring her to me."

*~*~*

Richard stood outside his tent, fury burning in his veins as Alix trudged toward him. Her mud-slathered dress was soaked, and her hair was plastered to her shoulders and back. His heart clenched at her drenched, forlorn appearance, reminding him of how close he'd come to losing her.

"What were you thinking, Alix?" he bellowed once she came into hearing distance. "You put yourself in danger needlessly. How can you be so reckless?"

He moved to tower over her, his fists clenched as hot anger coursed through him. If she offered a glib excuse for her actions, his control would shatter.

"The boy was going to drown. I couldn't stand by and watch him die."

"You could have died as well."

She looked up at him, her eyes wide in her pale face. "I truly thought I was going to die. When the current dragged me down that last time, all I thought of was never seeing you again. That alone gave me the strength to fight back."

The fear in her voice shook him to his very core. He'd never seen her so vulnerable before. Tenderness toward this woman who had put her life in jeopardy to help another fused with the searing anger that still gripped him in a blinding rage. He ached to crush her in an embrace, but she had to know that her actions today affected him. The thought of her dying ripped his soul to shreds.

"If you ever put yourself in danger again, you'll answer to me. Do you understand?"

She dipped her chin and focused on the ground, but not before he saw crystal tears seep from under her lashes. Once again, the need to hold her in his arms and protect her overwhelmed him, but he steeled himself. She couldn't be so careless with her life.

Alix nodded and rubbed her arms, shivering in the cool dusk air.

"Now, go inside and take a bath." A quick motion of his hand to Jacques, who hovered near the tent door, sent the boy inside to ready the water.

She nodded again and hurried into the tent.

"Maud, wait." His words stopped the girl as she attempted to follow Alix.

"Y-yes, Your Grace?"

"How is the lad? Will he survive?"

"The doctor said he should recover. When men dragged them from the water, the boy was bluish and not breathing, but Alix kissed him, and he started to take breaths on his own." Maud's eyes shone in admiration.

"Alix did *what* to the boy?" Richard demanded.

Maud stepped backward at his outburst.

"Richard!" André strode toward them.

Taking the opportunity to escape Richard's interrogation, Maud curtsied then scurried toward the tent.

"How is it that Alix can wreak havoc wherever she goes?" André asked.

"She does seem to have a talent for that." Richard sighed, then narrowed his eyes. "What is it, cousin? You look troubled."

André rubbed the back of his neck. "Gossip is spreading through camp that Alix brought the boy back from the dead."

"That's preposterous!"

"I know that, but most of the men are simple and uneducated. Alix healed the boy in a way that . . . isn't easily explained."

"Then they think she's a heretic? Or worse?" Fresh fear congealed within him for Alix's safety. What had she done to arouse their suspicions? Maud's explanation was outlandish, but the boy was alive.

"For certes, they're wary of her."

Richard's eyes steeled. "I'll find a way to alleviate the situation."

"Alix didn't suffer any ill effects from saving the lad, did she?" André asked.

"She didn't appear to, but I'll check to make certain."

He entered the tent and glanced at Maud and Jacques, who jumped up from the table.

Jacques bowed. "Your Grace, your lady is asleep. I didn't want to disturb her, so I left the tub in the room."

Richard cocked his brow and lifted the curtain. Alix lay sprawled on top of the cot, clad only in one of his shirts. He picked up a blanket that lay on his trunk and covered her. Warmth filled his heart as he gazed at the woman who instilled more conflicting emotions in him than he'd wanted to explore. In the dim light of the lantern, she looked younger than her five-and-twenty years, and a fierce protectiveness gripped him. As long as he had breath in his body, he'd do everything in his power to keep her safe, no matter what it might cost him.

*~*~*

Richard drank deeply from his cup, watching the shadows from the flickering lanterns dance and weave throughout the room. He was drained from the stress of the day, but his mind churned. Sleep would prove elusive, so he drained his wine and lifted the door to the tent.

The cool breeze off the water was a welcome break from the heat of the day. Cooking fires glowed across the plain, but the only noises were the barking and scuffling of dogs over leftover scraps and the heavy snores of the men. Intermittent clouds swallowed the silvery half moon, but it shone bright enough for him to locate the path to the river in the darkness.

The pitch-black water of the Rhône gurgled and splashed in the shallows. Richard relived the heart-stopping moment when the bridge's timbers had cracked, spilling all who were crossing into the depths below. Frustration twisted his gut. He'd meticulously planned for this journey and to be thwarted by a wooden bridge infuriated him. The river was too deep and swift to ford, and traveling downstream to another town would be a waste of precious time.

He paced along the shore, just able to make out the large, dark trees etched against the darker sky. The wind rustled the leaves of the groves along the banks. He stilled and smiled as the answer came to him.

*~*~*

"You've been busy!" Alix took in the sight before her. Along the riverbank, dozens of men hewed tree trunks into rough planks, then carted them to areas where they were sanded. Some planks were already tied together, forming a large flat surface. She frowned at the workers, then her brow cleared. "Boats. You're building boats to cross."

Richard turned and gave her a curt nod. "The men can hardly swim across with their armor and belongings."

She hadn't seen him since last night, and from his tone and attitude, he was still furious. Her breath caught as his words brought yesterday's events flooding back. "How many were lost?"

"Two, although more were injured."

His eyes narrowed. Something other than the collapsed bridge was weighing on him.

"How exactly did you save the lad? Maud didn't fully explain your actions."

Alix's mouth went dry. What could Maud have said? "If someone is drowning and stops breathing, there's a procedure by which you force air into the person's lungs and compress their chest to resuscitate them. Their survival recovery depends on how long they've been underwater."

"I see." His voice was remote. "Are there other methods?"

In her time, she could depend on advanced medical treatments, but in the Middle Ages, there were only herbal remedies and questionable practices. "No, in this type of life-or-death situation, speed is of the essence. Richard, why are you so troubled?"

He was still upset with her, but this aloofness was different. Surely, he didn't believe the men's claims that she had supernatural abilities?

His arms crossed over his chest, he pressed his lips into a thin line. "The men believe that the boy was dead and brought back to life. It doesn't help that the physician is unfamiliar with this type of medicine. You do understand what this means."

"They think I'm a witch." Alix's stomach churned. "Now what do I do?" Witches were considered evil, and anyone found to be one was put to death.

He glared at her. "First and foremost, stay out of trouble and out of sight, although it's too late for that now. If you can tell me how you knew what to do to save the boy, it might help change their views. There are a number of clergymen traveling with us. If one man should breathe a word of his suspicions, even I can't save you."

Alix's mind spun as she tried to concoct a reasonable explanation that didn't foster more doubts. She began a rambling story about a doctor in her hometown who had stumbled across a young child floundering in a pond.

Richard glared at her. "I know you're avoiding answering the question." He marched up to her and leaned down, his warm breath stirring her hair. "I'm tiring of attempting to wrest the truth from you. Do you not care for your own safety? I damn well do." His hard voice contradicted the protectiveness that flashed in his eyes.

A burst of laughter interrupted him, and he focused upon several men who were loitering in the sun. "God's legs. At this rate, by the time we cross the river, Philippe will have reached Outremer." He started toward them, then swung around. "Return to my tent now. That's an order."

Sharing a deep, intimate connection with Richard had its downside. He knew her almost as well as she knew herself, and could always tell when she was skirting his questions. But she also knew his mind. He wouldn't let his inquiries go unanswered, and she couldn't fault him for that. No one in this time knew of CPR, and to them, bringing the boy back from almost death was magic, witchcraft, the Devil's doing. In his place, she'd be just as suspicious.

Raised voices floated to her as Richard stalked along the bank, gesturing and motioning to the men. By the look of things, he'd be occupied for quite some time.

Alix hurried back to Richard's camp, thinking about her actions concerning the boy. She'd put herself in danger more than once without giving any thought to what might happen. But this time the possibility of death had been closer than ever. If she had drowned, would she have perished in this time or returned to her own to die?

She swallowed the lump in her throat. She missed her family and friends. Did they know she was absent once again? The first time she had been transported from the twenty-first to the twelfth century, she'd stayed about four months, which equaled minutes in her time. Two years had passed since her latest return. How long did that account for at home? What would she return to? Her stomach was in knots by the time she arrived back at camp. She lifted the door to Richard's tent and paused to let her eyes adjust after the searing brightness outside. Low voices and smothered laughter issued from the shadowed corner.

Alix cleared her throat, and Maud and Jacques spun around. Her eyes widened as she took in the younger girl's flushed cheeks. Concern surged through her. It was on the tip of her tongue to say something, but Alix had no experience in disciplining teenagers.

"Do you need anything, miss?" Jacques rose to his feet.

"No, thank you."

He nodded to her and exited the tent. Maud hesitated a moment before following him. Alix chewed her lip. She knew what Maud was feeling—the blush of first love and all the excitement and fear that went with it. Interrupting Maud and Jacques reminded her of the countless nights she'd spent with Richard. Even now, his touch still sent electric shocks through her, whether his hand brushed hers while handing her a cup of wine or caressed her during lovemaking.

She needed to keep a closer eye on this potential romance before raging hormones obliterated all rational thought. Maud was her responsibility. If she became pregnant, any prospect of a good marriage was destroyed. Alix also didn't want her to experience the stigma of raising an illegitimate child.

Alix went to the sleeping area and changed into a clean dress. She couldn't get used to wearing the same unwashed clothes multiple times, especially in the heat of summer. She entered the main room to find it empty. Exiting the tent, she saw Richard sprawled on the ground in front of the crackling campfire, leaning on one elbow, his long legs stretched out. Her heart filled with love for him. She smiled and he returned it as she approached.

She took that as a sign his anger with her was abating and sat on a log bench near him. "Are you making progress on building the boats?"

"Yes. I hope to cross in a week. Then we can be on our way. The longer we wait, the more chance we have of encountering bad weather during our sea crossing to Outremer. Not to mention I'm expecting my galleys to arrive in Marseille, and I'd like to be there before they do."

He rose fluidly to his feet and swiped the dust from his pants.

She scooted over to make room for him. "I imagine it will take several weeks to reach Marseille?"

Richard grimaced. "With the number of men and carts I have, we'll be lucky to manage three miles a day." He leaned forward to rest his elbows on his thighs. "I find it passing strange that you've made no mention of returning home and seeing your family. Alix, you've experienced every facet of my character—including my less honorable ones. I've always been honest with you."

Alix turned and stared into the fire. She couldn't tell him the truth, that she was from a different time, eight hundred years in the future. He'd likely think her delusional, or that she was a witch, especially coupled with bringing the boy back from certain death. But what if he did believe her?

If she were in Richard's place, she'd want to know all the notable events of her life. The good as well as the bad.

History had been altered once because of her. If he discovered that she had knowledge that could turn his defeats into victories, protect him from imprisonment, and even save him from death but stayed silent, he'd never forgive her.

He shifted on the bench to grip her chin in his fingers, forcing her to look at him. Hardness flashed in his eyes. "You're keeping something from me. Is it true what the men say? Are you a witch? Tell me the truth. Now."

Trickles of fear snaked through her. She wanted him to know every aspect of her life, who she was and where she came from, but if it became known that she believed herself to be from another time period, she'd be imprisoned. Or worse.

She had to tell him something. "I don't know if you could call my grandmother a witch, but she was proficient in the art of healing and had the gift of sight. She taught me about medicinal herbs. My mother wanted nothing to do with that way of life, which is why we left England." She pushed down the panic growing inside her. What would he do to her?

"You have the gift, too, don't you?"

"When I was younger, I had dreams about events that sometimes came to pass, but I haven't had one in years," she murmured. Another lie, but it was more plausible than being from the future.

"Alix? Alix, stop." Warm hands pulled apart her gripped ones.

She took a shaky breath and unclenched her hands to see crescent moons imprinted into her palms. He traced them with his finger, then pressed a kiss into her palm.

"What happens now? I know how witchcraft is viewed. Will you send me away?"

"This does add an unexpected complication, Love, but no." He laughed softly. "I'd never send you away. I'm glad you finally told me the truth."

"You're not angry?"

He shook his head. "I wish you'd told me sooner, but your secret is now mine." He brushed his lips across hers. "I'll protect you, always."

Relief overwhelmed her. She'd hated deceiving him, but this lie helped explain her reluctance to tell him more about her past. Perhaps, one day, she'd find the courage to tell him the real truth.

## ~ *Chapter 11* ~

UPON THEIR ARRIVAL IN THE port city of Marseille, the over one hundred ships Richard expected to see anchored in the sea hadn't arrived. Angry at another delay, he separated his troops. One group sailed to Outremer on hired ships to aid the French already fighting the enemy in the Holy Land. Richard chartered his own ships to travel south. He departed Marseille with his fleet, comprised of ten busses, a type of longship and twenty oar-powered galleys.

Alix leaned against the railing of Richard's private galley, entranced by the myriad of colors that painted the Tyrrhenian Sea. Light turquoise and cerulean dominated the prismatic shallow coastal waters while cobalt blue marked where the seafloor deepened. A gentle wind stirred her hair and sea spray tasted salty on her lips. Droplets flung into the air by hundreds of rowers' oars sparkled in the sun like diamonds gifted by Poseidon.

The undulating, pale rocky outcrops of Southern France merged into the smoother northern coastline of Italy. The further south they traveled, the more rugged the shore became, and small, jagged islands littered the sea.

They had stopped in Genoa, where they were to rejoin Philippe, but Richard had found the French king suffering from seasickness. So, instead, they made their way to Portofino, where they had a chance to disembark and feel solid land beneath their feet for the first time in weeks.

Maud joined her at the railing. "I wish we could have stayed longer in Portofino. The city was quite different from ones in France. The market had so many fruits and vegetables, I didn't know the names for half of them."

"Me too. Hopefully, we'll reach Messina soon and can spend more time there. Traveling by sea is enjoyable, but quite a few of the men are wishing we'd taken a land route."

Maud's eyes filled with sympathy. "Jacques still isn't able to rise from his bed for longer than a few minutes before he becomes dizzy and ill. I wish I could tend to him, but with the heat and the . . . odor . . . I can't stomach it."

"When we stop at the next port, I'll see if there's fresh ginger in the markets. That can ease seasickness."

A strident voice resounded behind them, and they turned to see Richard pacing the deck and gesturing while Rob and André stood silent.

"The king's been in a mood since before we left Portofino. You must know why, Alix."

"Philippe hired ships in Genoa to transport his army to Outremer, but he miscalculated the number he required." Alix exhaled and tried to keep her voice neutral to hide her exasperation with the French king. "He sent a letter requesting that Richard loan him five of his galleys. Richard counteroffered three, but that was refused and now he's furious. He feels that Philippe should've planned better, yet he spurned the offer of the ships that could be spared. By the look of things, I fear this is the first of many disputes between the two kings."

*~*~*

The galley rocked gently on the calm waves, but Jacques's face was still peaked as he served plates of fish and shrimp cooked in a seasoned broth. Oranges, figs, and tart lemons for flavoring the fish filled wooden bowls on the table. The fresh fruits were a welcome change from the dried, salted meat and limp, boiled vegetables which had been their staple meal since France.

Richard's tent was erected on deck, but it was smaller than the one he'd used on land. Alix had little room at the table with the addition of Rob and Georges.

"Did you see anything of interest on your journey?" Alix reached for another orange section.

When he could, Richard liked to travel by land and rejoin the fleet further south. She'd spent over a week exploring Naples with him. This time, though, she'd chosen to stay on board while he visited Salerno, accompanied by Rob. The doctors in the city were some of the most learned in Western Europe and he'd wished to consult with them concerning his fevers.

Richard shrugged. "Not particularly."

Rob and Georges chuckled, but swallowed their laughter.

Alix looked at them, suspicious.

"However," Richard continued as he reached for an orange and began to peel it. "I received news that the rest of my fleet has arrived in Messina. I can't afford to tarry any longer. Philippe slipped into the city a week ago with only one ship, but apparently nobody took any notice. He avoided the crowds and went straight to the palace."

"He must still be suffering from seasickness. Philippe enjoys being the center of attention almost as much as you." Rob laughed.

"I look forward to showing him how a king should enter a city." Richard smiled and motioned to Jacques to pour more wine.

He reached for his cup, and Alix frowned at the angry bruise which purpled his inner arm.

"Richard, what happened?"

"He hasn't told you about Mileto, Alix? It was a most enlightening visit." Rob gave her a cheeky smile.

Richard choked on his wine while Georges laughed.

Alix's eyes narrowed. "No, he's made no mention of it. I assume it has to do with the bruise?"

"It's quite amusing now, but at the time, I wasn't sure we were going to get out alive. May I?" Rob raised his brow at Richard and, at the latter's nod, he smiled, his eyes alight with humor.

"After meeting with the doctors, Richard decided he'd rather spend a bit more time on land, so we visited a few towns. The citizens were interested in our arrival and very accommodating. Women streamed out of houses to sell us fruit, baked bread, and sweet wine. I haven't eaten so well in months. We'd planned to return to the ship, but Richard wanted to visit one more town. Mileto."

Rob paused and motioned to Jacques to bring him some wine. He took a long drink, then leaned back in his chair, relishing every eye upon him. Alix had to force herself not to throttle him for taking his time.

"We were minding our business until we heard the cry of a hawk. Of course, Richard had to discover the source of the bird. We heard it again. He leapt off his horse and pushed his way into a house."

Alix's mouth fell open. "You forced your way into someone's home?"

"Only noblemen are allowed to own hawks, Alix. These were commoners. They must have stolen or captured it." Richard slammed his cup on the table.

"This isn't France. Maybe it's legal here." Alix studied him. "Knowing you, I can only imagine what happened next."

Rob laughed. "And you'd be correct. The woman inside stared at him, but when he grabbed the hawk, she yelled at him. Richard moved toward the door and that was when she hit him."

Alix gasped. "She hit you? In God's name, with what?"

"I'm not sure." Richard's brows knitted. "What was it, Rob? An orange or some other type of round fruit? At any rate, it seemed as if she had an arsenal of them. I left the house only to encounter an angry crowd of villagers outside who started throwing rocks and hitting us with sticks. One man even drew a knife. Needless to say, I was forced to release the hawk to defend myself."

"What happened then? How did you manage to get away?"

"I hit the man wielding the knife with the flat side of my sword, but it snapped at the hilt. Left with no recourse, we had to pick up whatever we could find and throw it at them to make our escape." Richard looked at Rob and they both burst out laughing.

"I fail to see the humor in this situation, Richard. What if you had been injured or worse?" Vexation coiled through Alix. Although Richard was amused, the outcome could've been quite different. And disastrous.

"Imagine this, Alix," Rob choked out between gales of laughter. "The King of England reduced to pelting poor villagers with clods of dirt, rocks, and offal. Did I mention they happened to have quite good aim? We managed to mount our horses, but not before an orange smacked me in the head. I should be gladdened it wasn't refuse."

As much as she tried to stay angry, Alix had to laugh at the image of Richard ducking and throwing pieces of filth at angry townspeople. How could she have no knowledge of this anecdote? She made a mental note to use this in her dissertation when she returned home.

"Next time, go with Georges, Richard. Maybe he can keep you from trouble."

Rob laughed. "Alix, I doubt even you can stop Richard when he has his mind set on something." He stood and beckoned to Georges. "Until tomorrow." He nodded to Richard.

Alix took a sip of wine as their footsteps receded. "What *were* you thinking? You can't act first and consider the consequences later."

"I seem to recall you doing the same thing with the boy who almost drowned."

"That was different. His life was at stake."

"I agree my actions were rash." Richard leaned forward and fixed her with a stern gaze. "But you put your life in danger without considering who it affected."

She raised her chin. "You could have been injured too. Perhaps we both need to realize there are ramifications to our actions. Please be more careful in the future."

"I plan to. The villagers fought more skillfully than I expected." He rubbed his jaw. "Perhaps I should have recruited them for my army."

Alix shook her head, then broached the topic that she knew weighed on his mind. "Do you have any news concerning Joanna? I know you're worried about her."

Richard's amusement vanished like the sun behind a thundercloud. "It's been relayed to me that Tancred has been holding Joanna prisoner for over a year. When her husband, William, died without an heir, the crown should have passed to his Aunt Constance, but Tancred, William's illegitimate cousin, seized power and Joanna's dower lands, and imprisoned her. When we arrive in Messina, I'll send envoys with a message for him—release my sister and return her lands. If he doesn't meet my demands or has ill-treated her, then by God's bones, he'll pay." Richard clenched his fist and his voice rose.

"I'm sure he hasn't mistreated her, Richard. With you being Joanna's brother, he wouldn't risk a war with England." Alix attempted to soothe his heavy heart.

Richard leaned back in his chair and studied the contents of his wine cup. "I have no idea what manner of woman my sister has become. She was but a child of twelve the last time I saw her. I remember a vivacious, mischievous girl who lit up the room with her laughter and loved to play jokes on our father. What if imprisonment has changed her? Made her cold and hard, or worse, destroyed her spirit?" He rubbed his eyes with his hand. "What if I've arrived too late?"

Alix stood, walked to him, and knelt by his side. "Richard, she's Eleanor's daughter." She caressed his cheek. "Joanna was raised to be strong and independent. She's been the queen consort of Sicily for thirteen years. You'll find her changed, but not broken."

He pulled her into his lap and wrapped his arms around her. "I pray you're correct."

# ~ *Chapter 12* ~

RICHARD SAILED INTO MESSINA'S CIRCULAR harbor with his entire fleet, his personal galley leading the procession. The cerulean Mediterranean waters frothed white as the oarsmen dug deep, propelling the ships forward.

People lined up along the shore to catch a glimpse of the king of England. The deafening cheers resounded as the brightly painted galleys hung with gleaming shields drew nearer. Trumpets rang in the ears of the spectators, and banners and pennons attached to spearheads snapped and fluttered in the wind.

Richard stood on a raised platform at the front of the ship. His polished armor glittered in the bright sun, but his head was bare, the better to see and to be seen.

The crowd undulated and pressed nearer to the shore as the galley drifted closer. Alix's hands tightened on the railing. Her heart pounded in time to the drums that accompanied the rowers' strokes. She tried to commit every sight and sound to memory to infuse into her dissertation.

"This is how a king should enter a city," Alix shouted to Maud, her words almost lost in the din of noise.

"I've never seen so many people in one place. I can't wait to get ashore and see the city." Maud bounced on her toes, her blond ringlets blowing in the breeze. "I wonder where we're going to stay. I hope it's nearby."

Some of Richard's barons who'd arrived earlier, guided massive warhorses bedecked in shining armor through the crowd. Moments after the ship docked, Richard and his men disembarked and strode through the raucous crowd. Once mounted, Richard turned and nodded to the townspeople, his smile as radiant as the sun.

"Miss?" Jacques rushed toward them. "I was informed that the two kings are planning to meet. I'm to escort you both to King Richard's camp in his absence."

Alix's stomach twisted and her pulse raced at the mention of the French king. Since Philippe's early departure, she'd been able to put him out of her mind, but now his presence resurfaced. He was still in the dark as to Richard marrying Berenguela. After he learned that his sister had been put aside, his fury would have no limit. He could abandon the crusade. Once back in France, Richard's kingdom would be the object of his ire.

Jacques beckoned to them to follow. They quickened their steps to keep him in sight. The citizens dispersed now that the spectacle was over. The blend of different languages—Greek, Arabic, and French—tumbled melodically over each other as they wove their way through the milling throng.

Alix clutched Maud's hand so as not to lose her as Jacques navigated them through the melee. Vendors selling fresh seafood, meats, fruits, and vegetables lined the maze of streets. The scent of freshly baked bread mixed with that of sweet citrus fruits and the pervasive tangy sea air. Maud's blue eyes widened at the colorful vegetables and fruits the vendors waved in the air to attract buyers. Alix wasn't surprised to see women wearing dresses similar to those worn in France. Since coming under Norman rule in 1061, the French had influenced Messina, but she didn't expect to see so many ladies wearing veils in the Arabic fashion.

A group of children crowded around a small, curtained kiosk, their squeals and exclamations filling the air. Maud hurried to see what the excitement was, dragging Alix along behind her.

"Oh, Alix, look!" Maud clapped her hands as they reached the crowd. A little dog jumped up on a small wooden bench, stood on his hind legs, and turned in circles in response to its owner's commands.

"He's adorable. We can stay a bit longer. I'd like to see what other tricks he can do." Alix made room for Jacques, who seemed as entranced by the dog as Maud was. All too soon, the show ended and the crowd melted away.

"Can we return, Alix? There's so much to see."

"Of course. I'm sure we'll need to buy provisions and I'd like to visit the city."

Richard's army was camped outside the city's stone walls. Hundreds of men's voices mixed with the whinnies of horses, and the jangle of metal filled the air. Tents covered the wide-open plain and the breeze carried the aroma of smoke and cooked meat from the blazing cookfires.

Jacques led them around tents and small copses of trees until they reached a huge conical pavilion. An unfurled banner blazoned with two lions flew from the center tent pole. Smaller tents flanked Richard's, which Alix assumed belonged to his household knights.

"Where are we to sleep?" Alix asked.

"You both will stay in the king's quarters." Jacques lifted the canvas flap to the tent and motioned them inside.

An immense wooden table set with chairs to seat about a dozen dominated the main room. Richard's squires carried coffers into smaller rooms cordoned off by hanging fabric. Oil lamps burned in stands about the room and on the table. Tendrils of smoke wafted up to the circular vent in the ceiling and the air was redolent with the scent. Pages rushed about, setting flagons of wine and bowls of fruit on the table.

"Miss, you will share His Grace's room." Jacques led Alix to the back of the tent and pointed out a room. The cloth curtain was tied open to reveal a cot, coffers, and a small washbasin placed against the tent walls. A table and two chairs occupied the middle of the area. "I hope this is acceptable?"

"It's quite comfortable, thank you."

Jacques smiled and brushed a fall of brown hair from his eyes. "Maud, you'll sleep here." He motioned to a smaller room with another washbasin, Maud's personal coffer, and one pallet piled high with blankets.

"This is all mine?" Maud placed her hand over her heart. "I've never had a room for myself before."

"The king said you were to have your own sleeping area. I'll make certain you'll have your privacy," Jacques stated loftily.

Alix hid a grin at his vow, but her heart warmed at Richard's thoughtfulness and protectiveness.

Richard's strident tone heralded his arrival. "He's acting like a petulant child, but far be it from me to stop him. Let him travel to the Holy Land. I have far more important matters to address."

Alix peered out from behind the curtain. Pages rushed to pour wine and offer bowls of fruit to Richard and his men.

"For certes, Philippe wasn't happy that you upstaged him with your grand entrance this morning." André chuckled and reached for his wine cup.

"He's the king of France. He should act the part!" Richard burst out. "Instead, he skulks into the city like a petty thief."

"It's no secret that you have a flair for the dramatic, Your Grace." Alix entered the main room.

Richard laughed, reached out his hand to her, and pressed a kiss into her palm. "You know me too well, Love. I have no doubt that my entrance into Messina will be remembered for years."

"If not centuries." Alix gave him a half smile as she took a vacant seat beside him. "I take it from your earlier words Philippe means to depart soon?"

"Today, apparently," Rob informed her. "When the two kings met, Philippe looked like he'd rather be tossed into a dungeon, but he managed to choke out a greeting. He then announced his intent to leave immediately for the Holy Land." He took a gulp from his cup. "It might be for the best, however, in light of Queen Eleanor escorting Richard's fiancée to Sicily. He won't take too kindly to his sister being spurned, but once the marriage with the Spanish princess takes place, there's little he can do."

"Soon you'll be a married man, sire. One thing I've learned over the years is to always agree with your wife." Georges smiled. "It makes for a happier home life."

"He's correct. I've no idea what your fiancée's disposition might be, but I know yours, cousin. I imagine your union will be fraught with quarrels." André laughed.

Alix took a sip of wine to swallow the ache in her throat. Each day brought Berenguela closer, and the end of her time with Richard. When Queen Eleanor returned to France, Alix planned to travel with her. Once there, she would use the brooch to go home. With Richard married, she doubted anyone would be surprised at her disappearance. Leaving her close friends and the life she'd carved out would be painful, but she didn't belong here.

"I'll bear that in mind. My first priority is to deal with Tancred." Richard's brow furrowed, and he looked toward the flap of the tent. "I requested a scribe when we arrived. Where is the damn man? Jacques! Find one and tell him if he values his position to make haste."

Jacques bobbed his head and scurried to the door, sidestepping to avoid a dark-haired, muscular man who lifted the tent flap and strode in.

"Sire, I heard you're in need of a scribe. Might I offer my own? He is fluent in French and Latin," stated Baldwin de Bethune, a knight previously in

Richard's father's service. He bowed to Richard, straightened, and propelled a gaunt man before him. The man bent a knee, the worn leather sack slung across his chest swinging forward.

Richard beckoned to him. "I need to dictate a letter."

The scribe took a seat across the table. With ink-stained fingers, he removed a piece of parchment and pen and looked at the king.

"I demand that my sister Joanna be released at once from your prison and escorted with all due courtesy to Messina. Furthermore, you'll restore her dower lands and the money that she should've received upon the death of her husband, William."

The scribe copied the orders, then handed the parchment to Richard. "Your Grace."

Ricard scanned the letter and nodded. "That will be all."

"Do you think that Tancred will acquiesce to your demands?" Baldwin asked while Richard folded the letter. "He's no fool, Your Grace, but he considers himself to be the king of Sicily. He won't welcome threats by you."

"I'm hardly threatening him, but my army *is* camped outside the city walls. He'd be foolish not to agree to them." Richard's eyes turned icy. "However, if Joanna has been maltreated, in any way, Tancred will answer to me." His voice was deadly soft.

"Were my sister in the same predicament, I would be as wroth as you. Tancred's illegitimacy creates a tenuous claim on his throne. He will use whatever leverage he has to keep it."

"Let's hope he realizes that my sister isn't leverage."

Baldwin bowed his head and left with his scribe.

The sun's rays dimmed, and shadows reached out across the ground as the light in the tent waned. Squires lit lanterns and candles that flickered as their movements stirred the air.

Richard picked up a candle and tipped it so the wax dripped onto the parchment. He took his seal and stamped it into the soft wax. Alix's heart skipped each time she saw the image of her brooch.

"He makes a valid point, Richard." André took the scribe's recently vacated seat. "With William's death, his aunt, Constance, by all rights, has claim to the throne. Tancred is fully aware that holding Joanna prisoner is to his advantage. Constance would never wage a war and jeopardize Joanna's safety."

"I'm aware of that. I also know that having two kings with well-trained armies within striking distance would make even the foolhardiest man take notice. He'll agree to my requests."

Alix frowned at Richard's cavalier attitude. Historically, Tancred wouldn't give in to the demands as easily as Richard surmised. He had to be careful in his negotiations. Tancred wanted to rule Sicily and Joanna's wealthy dower lands would be quite useful to him.

Also, Joanna's deceased husband, William, had willed a large legacy, including gold, money, and war galleys to his father-in-law, King Henry, to aid with the crusade. But since Henry was dead, Tancred considered this part of the will void and had claimed it. Richard thought differently. He was Henry's heir, and as such, deserved it himself.

"The only question is, how much is he willing to relinquish?" André queried.

"We shall see. I'm sending envoys tomorrow to Palermo, and I expect an answer soon."

## ~ *Chapter 13* ~

THE ENVOYS HAD RETURNED FROM Palermo with the news that Tancred had agreed to Richard's demand to release Joanna without complaint. However, he'd kept her dower and William's legacy. For Richard, Joanna's release took priority.

Townspeople scurried out of the way as the armored knights cantered toward the harbor. Richard's hands tightened on the reins as his stallion surged forward. Squinting in the glare of the brilliant sun, he could just make out the ship carrying his sister inching closer to port.

Voices rose in excitement as the people recognized the English king, but Richard's gaze was fixed on the azure sea. His gut knotted. The memories he had of his youngest sister were of her as a child. She loved to play hide-and-seek. She always chose the same hiding places, but he took his time finding her, then acted amazed when he did. Despite their eight-year age difference, her antics had always lifted his spirits and helped him forget his obligations for the moment.

Every time he returned to Poitiers Palace, she'd begged him to play with her. Until the summer she turned eleven. She told him she was too old for childish games. For the first time he'd seen her not as a child, but as a young lady. Would he even recognize the woman she'd grown into?

The ship docked and men hurried to lower the gangplank.

"Jacques, take my horse." Richard dismounted and tossed his squire the reins.

Several women appeared on deck, but only one captured his gaze. His fears melted away and he smiled as he strode through the crowd toward the ship. He would know his little sister anywhere. She walked decorously down the wooden gangplank, but, reaching the dock, she covered her mouth with her hands and raced into his waiting arms. He pulled her close to his chest. Now that she was here, he didn't want to let her go.

"Joanna, I wish I'd known what Tancred had done to you." He finally released her, keeping his hands on her shoulders. He peered down into blue-gray eyes so like his own. "But you're safe now."

"I never imagined that you'd come for me, but I'm so thankful that you have." She swiped tears from her cheeks. "How is it you *are* here? I see all your galleys in the harbor, but surely you didn't expect to battle for my release."

"As it happens, Sicily is on the way to my destination." At her knitted brow, his deep laugh filled the air. "There is much to tell you, little sister."

"I have so many questions too. I've been away for so long, sometimes I fear my memories of life in France will fade and become nothing more than dreams." A sad smile crossed her lips. "So much has happened in twelve years. I was sorry to receive word of Hal and Geoffrey's deaths, but when Father died . . . I can't imagine the pain Mother went through. Not to mention being imprisoned at the time. My own imprisonment was dreadful, but at least it wasn't sixteen years."

He put his arm around her shoulders and led her to where Jacques stood with an extra horse.

"It's over now." He stopped and faced her, his heart plummeting at the question he must ask and the answer he might receive. "Tancred didn't hurt you, did he? If he or any other man laid a hand on you, I will hold them accountable."

"No. Although he was my jailor, he treated me with the utmost respect."

Fresh relief flooded through him. "I'm glad to hear that. Tancred made an unwanted enemy of me, but he's kept his life a bit longer." He helped her mount the horse, then swung lithely up into his own saddle.

"I'd hoped to have a residence for you, but for now, you will stay in the nunnery. It's more comfortable than staying at my camp."

"Richard!" Dismay filled her voice. "You're not leaving me already, are you?"

"Don't fret. We'll have plenty of time to visit. There's someone I wish for you to meet."

"Who is this person?" Her eyes narrowed. "You're not trying to marry me off so soon, are you? Although I'm widowed, I was the Queen of Sicily. I do have a say in how I lead my life."

"That thought hadn't occurred to me, but since you brought it up . . ." Richard laughed aloud as Joanna playfully swatted at him. "I think you and Alixandra will find much in common."

"You brought a woman with you?" She spun in her saddle to face him. "I wonder what *Mamà* would say about that."

"You can ask her yourself. She arrives in a month's time."

"Mother is coming?" Her voice vibrated with excitement. "Is she to escort me home?"

"Actually, she's bringing my fiancée."

Joanna's mouth fell open. "Alys is traveling here?"

He cocked his brow at her. "We do have much to catch up on. Fortunately, we've reached our destination and I can escape your inquisition. I must return to camp now, but the nuns will make sure you're comfortable."

She frowned as he motioned to Jacques to help her down from her palfrey. "When will you return?"

"I will see you this evening and answer all your questions. Until then."

*~*~*

Richard returned as promised, greeted his sister with a kiss, then moved aside to let Alix step forward.

"Your Grace." She curtsied to the queen of Sicily. Her heart pounded. She had no doubt Joanna knew who she was—Richard's lover. What would she think of her?

Joanna took her hands. "Rise, please."

Alix studied the slender woman, who looked to be about twenty-five. Joanna had the characteristic gray-blue eyes of the Plantagenets and waist-length, reddish-gold hair slightly darker than Richard's.

"I hope I didn't keep my brother too long last night. We had so much to catch up on." She motioned for Alix to take a seat at the long trestle table covered with various dishes of meats and vegetables.

"I'm sure you did. Richard told me you've been away from France for quite some time."

Joanna nodded. "The last time I saw my family was when they put me on a ship to Sicily. After I married William, I never returned home."

Richard took a seat next to Alix and put his arm around her shoulders. Heat rose in Alix's cheeks. She tried to shift away, but Richard tightened his arm.

Joanna's eyes widened and her cool gaze cemented the knot in Alix's stomach.

"I remember that day very well, little sister. You were trying to be brave for Father, but I could see that you were terrified to leave." Richard gave a rueful grin. "I wish we could've seen you marry."

"I as well. The hardest part was not having Mother by my side to give me advice. Marriage at any age is difficult, but at twelve, it's overwhelming." A sad smile crossed her lips. "William was a good man and I do miss him."

Once again, Alix was reminded that royal children married to create alliances between countries, regardless of age. "I can't imagine how hard it must have been at such a young age. Commoners get a little more say in whom they'll marry."

Joanna raised her brow. "I'm certain they do."

A servant stepped forward to refill their cups and Alix took a sip to hide her discomfort. Richard's most trusted men might accept her, but Joanna's words were a sharp reminder that she wasn't her peer.

"Richard has told me quite a bit about you."

Alix choked on her wine and cast a glance at Richard. He'd turned away and was deep in conversation with André and Rob who'd joined them. What had he said? "Has he?"

Joanna reached for an orange. "It's strange how the most insignificant event can change lives. If Richard and his men had taken an alternate road, or arrived in Poitiers earlier, your paths might never have crossed. How fortunate for you." She gave Alix a pointed look.

Alix stared at her plate. No doubt Joanna suspected that she was sharing Richard's bed for her own gain.

"I'm still in disbelief at what's happened these past several years." Joanna peeled the fruit. "I wish my brothers hadn't warred against each other, but when a crown is at stake, alliances change as quickly as the wind. I know that very well. Who would have imagined that a third son would become king? And in several months, he's to be married."

Alix barely breathed as Joanna finished eating an orange section.

"I'm surprised at his change of plans," Richard's sister continued. "Philippe has no idea that Richard won't marry Alys?"

Alix's heart slammed against her ribcage. "No, not yet," she managed to say in a steady voice. "Once his fiancée arrives, King Philippe will have little recourse but to accept it. He'll be able to keep his sister's dowry, which hopefully will temper his anger a bit."

"I hardly remember Alys," Joanna mused. "I only met her once or twice during my father's Christ's Mass courts, but she seemed ill-suited for my brother. Richard was my favorite, although he used to tease me mercilessly. But he was always there to protect me." Her eyes glistened. She grabbed her cup and took a deep drink.

Alix's brows drew together. Was she reminiscing about the past or alluding to something else?

"Is it true that Philippe planned to leave for the Holy Land the day Richard arrived?"

The change in topic threw Alix, but she managed to nod. "Yes. He was quite vexed with how the townspeople cheered the pomp and splendor that accompanied your brother's arrival and decided to leave that evening. However, the weather changed for the worse and he was forced to stay."

Joanna laughed. "Richard does enjoy pageantry. I hope their alliance isn't strained over this."

"It would've been best if King Philippe had left, but perhaps relations will remain civil."

Once Philippe learned that Richard was marrying Berenguela, Alix was sure what little civility remained would be destroyed.

Her stomach clenched. She admired Eleanor and they'd become quite friendly. Joanna, although pleasant, perhaps for Richard's sake, had made it clear that Alix wasn't her equal, and never would be. If it became common knowledge that Alix had been the instigator, and implicated Henry in such a sordid scandal, Richard's family would despise her.

"Alix." Richard leaned close to her ear. "It's growing late. Rob and André will escort you back to camp. I'll return later. I still have many things to discuss with Joanna."

Alix stood and curtsied to Joanna. "It was a pleasure to meet you."

"And to meet you too. I look forward to seeing you again, Alixandra."

## ~ *Chapter 14* ~

"RELATIONS BETWEEN US AND THE townspeople are souring." Richard paced the outer room in his tent. "We arrived less than a fortnight ago and fighting has already broken out countless times. We need to put an end to this."

"It's getting much worse, sire," Baldwin de Bethune stated. "Recently several shopkeepers brought goods to sell to the soldiers. A woman had some bread, but the price she quoted was outrageous. One of the men attempted to haggle for it and she took offense. She struck him and then the townspeople joined in. He was savagely beaten. The Griffons . . ." Richard's brows drew together at the insult.

"The Greeks," Baldwin amended, "have raised food prices in the markets." He glanced at the other men in the room. "Grumblings amongst the soldiers are that if this goes on much longer, we'll have to sell our horses to be able to afford to eat."

Richard's lips thinned. "I'm aware that we're being taken advantage of."

"I don't think that's the only issue that the citizens have against us," André pointed out.

Richard frowned for a moment, then his face cleared. "My taking over Saint Saviour."

"You must admit, cousin, evicting the monks and using the grounds of the Greek monastery as a storage facility for the horses and the goods from our ships did little to promote goodwill between us. Not a day later, fighting broke out and has continued since."

Richard shrugged. "I needed the space and it's situated in a useful location for loading and unloading the ships. Yes, I'm aware of what it must look like to the citizens, but I'd rather my provisions not rot on the galleys."

"The people also fear for the safety of their wives and daughters," Andre continued. "The soldiers like to make advances toward the women, although they have no intention of seducing them. I hope."

"Men will be men." Richard arched his brow. "Hopefully, that's the least of our worries. I've arranged a meeting with Philippe and the Sicilian governors of Messina tomorrow. I intend to rectify this situation."

*~*~*

The warm breeze was heavy with the aroma of citrus, spices, and baked goods, blended with the pervasive scent of the tangy sea air. Richard's galleys floated on the azure sea that sparkled like sapphires in the bright sun. Fishermen unloaded their fresh catches from small boats bobbing in the crescent inlet.

"Tell me more about Queen Joanna. Is she as beautiful as the men say she is?" Maud asked as she and Alix wound their way through the throngs of people in the market.

After meeting Joanna, Alix couldn't help replaying their conversation over and over. She mistrusted Alix's motives toward Richard. Her thinly veiled remarks were testament to that. Alix admired that aspect of her. Joanna clearly adored her brother and was just as protective of him as he was of her. Perhaps in time she could convince Joanna that she loved Richard and wasn't using him to her advantage.

"She is. Richard said that when Philippe saw her, he was completely smitten, which amused Richard not at all."

"I feel sorry for her. First her husband died and then she was imprisoned. She scarcely had a chance to mourn."

"The queen has her freedom now."

Maud paused in front of a stall that sold an array of citrus fruits. She picked up an orange, sniffed it, then selected two more.

"I wonder if she'll stay with the king or return home? What will happen to us?" Maud's blue eyes widened. "I'm sure the king won't let us travel to Outremer with him. Will we go home?" Her gaze darted to Jacques, but the squire was talking to a couple of soldiers. "I'll miss Jacques if we leave, but traveling to that unholy land terrifies me."

"I thought you wished to see Jerusalem."

"I do. I did. Messina is wonderful, and although it's different from anything I've ever seen, there is still a sense of home. From what I've heard from the squires, Outremer is a barren land of almost certain death."

"They're repeating hearsay and embellishing it. I'd love to see Outremer, but it's probably for the best that we don't go. I'm sure we'll be allowed to return home with Queen Eleanor." She couldn't stay with Richard. Returning to France with Eleanor was her only real option to save herself from heartbreak.

Maud arched a brow. "Is that what you want, or are you trying to convince yourself?" She spun on her heel and went to make her purchase.

Alix sighed. Sometimes Maud was too perceptive. More than anything, Alix wanted to travel with Richard and witness history being written firsthand. But seeing him with his wife would be too painful.

"Alix, I spent the last of our coins on the oranges. It seems like prices are rising daily."

"Richard's meeting with the French king and the Sicilian governors as we speak. Hopefully, they can remedy the situation."

A woman dragging a shrieking child bumped into Alix. With no apology, the woman continued on her way. Alix stared in shock at the retreating figures. Maud was saying something, but shouts and yells drowned her words.

More people rushed past them.

*What's happening?*

The once-tranquil square erupted into a frenzy as panicked citizens fought their way through the crowd.

Loud voices and the clash of steel rang out on all sides of them. Townspeople screamed and scrambled out of the way as armed soldiers with swords drawn marched through the street. Alix didn't recognize any of the emblems on their shields. The men weren't part of Richard's army. A battle was about to erupt, and she, Maud, and Jacques needed to find shelter.

Alix's heart pounded, and adrenaline shot through her. "Run!"

*~*~*

The stifling heat in the tent exacerbated Richard's temper as the governors of Messina and Richard's men aired their grievances.

Angry words tumbled over each other until Richard raised his hand. "Both sides are at fault. I concede that insults have been traded, but I'm more concerned with the continuous fighting and the rising food prices."

"Your Grace, you must understand that supplying provisions for two large armies has put a strain on our resources," one of the governors of Messina stated. "The sellers are only acting in response to greater demand."

"The way I see it is they are acting out of greed. I suggest we fix the prices."

The governor leaned forward, his lip curling in derision. "And what of your men brawling in the streets? What's your solution to that?"

Apparently, the Sicilian leaders were more concerned with the fighting than the price of food. Richard swallowed his retort with difficulty. "Your men roam the streets looking to fight as well. I don't see you keeping them in check."

"Sire!" Rob burst into the tent, his chest heaving. "The townspeople are attacking Hugh de Lusignan's lodgings. You must come at once."

Richard threw a contemptuous look toward the governors. "I'm putting an end to this if I have to seize control of Messina myself."

The streets were filled with people as Richard and his men raced into town. The first unarmed civilians they came across fled like rats from a sinking ship. He grinned at André. But soon his amusement faded. Angry townspeople advanced toward them, hurling insults and brandishing sticks and rocks.

"Fall back! We need to arm ourselves."

"How do you want to handle this?" André asked as they returned to camp. "Attack with siege engines?"

"No. There are too many archers on the city wall. We'd be slaughtered like sheep while we moved them into position. We split up. Take the soldiers and attack the gates to keep the defenders occupied. I'll approach from the sea. Hopefully we can launch a surprise multidirectional attack."

"That won't be possible." Baldwin bounced his sword in his hand. "Philippe has blocked your galleys from attacking. In order to save his own skin, it appears that he's helping the Griffons more than the English army."

"Why am I not surprised?" Richard narrowed his eyes and studied the walled city. "The main gate is heavily guarded, and with our galleys unusable, we need another entrance. I'll circle around the western part of the town. There's a chance the back gates will have been overlooked. We strike there."

Richard mounted his destrier. Adrenaline coursed through his veins at the prospect of battle.

"Rob, you'll ride with me. But first go tell Jacques not to let Alix out of his sight. I don't want her anywhere near town."

Rob's gaze shifted and he looked down. "Sire, you should know that Jacques accompanied Alix and Maud to the market. As of now, they haven't returned."

Richard's heart hammered. "Why wasn't I informed earlier?"

"I ... uh ... thought they would've returned by now," Rob stammered as Richard's cold gaze pierced him.

The clang of steel rang out in the distance amidst the screams of men and women.

"If anything happens to her ..." Richard's chest tightened, and his gut twisted. He knew all too well what could happen to women when soldiers occupied towns.

"Cousin, I'm sure she'll come to no harm," André said. "Go. We have a city to take."

*~*~*

A cascade of dirt and small stones skittered and bounced down the steep slope. Richard and his men crouched on the ground, prepared to attack if discovered. He listened intently, but the only sounds were the clattering of settling stones and the whine of the ocean breeze.

Inching upward, he reached the wooden postern gate. He motioned to Rob to move to the right side of the gate and waited until the rest of his knights were situated below him. Two men stood on the wall above, their backs to him.

Richard held up his fist, then brought it down in a chopping motion. Rob swung his axe at the gate. Shouts from within mingled with the cracking of the weathered wooden door. The wood splintered. Richard kicked the remaining frame open and burst through the small opening. He ran his sword through the first man's chest and spun away as the second man lunged toward him. Rob hit the man's shield with his axe, and as his foe stumbled backward from the attack, he swung again. The man fell, Rob's blade embedded in his neck where his armor offered less protection.

In minutes they were confronted by armed soldiers streaming toward them, but Richard's men were well-versed in the art of combat. The steel of their swords flashed in the sun and clashed against shields and armor. Richard parried an attack, the man's blade bouncing off his shield as he crouched low. He stabbed upward, slicing the man's thigh, crippling him. The defender's screams cut the air, then were silenced as Richard dealt the death blow.

Soldiers' bodies soon littered the street. A man armed with a knife lunged at Rob. He leaped out of reach, stumbled over a broken shield, and threw his arm up to protect himself. The sharp knife sliced into his forearm. As the man readied himself for another charge, Rob grabbed the shield and flung it. The attacker dodged out of way, but by the time he regained his form, Baldwin de Bethune's sword was buried deep in his chest.

Baldwin gave his hand to Rob and pulled him to his feet. On top of the postern gate an old banner fluttered in the breeze. Baldwin pulled it down, ripped it into long swaths, and tied it around the bleeding wound.

"Can you fight?" Richard asked. "I don't need you as a casualty. Alix might have my head for it."

Rob flexed his hand, grimaced, and nodded. "It will take more than this to stop me."

Richard laughed and clapped Rob on his shoulder. "Follow me." Richard led his men down the street, the survivors fleeing before them.

Alix grabbed Maud's hand and dragged her away from the center of the square. Women and men raced by, pushing and shoving them to escape the arrows and rocks that rained down on the English king's soldiers from the city walls.

A man screamed as an arrow struck him. Maud froze, her eyes wide as crimson spread on his shirt and he collapsed to the ground in front of her.

Alix's heart pounded, and her chest constricted. What if they couldn't escape?

"Miss," Jacques gasped. "We need to get back to camp. I don't have a weapon and I can't protect us."

Alix searched for an exit, but she couldn't see through the mass of panicked townspeople. "Can we get to the main gate? We might be able to leave that way."

Jacques looked in the direction of the gate. Armed soldiers from both sides battled in the street while archers on the wall shot volleys of arrows into the melee. He shook his head. "We must find another escape."

He gripped Alix and Maud's arms and propelled them toward the small houses and shops that bordered the market.

They ran until Jacques threw out his arm to stop them. "Get back!"

A soldier fell from the wall, and Jacques darted over to grab his sword. An overturned cart lay between them and escape. They ducked behind it.

Maud shrieked as an arrow thudded into the flimsy wood inches from her head.

"We need to get into one of the alleyways for protection," Jacques yelled, his voice almost lost in the sounds of battle.

Cold sweat congealed on Alix's skin. She had to move, but her legs were leaden and she couldn't stop shaking.

Maud's eyes were squeezed shut and tears rolled down her cheeks.

Jacques peered out from their defenseless cover. "Now!"

Alix forced her heavy limbs to move. She hauled Maud after her and stumbled after Jacques. The distance to the small alleyway stretched longer as they ran. A rock struck Alix in the thigh. She cried out as a sharp pain coursed down her leg, and she fell to her hands and knees. Screams and the clash of metal surrounded them.

What if they couldn't make it to safety because of her? She lurched to her feet and almost lost her balance, but managed to stay upright. Jacques turned to help. His mouth opened in a silent scream and he fell backward. Blood seeped from the protruding arrow in his shoulder.

"No! Jacques!" Maud ran to where he lay. "Help him, Alix, please."

"We need to get him to safety. Grab his feet."

Alix put her hands under his arms and they dragged his limp body into a darkened, narrow alley.

"I'm going to check further down the alley. We might be able to find help or a way out."

She ran deeper into the bowels of the passageway, expecting to find an exit, but it dead-ended into a stone wall. "Damn it." Alix smacked her palm against the wall in frustration. She returned to Jacques and pressed her fingers to his wrist. His pulse was thin and feeble, but beating.

"Is there a way out?" Maud's voice shook.

Alix shook her head. "We need to move . . ."

Cheers filled the square, and she spun around to see Richard's men waving their swords and clapping each other on the back.

Panic surged through her. Now that the soldiers had their victory, the plundering . . . and worse . . . would begin.

# ~ *Chapter 15* ~

RICHARD STOOD IN THE SQUARE with his men, the shouts and roars of the victors growing louder. The center of town was littered with the dead and wounded. Soldiers were already breaking into unprotected shops, looting whatever they could carry.

"Cousin!" André called out as he threaded his way to Richard's side. "I believe we took Messina in less time than it takes a priest to say Matins."

Richard laughed. "I daresay we did. Now it's time to claim my town."

"What made you decide to enter through the back postern gate? How did you know it even existed? I hope it wasn't a lucky guess."

"A couple of days after our arrival, I took Rob and Jacques and scouted the area. I noticed the gate and hoped it would be lightly guarded."

André's eyebrows lifted. "I must say I'm impressed."

Richard shrugged. "I like to know my escape routes, should they become necessary."

A woman's hysterical shrieks replaced his thrill of victory with icy tendrils of dread. Richard grabbed André's arm. "Did you see any sign of Alix?"

"Ah, no. There's a chance she made it back to camp before the fighting began."

"If anything happens to her, I will find the culprit and kill them." Richard clenched his fist.

"Your Grace, I'll search for her," came a man's weak voice.

Richard swung around. Rob swayed on his feet, his face ashen. The bandage covering his wound was drenched in blood, the crimson liquid steaming in rivulets down his hand.

"I appreciate the offer, but I think not. I'll send someone else." Richard motioned to one of his men. "Take Rob back to camp and find a doctor. Once you do, return with my banners."

"Are you going to share this victory with Philippe? Where is that man, anyway?" André asked, a smirk curling his lips. "I didn't expect to find him in the thick of battle, but now that it's over, I would've thought he'd make an appearance."

Richard gave a short laugh. "I'm sure he's watching from the safety of his chambers. Why should I grant him the satisfaction of seeing his banners fly from the walls of my city?"

"Don't make more of an enemy of him than you already have."

"Philippe does hold grudges." Richard pulled off his helmet and wiped his brow. "I do as well. For his sake, let's hope that's a lesson he never learns."

*~*~*

"Maud, stay with Jacques."

"Don't leave me." Maud clutched Alix's arm. "What if we're attacked? What if he . . . he dies?"

Alix squatted and felt for the boy's reedy pulse again. His face was waxy, but he was still alive.

"Look, Maud. The arrow is in his upper chest. Nowhere near his heart or lungs. He'll recover, but I need to find some of Richard's men to help us move him. We must get him to the doctor as soon as possible. I won't be long." Hopefully, their presence would go unnoticed.

Maud looked at Jacques, eyes brimming with tears. "Go, then. We'll be fine. But please hurry."

Alix turned to leave but stopped at a flash of silver on the ground. She picked up a long sword and tried not to think about where its owner was or what had happened to him. With men's adrenaline heated with bloodlust, a weapon could prove useful.

"Ah, just what I was looking for."

The gravelly voice sent chills down her back, and she jerked her head up. A short, dark man covered in dried blood leered at her, barring her way. He wore leather armor, and from what she could tell, he could be from either the English or French army.

His eyes traveled up and down her body. "Yes, you'll do for me." He licked his lips and stepped toward her.

Alix raised the sword, struggling with the weight. "Stay away from us." She backed away.

"Or what?" He moved forward.

Alix swung the sword. It missed him by several feet.

He laughed. "Be nice now. It will go much easier for you if you do."

Maud whimpered behind her, and Alix lifted the sword again, arms shaking with the weight. Her throat dried and her heart threatened to explode out of her chest.

The man lunged. She jumped back, took an unsteady breath, and reinforced her stance. Her knuckles whitened as she clenched the weapon, her muscles tense as she waited for his next move.

If she could keep his attention fixed on her, Maud at least would have a chance of escape. He moved closer and she swung. Metal thumped as she contacted with his thigh. He grunted, but his thick leather armor protected him from the blow.

"I was going to let you live, but I've changed my mind."

He stepped forward, and Alix hit him again, this time with the sharp edge of the sword. He stumbled to his knee. She raised the weapon, preparing herself. He pulled out a knife and threw it.

She ducked.

He lunged again, grabbed the bottom of her skirt, and tugged. The sword thudded onto the ground as she lost her balance. Her feet flew up and she fell backward, her shoulders and head smacking hard on the ground. Pain exploded behind her eyes. Dazed, she stared up at him as he picked up the dropped sword and pointed it at her.

The man knelt over her, smiling in victory. She twisted, trying to escape, but he pressed the sword against her throat, the edge pushing the metal into her skin. Warm liquid trickled down her neck.

Images of that night in Austin when the mugger accosted her filled her head. When she'd refused to give him money, he'd struck her. Lying on the ground, stunned and paralyzed with fear, she'd been helpless to do anything.

She'd taken self-defense classes after the mugging and was confident in her skills, but practicing in a controlled environment was different than in the real world. Resolution flowed through her. Her life wasn't the only one on the line. She had to try to protect Maud and Jacques. This time, she would fight.

Her attacker ground his mouth on hers and pushed her skirts up. She gagged at his fetid breath and her stomach lurched. Her hand clenched on the sandy ground, her fingers scratching deep into the loose earth.

"Mmm, I'm going to enjoy this." His evil laugh echoed in the alleyway.

Maud screamed and the man looked toward the sound. Alix flung a handful of dirt into his face.

"Damn you, whore." He leaned back, wiping the grit from his eyes.

Alix kicked him in the chest with all her strength, and he staggered backward, dropping the sword. Scrambling to her knees, she grabbed the weapon.

"What do we have here?"

Her heart plummeted. The new voice erased any hope they had of escape. She looked up to see an armored soldier and a sob burst from her lips.

"They're mine," her assailant growled. "You can have them after, if they're alive."

"If you value your life, leave. She's under the king's protection. He will hunt you down and kill you should any harm come to her."

Cautious hope and relief flooded through Alix's veins at his words.

"The French king?" The man sneered and spat on the ground. "I don't fear him." He advanced upon Alix again and she scrambled backward.

"I should have clarified. King Richard."

The man stopped and stood slack-jawed as he stared at Alix's savior. "Take her then, but leave me the other one."

"No! Stay away from her!" Alix yelled.

He turned and bore down on Maud, but the soldier was quicker. The assailant grunted and fell face forward. The dry ground soaked up the crimson blood that pooled beneath him. The metallic scent filled the air. Alix's stomach heaved, and she turned away and retched. She looked up at their rescuer, who had removed his helmet.

"I know you." She tried to recall where she'd seen him.

"I'm Ralph Besace, the physician who examined the boy you saved when the bridge in Marseille collapsed."

"Of course. Thank God you're here. We need your help." Alix staggered to her feet, grabbed his arm, and led him to where Maud huddled next to Jacques. "I don't think the arrow pierced his lung, but it's lodged just below his shoulder."

Ralph wiped sweat from his round face and crouched down. He felt around the head of the arrow, studying the wound. "Luckily, it's a clean puncture."

He rolled Jacques over gently and nodded. "It didn't penetrate through, and it looks like it's not embedded too deeply. I should be able to make small incisions and pull the bolt out." The doctor straightened and walked to the entrance of the alley. "In here, quickly now!"

Three men pulled a cart into the passageway.

"Careful," Ralph warned as Jacques was lifted off the ground. "Don't jostle him."

Once the boy was in the cart, Alix and Maud fell in with Ralph as he trailed behind. Flies buzzed around the dead man, drawn by the scent of blood. Alix shuddered and stared at the ground in front of her.

As they passed dead soldiers and townspeople, Maud whimpered and covered her mouth with her hand. Alix looked at the gates where Richard's banners and pennons were mounted, the cloth snapping in the stiff breeze. Her throat tightened. If only she'd remembered.

She thrust the guilty thought away. "I never thanked you for rescuing us," Alix said as they exited through the gates. "I don't want to think about what would have happened if you hadn't found us when you did."

"You're very welcome, but I can't take all the credit. I was told that you might be in town and to look out for you."

Alix's forehead creased. "What do you mean? Weren't you fighting in the battle? You're certainly dressed for it."

"No, I wore this for protection while I checked the wounded. Once the battle was won, the king sent men to search for you."

Warmth filled her chest at his words. "How did he know I was here?"

He shrugged. "Fortunately, no true harm came to either of you."

The familiar camp sounds of men's voices and laughter, the whinnying of horses, and the ringing of metal were clear from several hundred yards away.

Ralph paused as the cart continued. "I'll leave you here. I must see to the lad."

"Please, let me come with you," Maud entreated.

"Lass, most likely there will be other wounded men in my tent."

"Maud, let the doctor attend to him," Alix said. "We can visit later."

Maud whirled to face her. "I won't leave him." She moved closer to Alix. "You'd do the same if it were the king."

Alix's heart thudded at the thought. "Of course I would." Alix looked at Ralph. "Is it possible for her to accompany him?"

He hesitated. "It's no place for a young lady."

"I don't think I can change her mind." She glanced at Maud's determined expression.

Ralph sighed. "Very well, then. Come along."

*~*~*

Richard's tent was empty except for a pageboy who bounded out of the chair he'd been lounging in. His eyes widened as he looked at her.

Alix glanced down. Her stomach lurched at the dried blood that darkened the top of her dress. She felt her neck and winced as she touched the wound from the sword. "Can you please bring me some water for a bath?"

The boy bobbed his head and hurried outside.

Once alone, the brave face she'd pasted on for Maud's benefit crumpled and a sob tore through her. She stumbled to the table and collapsed into the chair the page had vacated. Covering her face with her hands, she took shaky breaths. They'd almost been raped and killed.

Her breath hitched, and she pressed her fist to her mouth. Where was Richard? The battle had been quick, and that likely meant many casualties on both sides. She prayed that neither he nor any of his household knights had been injured, or worse.

Voices drew nearer, and she swiped tears from her eyes. Two boys lugged buckets into the tent, warm water sloshing over the sides, and carried them into Richard's cordoned off sleeping room. She stood on wobbly legs and bit back a cry. Her thigh throbbed where the sharp rock had struck her. Adrenaline and fear for their lives must have dulled the pain.

"Is there anything more you require?" one of the pages asked.

"Thank you, but that will be all for now."

She limped into the room, peeled off her filthy dress, and threw it into a corner.

"Oh God." Her thigh was covered with dried blood from a shallow, jagged cut. A dark purple bruise surrounded the wound.

Alix poured the water into the tub, then eased into it. She sucked in her breath as the water lapped against the laceration. Grabbing the bar of soap, she washed her skin to remove the dirt and blood and stench of her assailant. The cut on her neck stung as she plunged her head below the surface. She scrubbed her hair, then sat up, sluicing water off her face.

The tears she'd held in trickled down her cheeks, and she gave in to them.

She wrapped her arms around herself, her body wracked with sobs. Although the man hadn't had the chance to violate her or Maud, it had been too close, too real.

Alix squeezed her eyes shut and slid beneath the surface, feeling weightless as it surrounded her. The water cocooned her, blocking out the sights and sounds of the outside world. She stayed under until her burning lungs drove her to the surface.

When the mugger had attacked her in Austin, he'd only wanted money. This man had wanted to overpower and hurt them. Although rape was a criminal offense in Richard's time, during wars and raids, it wasn't unexpected. *To the victor go the spoils.*

Experiencing history firsthand thrilled her, but she'd been careless in considering the realities of this era. The brutality she'd experienced brought home how powerless she was here. Homesickness for the relative safety of her own time washed over her. Until she and Maud could return to France, she needed to be more careful. She couldn't put their lives in danger again.

## ~ *Chapter 16* ~

RICHARD STRODE TOWARD HIS TENT, but was redirected as André intercepted him, took his arm, and led him aside.

"Did my men find her? Where is she? Has she been injured?" Richard jerked his arm away. "André, tell me."

"Alix and Maud are fine, but they were attacked."

Richard's lungs tightened and fury erupted through his body. "God's bones! Who did this? I will find him and make him pray for death."

"He's already dead. Is that enough?"

"No! It's not." Richard raked his hand through his hair. "Tell me what happened."

"I only know that Ralph chanced upon them and killed the man before anything worse happened to them." André gripped Richard's shoulder. "I care about Alix, too, but Richard, there are other matters we need to discuss. Philippe is furious . . ."

"I must see to her. Philippe will have to wait."

Richard entered the tent and motioned for the pageboys to leave. He went to the cloth partition, lifted it, and let it fall behind him. Alix sat on the cot, her knees drawn to her chest, her head bowed. He ached to take her in his arms and ease her fear. As well as his own. His boot scuffed the ground, and she glanced up, her eyes red and swollen, her face blotchy.

"I'm so sorry," she choked out. "This is all my fault. I knew what would happen, but I did nothing to stop it."

"Love, what are you talking about?"

He walked over and sat next to her and took her trembling hands in his. She wore one of his shirts, and when she moved, the bottom pulled up, revealing an injury. Renewed anger coiled inside him. He touched her lacerated leg as he examined the raw cut. He'd sworn to protect her and instead had almost lost her.

"This wasn't your doing. You had no idea there would be a battle. Jesu, I hadn't planned to claim the town, but when my men were attacked, I had no option."

Alix shook her head. "You don't understand. It *was* my fault that I put Maud's and Jacques's lives in danger." She sniffed and grabbed his hands as if they were a lifeline. "If I hadn't decided to go to town, Jacques wouldn't have been injured and that bastard wouldn't have attacked us."

The fear that emanated from her gripped him. He knew what men were capable of. Every fiber in his being wanted to hold her and erase the horror of what she'd been through. The last thing he wanted was to hear what that savage had done to her, but he had to experience it with her.

"What happened, Alix? Tell me. I need to know."

She wiped her eyes and took a shaky breath. "When the fighting began, my only thought was to escape. We were looking for a way out when Jacques was injured. We managed to pull him into an alley. Then that man found us." Her voice cracked and her fingers convulsed on his.

"I tried to fight him, but he was stronger. If Ralph hadn't come upon us . . ." She collapsed in his arms, sobs tearing through her body. "There was so much blood and so many bodies . . . and the screams. Oh God, I keep hearing the screams."

Richard's arms tightened around her, his heart ripping into pieces. "You never should have had to witness that."

Tenderness warred with frustration. He wasn't surprised that once again she would put others' safety above her own, but damn it, the woman needed to think of herself as well.

He'd never been in this position before. In past battles he'd given no thought to what happened to the townspeople after victory. If the town was wealthy, he limited the amount of destruction and looting, preferring to keep the seized goods intact. What befell the women was of little to no consequence to him. But that was before Alix. Before she'd claimed his heart. He'd expected to worry about her safety in the Holy Land, but not in Sicily.

He smoothed her hair from her tear-dampened face. "You're safe now. As long as I have breath in my body, no harm will ever come to you."

"You can't guarantee that." Alix sat up.

"Love, I will do anything to protect you." He cupped her chin and brushed his lips over hers.

She recoiled from him and scrubbed the back of her hand over her mouth. His hands dropped into his lap as she jumped up and walked to the other side of the room.

"I'm sorry." She scraped her hands through her hair. "I just can't."

He stood, unsure of what to do and how to help her. Men's voices filled the outer room. He glanced toward the partition.

Her gaze followed his. "You must go, but please have someone check on Jacques when you can. I need to know he'll recover."

"For certes, I will. Alix . . ." He moved toward her.

She shook her head, crossed her arms in front of her, and stepped back. "Your men are waiting."

Regret, like a knife, pierced his heart. "As you wish. I'll send a physician to tend to your wound." He turned and left, the cloth partition settling behind him.

*~*~*

Alix stood frozen. The pain in Richard's eyes cut deep into her soul. She opened her mouth, but it was too late to call him back. She shuffled to the cot, curled up in the fetal position, and closed her eyes, but it was impossible to relax amidst the fear that swirled inside her.

She stared at the tent wall, listening as the rise and fall of voices faded to silence in the outer room. The cloth rustled in the air and a shadowy figure appeared on the other side. Alix bolted upright, shaking.

"Miss, the doctor is here to see you," a pageboy called out.

A small cry of relief escaped from Alix's lips. "Yes, please send him in."

She hoped it was Ralph so she could ask about Jacques. Instead, an elderly physician tottered in and proceeded to put salve on her wound while muttering that women should stay at home and not get involved in battles. She gasped as he wrapped a bandage tightly around her thigh, no doubt in the attempt to prove his point.

He examined his work, then stood and blinked his rheumy eyes at her. "If you come down with a fever, send for me, but you should heal in a couple of weeks."

The old man left, and Alix lay back on the cot. Her thigh throbbed, reminding her of what happened. No matter what Richard said, Jacques's injury and their attack was her fault. Forgetting that Richard and his men had taken Messina by force was another oversight she'd made. If the boy died, she would never forgive herself.

Her chest tightened. She couldn't forget her attacker leaning over her, his eyes cold as death, wanting nothing more than to take his pleasure and rob her of her dignity and self-respect. And afterward, potentially her life. If Ralph hadn't rescued them . . . she shook off the dark thought.

She fell into a fitful sleep, reliving the events. Jacques was struck by an arrow, but instead of crumpling to the ground, he stood, his eyes full of hatred and accusation.

*"This is your fault!" He pointed at her. "I could die, and Maud might have been raped because of you."*

*"I'm sorry, I'm so sorry. Please forgive me."*

*"You knew, Alix, yet you still put us in danger."*

*"I forgot, I—"*

*"You only thought of yourself. You vowed you would take care of Maud, didn't you?"*

*Alix's heart thudded. He was right. She'd sworn to herself that she would protect Maud and she'd failed. The sounds of fighting swelled, and she covered her ears as screams and the clash of swords echoed around her.*

*"I will take care of her, of both of you," Alix sobbed.*

*"It's too late . . ." Jacques's eyes turned glassy and opaque. He swayed backward.*

*"No! Jacques, you can't die."*

Alix stretched out her hands and tried to run to him, but was grabbed in a vise-like grip. She fought wildly, kicking and yelling.

"Alix, calm down! Stop fighting."

She lashed out with her fists and connected with something solid.

"God's bones," a deep voice growled.

She was abruptly released and fell backward. Her heart pounded as she prepared to face a new danger. Her hands clenched on the soft blanket, and she blinked as her surroundings shifted from the center of town to a darkened room. The warm glow from a lantern cast blurry shadows that danced and wavered on the tent walls. Long seconds passed while shapes grew more distinct. Richard leaned against the table, rubbing and working his jaw. The soft cot gave under her hands as she levered herself up.

"Richard?" Alix frowned. "What happened? What are you doing here?"

"I was planning to go to sleep, but you had other ideas."

She shifted on the bed and winced at the twinge in her hand. Her eyes widened. "Did I hit you?"

"That's an understatement. You fought like a tiger." His lips curved in a half smile. "Wherever did you learn to strike someone like that?"

"I'm sorry. I had the worst nightmare." She stood and walked over to him. The lantern illuminated the discoloration marring his skin, and she brushed her fingers over it.

"You missed dinner. Would you like something to eat or drink?"

Alix shook her head. "Did someone check on Jacques?"

"He'll recover. I thank God he was there to help protect you and Maud, although I wish none of you had been there."

"Is Maud still with him?"

"No. I escorted her back, but I had a devil of a time getting her to leave. She's not the meek and timid girl who left France."

A weak smile crossed Alix's lips. "No, she's not. I never asked . . . how many men did you lose?"

"Twenty-five of my household were killed. Rob was wounded."

Alix's stomach plummeted. "What happened?"

"He suffered a knife wound, but he's on the mend."

"Thank God. Sybilla would be devastated if anything happened to him."

"Come, let's go to bed. It's been quite a day."

He stretched, then peeled off his shirt and tossed it on the ground. The flickering light colored Richard's skin a golden hue. His boots soon followed. He untied the drawstring on his chausses and stripped down to his braies or drawers. His muscles rippled as he moved, accented by the shadow play.

Bile rose in her throat as she remembered her assailant's lips on hers and what his intent had been. She tried to erase the image, but it was imprinted on her mind. Richard held out his hand to her, but let it fall to his side as she remained where she was.

"Love? I won't touch you if that's what you're worried about." His tone was gentle, but hurt echoed in his voice.

She couldn't tell him that the thought of any man's touch now caused revulsion and fear to swirl inside her. Even his. "No, it's not that. I'm afraid to go to sleep. I don't want to relive the horror over again. I can't."

"Then we'll stay up until the sun rises."

Alix gave a small laugh. "That's a kind offer, but you're exhausted." She forced herself to cross the room and climb into bed.

He sat beside her, concern in his eyes as he looked at the cut on her neck, then at the bandage on her thigh. "I see the doctor has been here. What did he say?"

"Well, after scolding me for being in the middle of a battle, he said I should recover."

A smile of relief crossed Richard's lips. "That's welcome news. When I discovered you were in town during the fighting, I thought I'd go mad with fear." His voice hardened. "I wasn't there for you."

"You're here now, and that's all I need."

Alix lay back on the bed and he settled next to her. She inhaled the familiar scent of him, the soap and leather, and closed her eyes as the tightness and fear in her eased. She curled up closer to him, craving the security and protection he provided. "Have I told how much I love you?"

"Not today, and I never tire of hearing it. I love you as well."

# ~ *Chapter 17* ~

THE CACOPHONY OF VOICES FELL silent as Richard entered the outer room. Mediators from the French and English armies hovered like flies around Richard's most trusted men.

"Sire, Philippe has a message for you." Baldwin approached him, a piece of parchment in his outstretched hand.

Richard took it and cracked the seal. A cold smile stole over his lips. "Philippe has taken offense with my banners. He plans to remove my standards and raise his." He crumpled the letter and threw it on the ground. "Why should I allow his to fly when I was the one who claimed the town? God's blood, the man is insufferable!"

"I agree wholeheartedly with you," André said. "We lost too many men that day due to his refusal to help, but might I remind you of the agreement you made with him at Vezelay?"

Richard's face darkened. "How could I forget?"

He stalked to the table, poured a cup of wine, and took a long drink. Before starting this journey, he and Philippe had agreed to certain terms. After their triumphs over the infidels, they'd share equally in the plunder and glory, although Richard had little doubt that he'd be in the thick of more battles than the French king.

"By hanging your banners on the walls, you've taken Messina for yourself." Baldwin cocked a brow.

"I didn't see that coward lending his sword to our cause. He broke his oath and joined forces with the enemy by barring my galleys from attacking the city by sea." Richard's fingers whitened on the goblet.

André raised his hands in supplication. "Both armies know full well who defeated Messina. By all rights, the town is ours, but to placate Philippe, perhaps you should consider an alternative. We need to keep the peace between you two. Lowering your banners seems a small price to pay."

"Due to that cur's cowardice, I lost good men from my own household," Richard growled.

"Let Philippe have his way." André glanced around the room. "The men respect a king who stands beside them and joins his sword with theirs, not one who sends them off to war while he cowers in the shadows."

One of the mediators cleared his throat. "No one can doubt which type of king you are, sire, but by agreeing to the French king's terms, you're also showing how magnanimous you can be."

Richard crossed his arms and leaned against the table. His men were right. He could ill afford to alienate Philippe so early in their journey, but the cowardice of the man bit at him. "Give me one good reason why I should agree to his demands."

"He has a large army," Baldwin stated. "We need him if we want to claim victory against the Saracens."

Richard grimaced. "You have the right of that. I do need his swords and men to defeat Salah-ad-Din and reclaim the Holy Land. So be it. I'll lower my flags, but I will maintain control of the town until I can hand it to someone I trust."

*~*~*

"I hope that you will find your accommodations comfortable." Joanna led Alix and Maud down the well-lit hallway of La Bagnara.

Richard had claimed possession of the castle and moved his sister there to better protect her.

"I'm certain we will. Our stay here at the castle isn't an inconvenience, is it?" Alix asked, although she doubted Joanna had any say in the matter.

"No, not at all. I still can't believe Richard took Messina. I heard the commotion in the distance, but it was quite some time before I learned what had happened. My brother said you were in town when the fighting broke out and that his squire had been injured protecting you and Maud."

The memory of the attack rekindled Alix's ever-present guilt. "We were very lucky to have escaped, and Jacques is on the mend."

"Is it true that you fought your assailant?"

"I tried to." Alix gave a weak smile. "But it was an army medic who saved us."

"I'm glad you were unharmed." A distant look entered the young queen's eyes and her body tensed. "I can imagine how terrified you must have been."

Joanna stopped in front of a room and motioned for them to enter. Sunlight spilling in from the windows illuminated the immaculate chamber. It was small, but contained two cots, a table, and chairs.

"The room is perfect, Your Grace."

"Good. I'll send the pages up with your trunks. I'll see you tonight at supper." Joanna smiled and left.

"Alix, come and look." Maud motioned to her.

Alix walked to the window. The room overlooked a square courtyard edged with fruit trees and flowers beds. "It's beautiful. Perhaps later we can explore."

A soft knock sounded on the door and Maud hurried to open it. Two servants carried in their trunks, then withdrew.

Alix knelt by her trunk and opened it. The dresses that had been neatly packed had shifted during the move, so she took them out and laid them on the cot.

"Although I'm sure you'll miss the king, I'm glad we're staying here." Maud shook out one of Alix's rumpled dresses. "It ought to be more comfortable than the tent, especially in the heat of the day."

"That's why we were sent here." Alix ran her hands over one of the dresses to remove the wrinkles.

She didn't want to worry Maud by telling her the real reason they were here—that Richard feared for their safety. Even though a truce between the army and the townspeople had been enacted, he couldn't be certain that tempers on both sides wouldn't reignite. The castle of Bagnara was well fortified. Knights and a considerable number of men-at-arms were already in place guarding his sister.

She was also still on edge after the attack. The assailant was dead, but what if it happened again and next time she wasn't as lucky? During the day she could concentrate on other things, but at night the bad dreams came. She would wake trembling in a cold sweat and cower in Richard's arms until the nightmare faded. The slightest unexpected sound sent her heart racing, and she hadn't left the shelter of the tent in days.

The palace was safer than the camp, but it was Richard himself that made her feel protected. Without his presence, would her fears subside?

"I thought I might find you here," Richard called out.

When he discovered that Alix wasn't in the castle, he'd headed to the garden. Minutes later he found her seated on a stone bench in a shady area surrounded by fruit trees.

Alix looked up, her radiant smile easing the tension coiled within him. Between trying to pacify his disgruntled army and Philippe acting like a petulant child, he was juggling his priorities.

The assault on Alix in Messina was an added fear he hadn't expected. He wanted her with him, but her safety was more important. Especially after he discovered that Philippe had done nothing to help stem the fighting. Instead, he'd cowered in his rooms until it was over.

She gave him a teasing smile. "It's been almost two weeks since you've visited. I thought you'd forgotten about me. Tell me, how is Jacques doing?"

"He's almost fully recovered, as is Rob. How are you? Is your injury healed? What about the night terrors?"

"I'm fine, and the nightmares have stopped." She glanced down, a curtain of hair swinging forward to cover her face. "Being distanced from what happened has helped." She didn't want him to know that she still had them occasionally, but they were lessening in intensity.

Richard sat and drew her close. Guilt and exasperation crept through him. She wasn't telling him the entire truth, likely to avoid causing him more worry. Once again, she was thinking of his feelings and not her own.

"I'm aware I've been neglectful, but I'll make it up to you. Trying to keep the peace between my men and the townspeople is consuming my every waking moment. Not to mention my plans to leave this month have changed. It isn't safe to cross the sea in November. I'd rather not lose men and ships needlessly. We'll winter here and leave in the new year when the weather is more favorable."

"I know you want to reach Acre sooner than later. How did your army take the announcement?"

Richard laughed. "Not very well. The rising cost of goods in the market was taking its toll, and tempers flared again. I've met with Philippe and Tancred's messengers, and we managed to agree on stabilizing the prices. The men are appeased for the time being."

Alix stared out over the expanse of green grass. "I feel so far removed from what's happening in camp. I think the news we receive is portrayed in a far more positive light than the reality."

"I'd rather not concern you with the tedious issues I've had to deal with."

"By that you mean you don't want Joanna to worry." Alix twisted in his arms to look up at him. "Your sister isn't a little girl anymore. She's a grown woman."

"What she was put through—" His jaw clenched. He would never forgive or forget what Tancred had done to her.

"Yes, she was imprisoned. But Joanna is far stronger than you give her credit for." Alix caressed his cheek.

Richard caught her hand. "The voice of reason." He leaned forward to kiss her.

The crunch of approaching footsteps on the gravel path, followed by a discreet cough, forced them apart. Richard glared at his sister, who gave him an innocent smile.

"How kind of you to grace us with your presence, Richard. It's been days since you've visited."

"I apologize for my absence, but I've been quite busy. I can stay awhile, but then I must return."

"Good, come along then. It's almost time for supper." Joanna turned and left.

"Are you sure you can't stay longer?" Alix rubbed his forearm.

He stood and drew her to her feet. "I wish I could. Trust me, there's nothing I'd like more than to wake up with you in my arms, but I have a meeting with Philippe in the morning." He took her hand as they strolled back to the palace. "To keep the peace, I've decided, quite generously, to share part of Joanna's dowry with him."

Alix stopped midstride and stared at him. "Whatever for? This money belongs to Joanna, doesn't it? I thought that only spoils from battles were to be split."

Amusement flashed in his eyes. "She's willing to give her part to me to help fund our journey."

"I'm sure the fact that you're her favorite brother didn't hurt, either."

His laughter filled the air. "Not at all."

*~*~*

For the last couple of hours, Richard had been able to put aside thoughts of negotiations and peace talks. He was more relaxed than he'd been since arriving in Messina. He drained his cup and shook his head at the servant who moved to refill it. The hall was darkening as the setting sun cast long shadows across the stone floor.

"Joanna, as much as I would like to stay, I must take my leave."

"So soon?" She glanced toward the window and sighed. "It is growing late and I'm sure you want to get back before dark."

Richard leaned close to Alix. "Care to walk with me?"

"Do you have to ask?"

He waited while Alix curtsied and bid goodnight to Joanna, then he said his own goodbye.

"By the look of things, you and Joanna are getting along very well."

Alix nodded, her gaze focused on the ground. "Your sister has been very kind to me, and she's taken to Maud, as well, but I miss hearing you discuss strategy and politics."

Richard stopped and put his hands on her shoulders. "Your counsel is important to me, but protecting you is my priority. Especially after what happened in Messina."

Alix glanced up at him. "It will be dark by the time you arrive in camp. Are you certain you won't reconsider? You could leave early in the morning."

Richard laughed. "We both know that won't happen if I stay." He stepped back into a recess and pulled her toward him. The setting sun's rays illuminated her face. "But I think I can manage a few more minutes."

Sleeping alone tonight would be torture, but he needed to hold her, if only for a moment.

Alix moved closer and toyed with the hem of his shirt. Her warm fingers sent shocks through his body as she skimmed her hands up his chest. She moistened her lips with her tongue, and his heart pounded as he imagined her mouth on other parts of his body. No other woman affected him this way. He coiled his hand in her hair and tilted her head up. Her hazel eyes burned with the promise of a passion-filled night. His resolve was crumbling.

"Jesu, you're beautiful." Richard crushed his mouth on hers.

Her soft moan sent electricity coursing through his veins. He pulled her closer, desire erupting as his tongue tangled with hers. The fire within him grew until he tore himself away, his head spinning. "Now I must leave, Love. As much as I wish to stay, I can't be absent from a meeting that I requested."

*~*~*

Alix stood in the courtyard until Richard and his men vanished from sight in the gathering dusk. She turned, retraced her steps, and almost bumped into Joanna, who was leaving the dining hall.

"My brother left? Perhaps he'll stay longer next time." She frowned. "I thought I'd see more of him, but apparently, that's not to be."

"One thing I've learned about the king is that when he's focused on a task or idea, he forgets about everything and everybody else until it's resolved."

"I can hardly wait until Mother arrives." Joanna clasped her hands. "I'm looking forward to spending time with her. I'm still surprised Richard's not marrying Alys. There must be a reason for him to choose Berenguela."

"He's had trouble with one of his nobles in Toulouse for quite some time. An alliance with Navarre will help protect the southern part of Aquitaine, especially in his absence."

"That explains why my mother is making such a long journey to escort his fiancée." Joanna smiled. "She and Richard would do anything to protect Aquitaine. He also needs an heir to secure his realm, something I was unable to do."

She glanced at the window, which mirrored their reflections, then turned a hard gaze upon Alix. "I'm sure sharing my brother's bed is a boon for you. However, I wonder why you traveled all this way, knowing that Richard's fiancée will arrive soon. Do you think that after his marriage, you'll continue to be his lover?"

Heat crept up Alix's face. "No, I would never do that."

"Then what do you expect from him?" Joanna walked closer. "Money? The opportunity to better your position?"

Alix shook her head.

Joanna gave a short laugh. "You truly love him and want nothing in return?"

"I do love him," Alix whispered. "My relationship with Richard was never for personal gain."

"I wish I could believe that, because it's clear he loves you. But I don't trust you." Joanna spun on her heel and hurried away, her footsteps fading in the distance.

Alix let out a shaky breath. She'd hoped she and Joanna would become closer since they were together much of the time. But she'd sensed a distance in the other woman. She'd assumed it was due to their difference in stations, or the fact she was with Richard. Now she knew that it ran much deeper.

Maud finished lighting a candle on the table and looked up as Alix entered. "Oh, the king didn't stay?"

"He does have obligations other than me." Alix picked up the candle and tipped the burning wick to light the remaining ones.

Maud smiled. "I'm certain he does, but he seemed more relaxed tonight. Is there still fighting between his men and the townspeople?" Worry crossed her face.

"They've made progress in their peace talks, and I hope the worst is over. Oh, I didn't have the chance to tell you . . . Jacques is almost fully recovered."

"Is he?" Maud's eyes lit up. "I've been praying for him. I enjoy staying here, but I miss not seeing him. Perhaps that's silly of me." Color rose in her cheeks.

"Not at all. Now let's get ready for bed before the candles burn out."

Alix turned her back while the younger girl undressed.

"Has Queen Joanna said anything to you about traveling to the Holy Land?" Maud's muffled voice grew louder. "I know it won't be for several months, but I hope we can. I don't think I'm ready to go home quite yet."

Heaviness sank into Alix's heart. "We'll see what happens." She forced a brightness in her tone.

There was no reason for her to stay any longer. Joanna had been released and was now under Richard's protection. As far as Alix could tell, Joanna wasn't suffering from any lingering effects from her imprisonment. Alix's commitment to Eleanor had been fulfilled. But Maud's future remained in question.

# ~ *Chapter  18* ~

ALIX BENT DOWN TO STOKE the glowing embers in the fireplace. She rubbed her arms to ward off the chill of the March night.

Since Joanna had divulged her feelings toward her, Alix had spent the past few months trying to convince her she didn't have ulterior motives toward Richard. Joanna's attitude toward her had changed. She was more open, but Alix sensed she still didn't fully trust her.

The castle was comfortable, but she missed the liveliness of the army camp and seeing Richard daily. The last time he visited, he'd brought the news she'd been dreading. His mother and fiancée had arrived, but Tancred had refused to allow them to disembark in Naples. Instead, they were forced to sail to Brindisi. Furious, Richard had traveled south to Catania to meet Tancred and discover why.

The wooden door creaked open as Richard entered the room. "Now that I'm fit company to be around, I'm famished."

She turned and rushed into his arms, his still-damp hair cold against her cheek.

"If I knew I'd have this kind of welcome, I would have come sooner."

Alix gave him a kiss and stepped back. "I missed you and this is the one of the rare times I have you all to myself." She motioned to the table. "While you were bathing, I asked the servants to bring some food and wine."

Richard pulled out a chair, the legs scraping against the stone floor. He poured some wine while Alix filled their plates.

"Were you able to convince Tancred to allow your mother to sail to Messina?" Alix's stomach knotted as she waited for the answer.

"Yes, they'll depart Brindisi soon. As for Tancred, although meeting with him was an inconvenience, I discovered some interesting information." He paused to take a drink from his cup. "We were able to strengthen the peace treaty that we'd made last year, but upon my leaving, he gave me a document he'd received from Philippe. That French snake stated that my word wasn't to be trusted and that I was going to break the treaty and take Messina for myself. He even had the audacity to offer aid to Tancred should he wage war against me, which is what he was hoping for."

Alix nodded, but her racing thoughts took precedence. When would Eleanor arrive in Messina? Would she take her back to France? How much time with Richard did she have left?

Richard cleared his throat. "Have you heard anything I've said?"

She looked up into his narrowed gray-blue eyes.

"Yes, yes, of course. I'm shocked that he went to all that effort." Her voice was hollow in her ears, but Richard apparently didn't notice.

"I'm beginning to think this alliance with Philippe is more trouble than it's worth. The man is insufferable, but I was able to convince Tancred that was hardly the truth. As much as I enjoy Sicily, I have no plans to deprive him of it."

Alix's thoughts spun anew. She couldn't leave without making sure Maud was provided for. And what of her own fate?

"You appear to be more interested in your plate than in my company. Should I take offense?"

"What? No, of course not." She took a deep breath, preparing herself. "When do you expect your mother to arrive in Messina?"

Richard shrugged. "One or two weeks at most."

Her heart constricted. Time was running out. She knew how to return to her own century, but could she leave Richard in the past?

Richard paced outside the small church, waiting until morning Mass ended.

"Are you certain this is the best course of action?" André stood out of the way of Richard's path. "Telling Philippe you're refusing to marry his sister isn't going to be well received, especially in front of his men."

"That's precisely why I'm doing it." Richard gave a tight smile. "I doubt Philippe will concede to spreading the rumor of an affair between Alys and my father, but if he does, I want to make sure the conversation doesn't get misinterpreted."

"Do try to keep your temper, cousin. You need his army, whether you like it or not."

The door creaked and Richard swung around. Philippe exited, blinking in the bright sun.

"Richard, do we have a meeting that I'm not aware of?"

"We do now."

The French king glanced at his men and shook his head. "Why don't we go to my rooms and discuss it there. It's more private."

"I prefer to talk here."

Philippe cocked a brow. "What's this about then?"

"I had a very enlightening meeting with Tancred several days ago."

"Why would that be of interest to me?"

Richard held out the document. "Are you familiar with this correspondence?"

Philippe paled, then shook his head.

"You've never seen it before? Imagine my surprise when I was told that my word to Tancred concerning peace between us wasn't to be trusted." Richard opened the document. "Shall I read its contents?"

"Whatever is written wasn't by my own hand. This is a scheme, no doubt instigated by you, to avoid marrying my sister. Yes, I'm aware your mother arrived with your fiancée in tow." Philippe's jaw clenched. "If you dare put her aside and marry another . . . think carefully on this, for you don't want to make me your enemy."

"As much as your words pain me, I refuse to marry Alys. If what I've heard is true, she was intimate with my father and even had a child by him. I have many witnesses that I can bring forth who will swear to it." He walked to Philippe. "You understand my predicament? If Alys has already given herself to another man, how can I be certain she won't stray from my bed? I don't wish to question the legitimacy of any future heirs."

Blood suffused Philippe's face, and his stance shifted. "Those are untruths."

"I would very much like to believe that these are baseless rumors, but I need irrefutable proof. Can you provide that?" Richard let his words sink in.

Philippe's gaze darted toward his men, who avoided his eyes. "What is it you want?"

"Come to my residence tomorrow. I'm certain that we can negotiate a treaty to solve this dilemma. And know this—if you retaliate against me or anyone I care for, you will regret it."

Richard swung away from Philippe and strode back to André and his men. "That went better than I thought it would." He grinned.

"I can't believe he didn't admit to spreading the rumors himself, or at least put the blame on one of his men. Now his sister will be forever sullied," André mused.

Richard glanced back toward the group of men behind him beating a hasty departure. "He's never been interested in this marriage. He wants to reclaim her dowry; namely, certain lands, such as the Vexin. If he had any concern for her honor, he wouldn't have allowed the rumor to start in the first place."

"Alix planted the seed to help you form an alliance with him, but I worry about her safety. He won't attack you, but he wouldn't think twice about her, especially if he feels that he's being shamed by you marrying another."

"Philippe knows that if he threatens Alix, he will answer to me."

In preparation for his mother's imminent arrival, Richard had brought his most trusted men to the castle, and almost every seat at the tables in the dining hall was occupied. Alix had spoken to Rob, and he'd recovered, as had Jacques, who was attached to Maud's side and looked as if he had no plans to leave.

Alix leaned closer to Richard to hear him over the myriad conversations echoing in the room. "So, Philippe readily agreed to your decision to not marry Alys? Did he not argue?"

Richard laughed. "Let's say that I didn't give him the option to refuse. Thanks to you, Love, he had no recourse unless he acknowledged that he was behind the rumor." He shrugged. "He has too much pride to allow people to think poorly of him."

"Yes, he does have his pride, which Richard managed to wound during the negotiations." André's voice boomed from behind them. He bowed to Joanna, then smiled at Alix.

Richard cocked his brow. "I think I was quite fair. If Philippe felt differently, he should have spoken up."

André stepped nearer. "His sudden decision to travel to Acre shows that he's not happy with what he received."

"What exactly was in the treaty?" Joanna raised her voice as loud laughter broke out from a nearby trestle table.

"I'm to pay Philippe ten thousand marks for not marrying his sister, and upon our return to France, I will send Alys back to him as well as return her dower lands."

"That's very generous of you, and what do you get in return?"

"I get the Vexin." Richard chuckled. "If I don't have any male sons, which is very unlikely, it reverts to Philippe and his heirs upon my death."

Alix's muscles clenched.

Philippe had always wanted the Vexin. Being forced to give it to Richard had to have galled him. What if he took out his anger on her? She was the only other person who knew of his deception, and as far as he was concerned, expendable.

Richard enfolded her hand in his and leaned close. "I know you worry, but you have nothing to fear from him." He murmured for her ears alone. "I made sure of that."

"I'm glad you were able to end the betrothal with Alys, although I feel sorry for her." Joanna said. "When do you think Mother will arrive?"

"She'll be here in a day or two."

A smile lit Joanna's face. "I can't wait to see her. It's been far too long. I'm curious about your fiancée. I hope she meets your lofty expectations," she teased. "Have you ever met her or her family?"

"Once, when I visited her brother, Sancho, but it's been many years."

"I'll find out soon enough, I expect." Joanna glanced at Alix. "Richard wants me to travel to Acre as a companion to Berenguela. Has it been decided that you'll go back to France?"

Alix's hand tightened on her goblet. Nothing had been said about what would happen to her when Richard left on his crusade. She assumed she'd be allowed to return with Eleanor.

"I imagine I will. There's no reason for me to stay."

"I'm still not entirely sure if I can trust what you say are your reasons to be with Richard, but even so, if you leave, I'll miss you." Joanna gave a rueful smile and leaned close. "I don't envy you telling Richard."

Alix glanced at Richard, who was in deep discussion with André. She never tired of watching the play of emotions across his face, whether he was putting forth his point of view or simply glancing at her from across the room. This life she'd stumbled into had become just as important as the one she'd been born to in the future, but this wasn't her time. It would be painful to leave her friends, but losing Richard would create a vacuum in her soul that could never be filled.

*~*~*

Richard opened the door to Alix's room and followed her in. Maud was staying with Joanna this evening, so Alix had the room to herself.

He walked to the table and lifted the flagon of wine. "You were quieter than usual at dinner tonight. Is something troubling you?"

She sank into a chair and took the full cup that Richard handed to her. *Yes!* she wanted to scream. She swallowed the word with a gulp of spiced wine. "No, I'm fine."

"I know you're worried about Philippe, but as I told you, you have nothing to fear. I'll always protect you."

She'd give anything to only have to worry about Philippe.

Richard shoved his chair back and walked toward her. The candle flames wavered as his movements stirred the air. "The past few nights, all I could think about was holding you in my arms."

"Is that all you want to do?"

"Oh no, I have other plans as well." He pulled her to her feet.

Richard cupped her face in his hands, his thumbs stroking her neck. The mere touch raised the hair on her skin, sending shivers cascading through her. His light kisses became more demanding as their tongues tangled together. He twined his hands in her hair as he crushed his lips against hers. Heat flooded her belly and raced through her veins.

"Jesu, Love, will I ever stop wanting and needing you?" he gasped.

An ache seized her heart. This could be the last time she would ever be with him intimately. She wanted to imprint every moment, every look, every sensation.

"Tonight is my night." She stood on tiptoe and nipped his lower lip with her teeth. "I get to do whatever I want to you."

"I'm yours, as always," he exhaled.

She gripped the bottom of his tunic, pulled it off, and tossed it aside. Alix skimmed her hands over his stomach down to his chausses and braies, unknotting the ties. She pushed them down inch by inch until they slipped to the floor. Shadows thrown from the candles danced over his chest, highlighting the muscles and hard planes. Time stilled as she gazed at him. Jesus Christ, he was gorgeous, and for now, all hers.

"Are you going to simply stand there?" he murmured.

Alix gave a small laugh, put her hands on his hips, and pulled him close. The heat radiating from his skin washed over her and she melded into him. She pressed her lips to his neck, kissing the vein that pulsed wildly. His head fell back, and she gently sucked the sensitive skin below his ear, then exhaled, causing goosebumps to erupt.

Shiny scars snaked across his torso, and she traced them with her finger. A pang gripped her heart as it always did when confronted with them. In every battle he put his life in danger. One inch to either side and his wound could have been mortal. She trailed her hands lower, his stomach muscles shivering under her touch. Richard gasped. It amazed her that after all these years, she could affect him like this, and he, her. Simply touching him and imagining what would happen next sent tendrils of desire twisting through her veins.

Richard put his arms around her, feeling for her laces.

Alix allowed him to untie them, then stepped back. "What did I tell you? Tonight, you're mine."

Her fingers trembled as she reached behind her back and loosened the ties. The garment slipped off her shoulders to her waist. She slowly pulled it down until it puddled around her feet. Richard stared at her, his blue-gray eyes dark with desire. Alix entwined her fingers with his and led him to the bed covered with linen sheets and wool blankets. He lay down, his gaze fixed upon her. She curled up next to him, tracing the shape of his lips with her tongue before kissing him. He claimed her mouth again, conquering her senses. She inhaled spiced wine, soap, and the scent that was uniquely him.

Richard caressed her breast. She swatted his hand, smiling at the frustration that flashed across his face.

"You'll get your chance . . . later."

She kissed the hollow in his throat, then shifted position as she inched lower, trailing her lips down his chest. His heart pounded under her touch. Moving lower to his stomach, she flicked her tongue over his heated skin.

Richard sucked in his breath as Alix caressed his thigh, her light touches moving upward. She wrapped her fingers around him and swirled her tongue over the tip. His muscles tightened as she gripped him tighter and slid her lips down his length.

His hands clenched on the bedsheets. "Don't take too long," he gasped. "Even I have my limits."

She grazed him with her teeth as she lifted her head. "Hmm, shall I test them?"

Alix stroked him faster and tightened her lips around him, increasing the pressure. His ragged breathing turned to groans. He was on the edge of release. As his pleasure grew, her own desire crescendoed through her.

"Minx," he growled.

A squeal escaped her lips when he sat up and pushed her back onto the bed.

"You found my limit. Now where's yours?" His eyes smoldered with lust.

Richard captured her breast in his mouth, sucked, then lightly bit her peaked nipple. Heat coursed through her. He kissed her stomach, his tongue carving molten trails as he inched downward. An ache grew between her legs. She grabbed his hand and tried to move it lower.

Richard caught her wrists in one hand, held them over her head and pinned her legs with his muscular thigh. "Oh no, Love, you had your turn. Now it's mine."

He twirled his fingers over her throbbing core, then pushed one deep inside her. She whimpered and arched her back. He released her wrists and shifted position to kiss her inner thigh, moving closer to the sensitive area that ached for more. Desperate need overwhelmed her as he traced her nether lips with his finger. Richard tasted her and a moan escaped her throat. Alix grabbed his shoulder, her shaking fingers digging into his skin. Waves of pleasure roiled from her belly, growing as they threatened to consume her.

Richard parted her legs and settled between them. He slowly inched into her, then thrust deeply. Alix's cries echoed in the room as he moved faster, taking her once again to the edge. All thought fractured as raw pleasure seized her. Fireworks burst behind her eyes. Her legs clenched around him, her body shuddering in release. Richard stiffened, then collapsed, his harsh breathing loud in her ear.

"I love you." Through shortened breaths, the words flowed from her lips. "Always and forever."

"You're the only woman I will ever give my heart to."

She held him as their racing hearts slowed. No other man had ever brought her to the frenzied brink and sent her careening into ecstasy like he did. He kissed her, then rolled to his back and pulled her close. She nestled into him, wishing she had the power of Chronos to stop time and stay locked in this moment forever.

*~*~*

Alix turned over to escape the bright sun that streamed into the room. Cool air on her bare back reminded her of the night she and Richard had shared. She stretched out her arm, seeking his warmth, but found only empty space. She propped herself on her elbow and smiled at Richard, who lounged in a chair at the table eating a slice of bread.

"After last night I thought we were in need of sustenance. At least I was."

"I'm starving, but can you hand me my dress first?"

"I prefer you as you are now, but food takes precedence. For the moment," he teased and tossed her the dress.

"When was breakfast served? I didn't hear anyone come in."

"I ordered a servant to bring it earlier."

Once clothed, she padded to the table. Her stomach growled as she inhaled the aroma of fresh bread and cheese. Richard handed her a knife to cut the loaf. She sawed a thick slice, then bent over to cut a slab of cheese.

"I have some news. Philippe made good on his word to leave. He sailed for Acre this morning."

Alix laughed. "I imagine he still hasn't come to terms with losing the Vexin."

"Apparently not. I also received word that my mother is arriving this afternoon."

The knife fell from Alix's nerveless fingers and clattered on the table. Coldness washed over her, and the room spun out of focus. "She arrives today?"

Richard grinned. "Joanna doesn't know yet. I thought I'd surprise her."

Alix sagged into a chair, her thoughts scattering like marbles spilled on the floor. Historically, Eleanor had stayed a mere four days in Messina before returning home. She had to convince Eleanor to allow her to travel with her. As a cover for her disappearance, she could claim she wished to visit her family, and then use the brooch to return to her own time.

"It's for the best that Philippe left," Richard mused. "I can't predict what my mother would do if they crossed paths."

"I'm certain she'd have choice words for him." Alix focused on her bread. "I know you're going to monopolize your mother, but I hope to be able to speak with her in the coming days. I need to discuss returning to France."

Richard stilled, his goblet halfway to his lips. "I don't recall having that conversation."

"We both knew this was coming. Traveling with you to Sicily is one thing, but continuing to Acre, quite another. I can't stay. Not with your fiancée here. I need to go home."

"Your leaving is out of the question."

"You're going to marry. We can't be together anymore."

His eyes hardened. "You knew I was to be married. God's bones, you even supported it. I don't find this amusing, Alix." He shoved his chair back. It teetered on its back legs before settling on the stone floor.

Alix slammed her palm on the table, a stinging contact. "You never take my feelings into account."

"Your feelings? Not five hours ago, you said you loved me. Has that changed?"

"No, of course not. But everything else will."

As he stalked past her, she jumped up and grabbed at his sleeve. He didn't pause, didn't stop, and the fabric slipped through her fingers.

"I've done what was asked of me. Eleanor will be able to see for herself that Joanna is fine. Let me go back to France, I beg of you."

"You'll stay with me. I refuse to hear any more on this topic."

"Richard . . ."

The door slammed behind him, and she glared at the empty space before her. Richard knew how she felt about adultery, but she also knew that his views were at odds with hers. He didn't like the fact that his father had been unfaithful to his mother, but accepted it. He would think nothing of having his own mistress. He was stubborn and strong-willed, but so was she.

*~*~*

Richard strode into the dining hall and was immediately accosted by Joanna.

"Why didn't you tell me Mother is coming today? I had to hear it from André." She glared at him. "I'd like to go with you to meet her, but there's so much to do to ready for her arrival."

"I'd hoped to surprise you," he ground out.

She raised her brow. "I thought you'd be happier than this."

His jaw worked. "Not now, Joanna."

André appeared behind him. "We should leave soon. After Philippe's meddling, your mother is likely chafing at the bit to be on solid ground."

Richard nodded, glad to escape Joanna's inquisition.

Once they reached the courtyard, a groom brought Richard his horse and scuttled away. He waited until his men were mounted, then rode out ahead. Hoofbeats grew louder as a horse cantered up beside him.

"Jesu, I hope your mood improves or your fiancée might have second thoughts about this marriage." André's light tone faded. "What's going on? Have you received bad news?"

"No, nothing like that." Richard's grip tightened on the reins.

He knew Alix couldn't forgive her father for being unfaithful, but he hadn't considered that her views would extend to him. Or if he was being honest, he hadn't wanted to.

"It's Alix. She's being unreasonable." His horse shied and he passed a soothing hand down the steed's neck.

André raised a brow. "How do you mean?"

"She refuses to stay. She's asked to return to France with my mother."

"If Alix didn't intend to remain with you, why did she travel with us?" He glanced at Richard and sighed. "She wanted to stay behind, but you didn't give her a choice. If she's set upon leaving, let her go. Soon you'll have a wife you need to focus your attention on."

Richard's chest constricted. Being the king, no one would condemn him for taking a mistress, but Alix's views on adultery were carved in stone. As much as he hated to accept it, André was correct. He should allow her to return, but the thought of her leaving him cut into his soul.

He was saved from answering as they wound their way through throngs of townspeople that crowded the harbor, eager to catch a glimpse of the passengers as the large galley docked. He dismounted and handed the reins to Jacques. He smiled as his mother appeared on deck. Her auburn hair had silver woven through it, but at sixty-eight years old, her movements were as quick as a woman half her age.

He strode up the gangplank. "Mother, I hope the journey wasn't too taxing?" He kissed her on her cheek.

"It was pleasant enough, except for our unplanned detour. I hope you'll enlighten me as to what the reason was."

His lips twisted. "I will, but that's best saved for a later time."

A movement behind her caught his eye. A slight, dark-haired young woman approached, followed by three older duennas.

Richard walked to her and bent over her hand. "I'm not sure if you recall, but I met you many years ago, when I visited your brother. It's good to see you again."

Berenguela's eyes widened. "Certainly, I remember. You were quite kind to me."

He smiled at her. The one time they'd met, she'd been about fourteen and had seemed a bit in awe of him. He'd included her in conversations with her brother, but saw her as nothing more than Sancho's little sister. Now, as a young lady, she appeared poised and confident. Hopefully, she'd make a good queen.

"I brought carts and extra horses for the journey to the castle. Which do you prefer?"

She turned to the women, and they launched into a spate of unfamiliar words. "My ladies will take the cart, but I would like to ride," she responded in perfect, although accented, French.

Richard motioned to the grooms to bring the horses, then helped his mother and Berenguela mount. He instructed Jacques to make sure all their belongings were stowed in the carts, then swung lithely onto his horse and fell in beside Eleanor. The clamor of the townspeople as they crowded them made conversation and navigation difficult until they left the busy square.

"Joanna's at the castle, is she not?" Eleanor smiled as Richard nodded. "I'm looking forward to seeing her." She took a deep breath. "Tell me the truth . . . she wasn't ill-treated, was she?"

"She said she was treated with respect, but she takes after you and keeps things to herself. If anyone should know, it's Alix. They've grown quite close in the past few weeks."

Eleanor cocked her brow. "Alixandra? She's staying there as well?"

"I thought it was safer for her in light of the differences the armies have had with the townspeople." He was reluctant to tell his mother that Alix had been attacked, in case it swayed her decision to escort Alix home.

"Your Grace, is that where we are going?" Berenguela pointed to a castle perched on a hill.

"Yes. It shouldn't take too much longer. Since we're to be married, you can call me Richard." He smiled at her.

Her cheeks flushed. "The town looks interesting. Might we be able to visit it again?"

"Tell me when you wish to go, and I'll provide an escort."

His mother cleared her throat and gave a minute headshake.

"I would be happy to accompany you myself," he amended.

An hour later, they rode into the courtyard. While they were dismounting, Joanna ran out.

"Mother! At last, you're here."

Eleanor enfolded her daughter in her arms, then stood back. "You've grown up. You're not the little girl I remember. We have much to talk about, but I do need to speak with your brother about certain things first."

"I understand." Joanna spun around. "You can't keep her all to yourself, Richard."

He laughed. "You'll have plenty of time to visit, but let me introduce Berenguela."

"It's nice to meet you." Joanna smiled at the younger woman. "Please come with me. I'm sure you and your ladies would like to unpack and relax before dinner."

Once the ladies left, Eleanor tuned to Richard. "Aren't you the least bit curious about your soon-to-be bride?"

"She seems pleasant, unless that's merely a pretense."

"Oh, she's quite agreeable and, I believe, will make a dutiful wife." Eleanor took Richard's arm as they made their way to the castle. "You told Philippe you weren't marrying his sister, did you not?"

"Yes, we had that conversation."

"How did he accept it?"

He shrugged. "Surprisingly well, considering I told him I couldn't possibly marry a woman who'd had relations with my father."

Eleanor's lip curled. "I never believed that slanderous nonsense. Henry was many things, but stupid wasn't one of them. He'd never have taken her to bed, not when there were other women with no political ties. Someone took a risk in spreading that rumor. If Philippe ever found out who it was—"

"Well, it benefitted me, so I'm grateful to whomever was behind it," Richard interrupted. "I do have things to discuss with you, but allow me to show you to your rooms so you can rest before supper."

"Is Alixandra joining us tonight?"

Richard knit his brow. "I'm not sure if that's a good idea."

Eleanor laid her hand on his arm. "She'll meet your fiancée eventually. Sometimes the best-kept secret is one that's not hidden away."

*~*~*

The dining hall seemed cavernous, and Alix felt as if everyone's gaze was focused on her. She gripped her hands and forced deep breaths into lungs that seemed to shrink with each step she took as she walked up to the dais. Joanna turned and smiled as she approached. She took Alix's arm and led her to where Eleanor stood with Richard and a young woman.

Alix focused on Eleanor, not prepared to meet Richard's fiancée. "Your Grace," Alix murmured as she curtsied.

"Alixandra, it's lovely to see you."

"I trust you had a good journey?"

Eleanor nodded. "The majority of the time we had pleasant weather, but mountain passes in the winter can be treacherous. Fortunately, we came through unscathed." She turned to Berenguela. "I'd like to present Alixandra, a kinswoman of mine."

Alix's mouth dropped, and she clamped her jaw shut. Of course, Eleanor would have to explain her presence here, and being a relative would solve that. She'd told so many lies about her background, so what was one more?

She curtsied, then forced her eyes up. Richard's fiancée was petite and attractive, with waist-length mahogany hair and olive skin. Warmth shone from her dark eyes. She had expected dislike and even jealousy of this woman to engulf her. Instead, numbness spread through her body. From this moment on, everything would change.

Berenguela smiled at her. "I'm pleased to meet you. Joanna has told me about you. You're a cousin, is that correct?"

She glanced at Eleanor, who gave a small nod. "Yes, I am."

Once Eleanor sat down, Joanna took her place and motioned for Alix to sit next to her.

"I realize you've just met her, but what do you think?" Joanna whispered. "She's much younger than I thought she'd be."

"She speaks French very well, so she must be well-educated."

Joanna frowned. "You know that's not what I meant. I wonder if they will have a good marriage."

Alix shrugged. "That remains to be seen."

She reached for her cup and took a gulp. She risked a look down the table. Richard nodded at something Berenguela said, and then his eyes met Alix's. He held her gaze for several seconds before Alix forced herself to look away. Was this what their relationship would disintegrate into in the next few days . . . stolen looks from afar and creating reasons to be in the same vicinity as him, so she would have her memories when she left?

Alix pushed the chicken through the thick, fragrant sauce with the sharp point of her knife but couldn't swallow a morsel. The cooks had prepared a feast for Eleanor, but the food held as much appeal as sawdust. At last, dinner was over and the sanctuary of her room beckoned her. She curtsied as Eleanor, Joanna, and Berenguela walked past. Her throat tightened as Richard paused in front of her.

"Now is not the time, but there are things you and I need to discuss. Don't avoid me, Love." He gave her a steely look, then followed Eleanor.

Alix's heart plummeted. That was a discussion she wasn't looking forward to.

# ~ *Chapter 19* ~

ALIX STROLLED INTO THE GARDEN and wandered along the path until she found a bench near an olive tree. She raised her face to let the sun's warmth wash over her. Richard had escorted Joanna and Berenguela into town, so she'd taken the opportunity to venture out of her room. Up to now, she'd avoided the conversation that they'd have to have, and was more than willing to put it off for as long as possible.

"The garden is lovely this time of year. Don't you agree, Alixandra?"

Alix started and opened her eyes. She jumped up to curtsy to Eleanor, then retook her seat on the bench after Eleanor motioned to her to do so.

"I spend as much time here as I can, Your Grace." She smiled. "Are you going to stay awhile? I'm sure you and Joanna have much to talk about."

Eleanor shook her head and sat next to her. "I must return soon. I dare not leave Richard's kingdom for too long. There are too many nobles who would take advantage of his absence. Which brings us to the topic I'm sure you want to address. You wish to return home." She folded her hands on her lap.

"Yes, Your Grace. I've done what you asked, and as you can see, your daughter wasn't mistreated. Now that Princess Berenguela has arrived, I'm sure my presence won't be required."

Alix's nerves jangled as Eleanor remained silent. She needed to return to her own time. Her life in Austin might consist of a series of "if only things were different" and "what might have been," but then so many people's lives did. The thought of Richard marrying pierced her heart.

The fear of altering history again was another concern. Events had already changed with her accompanying Richard this far. She couldn't risk it by traveling to the Holy Land. Also, watching Joanna's interactions with her mother made Alix yearn for her own family. She needed to go home.

"Very well. I plan to leave in a couple of days, which should give you time to finalize things. Your decision won't be accepted easily. Joanna told me she has grown quite fond of you."

"I value her friendship as well. Perhaps one day our paths will cross again."

Eleanor raised her brow. "Have you told Richard yet?"

A breeze rustled the leaves, and Alix brushed strands of hair from her eyes. "I tried, but he wasn't willing to listen."

"Imagine that." Eleanor gave a soft laugh. "I understand your desire to leave. I hope this is what you truly want and not a choice you think you're expected to make."

"This is for the best."

Eleanor stood. "We shall see." She nodded to Alix, then left.

She had the answer she'd wanted. Once she was back in Austin, she could move forward with her life. This was the right decision. It had to be.

She sat, lost in thought until thunder rumbled in the distance, and dark clouds scudded across the sky to blot out the sun. Fallen leaves swirled in a chaotic dance as the rain-scented breeze picked up. Alix lifted her skirt and ran, reaching the castle seconds before the heavens opened. She finger-combed her windblown hair and waited for her eyes to adjust to the gloomy darkness of the hall.

Her footsteps echoed on the stone floor as she walked to her room. Jagged lightning illuminated the corridor and the imposing figure of Richard waiting outside the door. Her heart dropped.

"This storm was unexpected. I see you made it back before it broke." Alix smoothed her skirt. "Did Berenguela enjoy visiting the town? I'm sure it's more exotic than what she's used to." She was stalling for time, and Richard's crossed arms and drawn brows showed he was aware of it too.

He motioned toward the door. "After you."

"Maybe we could talk elsewhere? It probably isn't wise for you to be in my room, especially now."

"Alix, I'm tiring of this game." His voice was soft, an indication that he was close to losing his temper.

She turned the handle with shaky fingers and crossed the small room to stand by the window, putting distance between them. Her stomach was in knots by the time he entered and shut the door behind him.

"I spoke with your mother, and we're in agreement that I will return to France with her." The words solidified her decision.

"What if I disagree?" His lips twisted. "I was in hell the last time you left. This time won't be any different."

"I can't stay. It would be torture seeing you and not being able to be with you." She held up her hand to stop his next words. "I've told you how much my father's infidelity hurt my mother. You've seen it firsthand between your own parents. I refuse to be the cause of that pain to anyone."

Richard raked his hand through his hair. "I know your views on this matter, and I respect them." He crossed his arms. "But do my feelings count for naught? You've done what I thought was impossible—captured my heart."

Her soul soared at his words, but she steeled her resolve. "I love you, too, but I won't change my mind."

"This is a political marriage only, Alix. God's bones, you know that."

"I do, but it's still a marriage. I refuse to stay for . . ."

All expression faded from his face. "For me? Is that what you were going to say?"

"No! I fear that if I were forced to go on the crusade, I would resent the situation and everyone involved. I couldn't bear to feel that way about you." She gripped her hands until they reddened.

"I would never force you to do anything against your will."

"I know that." Her throat thickened. "This is one of the hardest choices I've ever had to make, but it's the right one."

His eyes turned to ice. "So be it." His tone was flat. He spun on his heel and left.

Those three words cemented the end of their relationship. Hot tears pricked her eyes and slid down her cheeks. Her heart exploded into shards of glass that ripped into her soul. She pressed her hand against her lips to stifle the sobs that tore through her. She was prepared for heartache, but this was a dagger twisting inside her. The last time she left hadn't been of her own accord, but she'd had a reason to return. This time was final. There was no coming back.

*~*~*

A knock echoed on the door, but Alix lay on her bed and remained silent, hoping that whoever was outside would leave.

"Alix, it's Joanna." A muffled voice filtered through the wooden door. She paused, then continued, "I saw Richard earlier, and I thought you might like some company."

Joanna deserved a response. "Thank you, but I'll be fine."

"I know this can't be easy for you. I'm an excellent listener if you wish to talk."

All Alix wanted was to be left alone, but she couldn't ignore Joanna. She unwound herself from the fetal position, swiped the remains of tears from her eyes, and went to open the door. "I must look a mess. I'm sorry."

"You have nothing to apologize for. Richard feels the same, although he shows it differently. I've seen thunderclouds more cheerful."

Joanna took Alix's arm and led her to the bed. "I'm sorry you ended your relationship with Richard. I know it wasn't easy." She gave a tight smile. "Mother told me that you'll return to France with her. Might you change your mind? I have misgivings about traveling to the Holy Land."

Alix's stomach clenched and her nerves prickled with rising panic. Was her chance to return to her own time in jeopardy?

"Berenguela has been entrusted to my care. Richard will do everything in his power to protect us, but there will be times when he'll be absent." Joanna gripped Alix's hand. "The tales I've heard terrify me. I value your wisdom and courage and would feel more comfortable if you came with us."

Alix's brows drew together. "I can't do that. Seeing Richard with his wife would be a reminder of what I've lost." Why would Joanna even want her to travel with them? This was her chance to allow Alix to return to France and not complicate Richard's marriage.

Joanna released Alix's hand and walked to the window. "When Tancred stormed the palace, my ladies and I were caught unaware. We hid in my bedchamber, praying we wouldn't be found. Four soldiers burst into the room."

Her voice was so low that Alix strained to hear it.

She turned around, her arms wrapped protectively around her. "A man grabbed one of my ladies and dragged her to the door. I tried to stop him. He struck me and pushed me down." Her face blanched. "He took her outside, then I heard her screams. I couldn't protect her. I couldn't protect any of us." Tears seeped from under her lashes. "I've never felt so powerless. I've been too ashamed to tell anyone this, not even my mother. She didn't raise me to be helpless."

Empathy rushed through Alix. "It wasn't your fault. They were soldiers. I'd be terrified too."

Joanna walked to the bed and sank down beside Alix. "But you had the courage to fight your attacker. I cowered on the floor until Tancred found us. You have skills that I don't. If we're attacked, I can't defend us, but you can."

Alix shook her head. "Joanna, I'm no match for an armed man. What happened in Messina is proof of that."

"I know you stood up to him, which is more than I did." She gave a watery smile and rose to her feet. "Please reconsider. I'd feel much safer with you with us."

The door closed behind her with a thud. Her final words reverberated through the room and sank like stones into Alix's soul. Blood pounded in her ears. Once again, she felt like a ship set adrift in a vast, uncharted sea, prey to other's decisions.

This was the perfect opportunity to return home. With Richard traveling to Outremer and marrying en route, her disappearance wouldn't be questioned.

Alix drew her knees up and rested her chin on them as despondence washed over her. Although Eleanor was willing to allow her to return to France, Joanna's plea tugged at her heart.

She understood the feeling of being vulnerable and defenseless all too well, but Joanna had an additional issue to overcome. She was a queen and used to deferential treatment. The man's callous attitude toward her and ladies had robbed her of her dignity and the sense of safety that came with being royal. Historically, the journey to the Holy Land had been fraught with danger.

Was Joanna strong enough to endure that?

*~*~*

Richard took a seat at the table in his mother's chambers, glad the room faced away from the bright midmorning sun. A servant approached with a flagon of wine, and he waved him off.

"You look the worst for wear." Eleanor's gaze sharpened as she joined him. "I assume you spoke with Alix concerning her return home?"

He gave a curt nod and winced as his head pounded from the movement. He rarely over imbibed, but last night, he'd dwelled on the conversation with Alix until frustration had erupted into anger. The aftereffects of too much wine and too little sleep had done nothing for his frame of mind or his physical health.

"You'll have a wife soon enough, so perhaps it's for the best your attention isn't focused on someone else."

Richard clenched his jaw and bit back the retort that threatened to burst from his lips. "I know where my duties lie, Mother."

Her eyes softened. "She'll arrive home safely."

"I appreciate that. I wish you could stay longer, but leaving the reins of my kingdom in John's hands worries me. I'll feel much better knowing you're overseeing it."

"I as well. When I reach Rome, I'll make sure that Geoffrey is consecrated archbishop of York, per your request."

He raised a brow. "To think I have more to fear from my half brother than John. This position will ensure that he has no chance of taking my kingdom."

"What plans do you have for Sicily once you leave?" Eleanor rested her arms on the table. "Joanna is a widow with no children. William left his kingdom to his aunt, Constance, in the event he died without an heir. Her husband is German, and the Sicilians don't want a German ruler. Can you trust Tancred to be a just king?"

Richard crossed his arms and leaned back in his chair. "I've met with him, and we've settled on agreeable terms. I've received Joanna's dower in full, which benefits me more than the arranged marriage between my named heir, Arthur, and Tancred's daughter. Philippe and I agreed to acknowledge Tancred as king of Sicily." He raised a hand to stop her expected protest. "I know this goes against William's will, but the people trust Tancred, and he is an honorable man who keeps his word. Unlike certain individuals."

Eleanor's lips tightened. "I assume you're referring to Philippe. He's proven to be quite duplicitous. I don't like the fact that you're going to need his aid in the Holy Land, but I'd rather he be there than scheming against you in France."

"You have the right of that." Richard gave a reluctant smile. "All you need to do is make sure John doesn't decide to meddle in politics. I wish to return to my kingdom as I left it."

*~*~*

Alix took her dresses out of her trunk and laid them on the bed until she found her pouch buried beneath them. She untied the laces and tumbled the contents onto the bed. The two pieces of jewelry that had changed her world—the brooch and the ruby pendant with an *R* and an *A* intricately entwined—glinted in the sun that spilled through the window.

Alix picked up the former item and smoothed her thumb over the delicate engraving of a knight riding a steed. This was her way home, but the desire to witness Richard's crusade for herself intensified. Traveling with him would give her the advantage of being privy to his decisions and thought processes. What if she discovered something that the chroniclers didn't know?

Their relationship was over, but was she really ready to leave this life—and Richard—behind forever? She could always use the brooch and return home later, at a time of her choosing, although it might create questions for those she left behind.

The door creaked open, and she dropped the brooch and pendant into the pouch.

"You're packing. Are we going home?" Maud asked in a tight voice.

"That was *my* original plan, but Queen Joanna can be very persuasive." Alix gave a half smile.

"You can't refuse a royal request." Maud walked to the window and looked out into the garden. Dust motes illuminated by the sun hovered around her like golden fairy dust. "What will become of me? Will I return to France? I miss Poitiers, but I enjoy traveling and seeing new places." Her voice was wistful.

Protectiveness flooded through Alix. She'd taken Maud from a place of familiarity to one that was unknown. If Maud returned, would she still have a position at the palace, or would Eleanor carry through with her plan to find a husband for her? Alix wouldn't leave her to fend for herself.

"I know you want to see the Holy Land. I can speak with Queen Joanna. Perhaps she has need of another lady's maid in her household."

Maud's face lit up. "Would you? I dread returning to France, not knowing what will happen to me. There are also certain people here I'll miss." Her cheeks flushed and she ducked her head.

Alix walked to her trunk and replaced the pouch under her clothes. "I know you have feelings for Jacques. And from the way he looks at you, I daresay he feels the same."

"I hope so. I do care for him." She bit her lip. "What about the king? What will happen between the two of you once he marries?"

A pang gripped Alix's heart. "What we have is over, but I hope we can remain on civil terms."

That was an understatement. She'd been prepared to leave Richard in the past and try to move on with her life. But now that Joanna had asked her to consider traveling with them, would civility even be possible?

## ~ *Chapter 20* ~

GALLEYS AND THE LARGER SHIPS called busses dotted the sparkling azure sea as far as Alix could see. Richard and his men had spent the last several weeks readying them to depart. He'd dismantled his siege engines and stored them in sections on his galleys. Townspeople crowded the shore, jostling each other for an advantageous position to watch as Richard's war horses were loaded onto transport ships.

Alix rode in one cart with Joanna and Berenguela while the queens' ladies, Maud, and Elisabetta, the laundress who had befriended Alix, traveled in another with their belongings. Knights rode beside them to keep the crowd from pressing too close as they inched their way toward the ships. Richard stood near the gangplank but strode toward them as they approached.

He smiled at Joanna as he helped her out, then assisted Berenguela. The last thing Alix wanted was help from Richard, but in her skirts, it was too difficult to clamber out on her own. His face was unreadable as she took his hand and tried to ignore the electricity that shot through her at his touch. Once on the ground, she gave him a small nod, then walked to where Joanna waited.

Alix curtsied. "Thank you again for allowing Maud to be one of your ladies. I was worried about what would happen to her if she returned to France."

"I've grown quite fond of her, and I would miss her, and you, if you'd decided to leave. I'm glad you changed your mind. It's inconvenient that two of Berenguela's attendants left with my mother, but they are older, and it will be a difficult trip. I believe Elisabetta is an excellent choice in their absence. She has a sensible air about her."

Joanna leaned closer and dropped her voice. "Berenguela is nervous about traveling to Outremer, not to mention marrying Richard. It's understandable.

She's young and has had a sheltered upbringing. We both know my brother isn't the easiest person to get along with. I think she's a bit in awe of him."

Alix chuckled. "He can be intimidating. But so far, he's been the perfect gentleman."

"You English do say the strangest things, but you're correct. He's being very chivalrous."

"Joanna, I want you to know that traveling to Outremer doesn't change anything between Richard and me. Our relationship is over. I won't do anything to come between Richard and his wife."

"I'm glad to hear that." She glanced at Richard, who had his arm around Berenguela's shoulder as he escorted her onto the ship. "I hope they find happiness together."

Alix rubbed her arms as a cool breeze swept in from the sea. "As do I, Your Grace."

Rob walked over, trailed by Maud and Elisabetta, and motioned for them to follow Richard and his fiancée up the gangplank.

The buss swarmed with activity. Servants carried coffers filled with coins and jewels. Barrels of water, wine, dried beans, and salted meat went to storage areas below deck. Knights kept watch on the crowd as the carts were emptied. Rob led them to the center of the deck, where Richard stood in front of a large tent.

Servants had placed cots near the walls with space for their trunks at the foot of them. A small table with several chairs was in the center. Lanterns hung from the ceiling provided the only illumination.

Joanna glanced at Richard. "I wish you were traveling with us. I'd feel safer with you close by."

"We'll only be half a day behind you. The galleys can travel more quickly, so I'm certain we'll catch up. I've entrusted your care to Rob, so direct any concerns to him." Richard tilted his head toward Rob.

Sailors pushed past as they readied the ship for departure. Alix turned to Maud and Elisabetta. "Let's get settled. Berenguela has chosen the far end, so closer to the entrance would suit me."

Elisabetta nodded. "It will get warm in here. Sleeping next to the open tent fly will be more pleasant." She planted her hands on her ample hips. "To think, yesterday, I was cooking and washing clothes for soldiers, and today, I'm attending to two queens. I don't know what made you think of asking me, but I'm much obliged."

Alix smiled. "You were the first person to befriend me. I've never forgotten your kindness to Maud and me."

As her relationship with Richard progressed over the years, his circle of friends and hers accepted it. Once he became king, there was more talk and whispers from outsiders, but she hadn't felt as much contempt aimed at her until this journey. It had bothered her more than she'd let on, but Elisabetta's friendship had made it easier to handle.

After their trunks were stowed, they exited the tent, followed by Joanna and Berenguela. Richard stood at the helm, conversing with a tall, barrel-chested man with tanned, weathered skin. He turned at their approach.

"This is Roger, the captain of this ship. In his hands, you'll be safe."

Roger bowed to the queens. "It's my pleasure. I've been sailing since I was a lad, so you've nothing to fear. Excuse me, but I need to finish preparations. We're leaving soon."

"I know you're apprehensive, little sister, but I've assigned many of my knights and servants to travel with you, so there's nothing to fear. Now I must go, but I'll see you when we reach Crete."

Richard enfolded Joanna in his arms, then drew Berenguela close and kissed her on the cheek.

Her cheeks reddened. "Which ship is yours, Richard?"

Alix's heart tightened as he draped his arm across his fiancée's shoulders and led her to the gunwale.

He pointed to a line of sleek, brightly painted warships bedecked with his standards that waved from the mastheads. "The first one is mine. Now, I must leave so you can depart." He smiled at her again, then shifted his gaze to Alix.

"Alixandra," he said with all the warmth of a glacier.

She inclined her head, hiding her hurt at his formality behind a fall of hair. "Take care, Your Grace."

*~*~*

After days of calm seas, light breezes, and blue skies, bruised clouds gathered on the horizon, dragging the tempest behind them. Sheets of icy rain heralded the storm's arrival. Salt spray stung Richard's eyes as the wind whipped the ferocious waves into a frenzy. His knuckles whitened on the gunwale as he was pummeled by the wind. The rowers had long since abandoned their efforts, since steering was impossible, and had taken shelter in the tent.

Jacques had stood with him as the sky darkened, but as the storm grew in strength, fear etched into his face.

"Your Grace, will we sink?" His question was almost lost in a crash of thunder.

The thought had occurred to Richard multiple times. "We'll make it," he said with forced confidence. "We've been through the worst of the storm and remained intact. Go back to the tent."

The boy turned to leave, then screamed as the ship dropped into a trough. After what seemed like eons, it struggled back up. Richard wrapped his arm around Jacques as a wall of water crashed over them. His heart froze until the ship righted itself. Lightning illuminated the darkness for mere seconds, but it was enough to show ships scattered across the expanse of water.

"Jesu," Richard breathed. Although he wasn't particularly religious, he crossed himself, praying Joanna and Alix's ship was intact and they were still alive. Jacques clung to him, his body shaking.

"Are you all right, lad?"

Jacques nodded, but remained attached to Richard's side.

Richard's stomach plummeted each time the ship floundered in the waves, but still, he refused to leave the deck. He needed to lead his men by example, not give in to the fear coursing through his veins. Hours crept by as the helpless ship groaned and pitched at the mercy of the elements. At last, the torrential rain and wind stopped, and the sea quieted.

"Is it over?" Jacques's voice trembled.

Richard gripped the boy's shoulder. "It's over. Never have I been so relieved to see the end of a storm."

"What about the others?"

Trepidation swept down Richard's spine. "We must hope for the best. Come, let's light the lantern. Any ships within distance should see it."

The sailors recovered first since they were used to treacherous waters, but Richard's soldiers were battling the effects of seasickness and how close to death they'd come.

Richard entered the tent, and Georges managed a weak grin as he slumped on his cot.

"Sire, you look worse than I feel. I was convinced we were going to meet our maker before we reached Acre."

Richard raked his hand through his wet hair. "I've never minded journeying by sea, but I'd give anything for solid ground beneath my feet."

"You have the right of that. I don't think I can stomach food or drink for a week."

Exhaustion hit Richard, and he staggered to his bed and collapsed onto his soaked cot. The tent was constructed to withstand light rain but not hours of constant deluge. He closed his eyes, thankful the pitching of the ship had stopped, but sleep eluded him. How many galleys had they lost? They'd been unable to catch up to his sister's ship before the storm hit. What if they hadn't survived? Had he traveled to Sicily to rescue Joanna, only to lose her?

Dread snaked through his heart. What of Alix? Joanna had been instrumental in changing her mind about traveling with them, but he'd done nothing to dissuade her. If he'd sealed her fate, guilt would torment him for the rest of his life.

Somehow, he managed a couple of hours of sleep and woke to find the winds had remained calm, and the rowers were able to steer the ship to their rendezvous destination. Richard sat at the table in the tent, bent over maps of Crete and Rhodes, but spun around as Georges entered. He'd sent scouts to search for his missing ships, but the longer they took to return with news, the more intolerable the waiting became.

"What island is this?" Georges looked at the steep, forbidding mountains thrown into relief by the setting sun.

"I'm told it's Crete. We'll stay here a couple of days to wait for any stragglers. I've sent rowers to count the ships that managed to keep up and see if any need repairs."

Georges laughed. "I don't mind. If the next half of the journey is anything like the first, I might be tempted to stay here."

Richard chuckled, then returned his attention to the maps. "I don't wish to sail too far ahead. This is the route the captain suggested we take." He traced his finger north, then east of Crete. "We'll travel to Rhodes, which will give the rest of the fleet time to catch up. If any ships are missing, we'll search for them."

"Your Grace," Jacques called out as he rushed into the tent. "One of the scouts you sent has returned."

Richard jumped to his feet. "Send him in."

The man entered and bowed.

"What news have you?"

"Sire, twenty-five of our ships are lost."

Anger rushed through Richard's body. These men were under his protection, and he'd failed them. The man's gaze flicked away, and Richard's chest constricted.

"What haven't you told me?" Richard ground out.

"There's been no sight of the buss carrying your sister and fiancée."

*~*~*

Alix's stomach heaved as the ship tossed to and fro. The lanterns had been extinguished as protection from fire, save one fragile candle which Maud guarded. Jagged lightning illuminated the tent and the terrified faces of the queens' ladies. Joanna leaned over her trundle and grabbed the privy bowl, her body convulsing as she retched.

"Elisabetta, can you wet a cloth?" Alix held Joanna's hair back. The ship pitched again, the winds whipping the cloth fabric of the tent like a billow.

Maud huddled next to Alix, her thin frame shaking. Her face was ashen and streaked with tears. "I'm scared. Will the ship go down?"

"It will be fine, dearie." Elisabetta handed the cloth to Alix, but the fear in her eyes mirrored Alix's own. "We have a good captain, and with God on our side, we won't come to harm."

Joanna retched again, then sank back on her soaked bedding.

"What can I do?" Berenguela murmured.

Alix motioned in the direction of her cot. "Can you bring me my small coffer? I have some medicine that might help."

Before they'd left, she'd had the opportunity to travel to town and found an apothecary that sold herbs. She opened and rifled through the small box until she found ginger syrup. Berenguela supported Joanna's shoulders while Alix tipped the bottle to Joanna's lips. She managed to swallow a bit and keep it down for the moment.

The ship rocked sharply to the right, and Maud shrieked. Alix clenched her eyes until it righted itself.

"*Por favor, Dios.*" Berenguela crossed herself.

The maelstrom raged for hours until Alix was certain the ship would be split in half by the waves and dragged down to a watery grave. At last, the violent tossing of the ship was replaced by gentle rocking. Hours passed until she was convinced this wasn't the calm before another round of violent storms.

She inched her way off her cot so she wouldn't wake Maud, who'd finally fallen asleep next to her, and walked out of the tent. The sun barely peeked over the horizon, but it was enough to show calm swells. Stars twinkled, then were eclipsed as clouds scudded by.

Rob stood at the front of the ship, staring at the great expanse of water. He mustered a smile as she approached, but exhaustion weighed on him like a heavy blanket. "The storm is over. We made it through."

"I had my doubts." Alix looked past him to the empty sea. Chills swept over her. They'd departed Messina in the company of several other ships. Now there was nothing except undulating waves for miles.

"Wh—where is the rest of the fleet?" Joanna asked in a weak voice.

Berenguela and Elisabetta stood on either side of her, holding her up. She stumbled to the edge of the ship, her eyes wide.

Rob knit his brows. "We must have been blown off course. Once we find land, we can determine where we are."

"The storm was terrible. What if Richard's ship didn't . . ." Berenguela's whisper tapered off.

"Don't think like that." Alix turned her head in Berenguela's direction. "I'm sure Richard is fine and waiting for us to join him."

Joanna nodded. "My brother is as protective as a mother hen with her chicks. He'll wait until the last ship is accounted for."

Rob laughed. "I doubt Richard would take too kindly being compared to a hen, but you have the right of it." He leaned close to Alix, worry still sparking in his eyes. "I'm going to speak with the captain to see if he knows where we might be."

Elisabetta helped Joanna back to the tent, but Berenguela remained with Alix.

"I've never been so far from my home. This is very unfamiliar to me," Berenguela said. "I was terrified we would perish in the storm." She gave Alix a shaky smile.

Compassion tugged at Alix's heart. Berenguela had lived a sheltered life, but now she was journeying to a foreign land and soon would be married to a man she hardly knew. She had every reason to be anxious and scared.

"The last couple of days have made me question *my* decision to come, but we survived. Once we establish where we are, we can rendezvous with the rest of the fleet."

Berenguela gave a tremulous smile. "Both you and Joanna are confident that we'll find them. I must hold to that hope as well."

"Alix! Wake up."

A hand gripped her shoulder and shook her.

"I'm awake." She rolled over and blinked in the dim light. Maud hovered over her, a huge grin on her face.

"Hurry, you must come and see."

Alix stumbled from the tent to where the others were gathered at the front of the ship. After two days of seeing nothing but the cobalt sea, a hazy smudge of green and brown in the distance became more detailed as the strong wind pushed them closer.

Joanna was still shaky from not being able to hold down food and water, but her eyes glowed with the hope of rescue. "I'm not sure where we are, but there's land ahead. Look, in the distance, you can see one of our ships."

"The captain says this is Cyprus. He can anchor next to the other ship, then we'll send men ashore to see if any survivors made it to the island." Rob's voice bellowed from behind them.

Joanna whirled around, her face whitening. "We can't go ashore. We must leave at once. I've heard stories of the ruler, and if they're to be believed, we'd be in grave danger."

"Who is this man?" Berenguela asked.

"His name is Isaac Comnenus. About five years ago, under false pretense, he claimed to be the new governor of Cyprus. The island's fortresses were handed to him. It didn't take long before his true nature was revealed, and he named himself Emperor. He plundered Cyprus, stealing from the citizens, enacting harsh punishments for those who committed crimes, and preyed on pilgrims who landed on shore or who were shipwrecked."

She paused and glanced toward Maud, who hovered nearby. "What he did to the women was despicable. Even highborn ladies and their daughters weren't safe." Her eyes filled with fear.

Alix's stomach plummeted.

Joanna's description of Isaac's actions was very similar to what Alix had read in books. Joanna had already experienced callous treatment in Sicily, but this would surpass that. If they fell into his hands, Joanna and Berenguela would be treated like chattel. She knew her life, along with Maud's and Elisabetta's, would be of little consequence to him. Once his use of them was over, she doubted they'd live much longer. Richard's men, on the other hand, would be put to death immediately.

They needed to make their escape.

Alix stepped closer to Rob as an idea took hold. "Richard's likely expecting us to come to him. Can we try to sail to Crete?"

"It's been two days since the storm. There's no way of knowing if the fleet is still there or are looking for us." Rob swept his hand toward the vast expanse of blue. "We could easily miss them."

Alix's nerves jangled as Rob's words sank in, but the danger they faced was too great. "I understand it might be safer to stay here until we're found, but I doubt Isaac would give up a potential conquest. If we try to leave, do we have supplies to last?"

"There's more than enough." He glanced toward the open sea. "And we're surrounded by water. We can fish for our supper if needed."

"Let's hope that's not the case." Alix smiled.

Conversation stopped as the rocky coast grew nearer. Several busses that had accompanied them from Messina lay smashed in the shallows. Torn sails hung from broken masts that stretched to the heavens like skeletal limbs. Wood and debris washed up on the beach.

"Those poor souls." Joanna crossed herself. "I hope some made it to shore."

Men waved and called out from the lone buss that was anchored offshore. In moments, longboats were lowered, then rowed toward them. Rob threw a ladder over the side of the ship. Once aboard, the men gathered around Rob and several other knights, fear drawn on their faces, appealing to him with emphatic gestures and raised voices. After several minutes, Rob led one of the men over.

"Tell me what happened," Joanna demanded.

"Your Grace, we tried to steer clear of the rocks, but the waves were too strong. Three of the ships were smashed to pieces. I was fortunate to make it ashore. Citizens appeared on the beach and greeted us. We thought they were going to bring help. We were mistaken." He glanced at Rob. "They took us to a castle and held us captive. All our belongings were stolen."

Joanna gasped. "How did you manage to escape?"

"When we learned that the emperor planned to kill us, we barricaded ourselves in the castle. The citizens laid siege to it, but to survive, we banded together and escaped. Unarmed, we were no match for the locals, and many were killed."

He paused, but at Joanna's nod, continued. "Roger de Hardecourt mounted a mare and rode into the crowd of Greeks, sending them fleeing. Somehow, a few of the knights had managed to hide their bows from their captives. They fired arrows at the citizens, allowing enough time for us to escape. The men on the ships saw the battle and made for the beach. The Greeks fought them with everything they had, but there were no losses on our side. We joined forces and routed the enemy, but many of the men are wounded."

"Thank God you and the others were saved."

The man frowned. "Your Grace, by now Isaac knows of your arrival. He questioned us while we were in captivity about who we were traveling with and where we were headed. I'm certain he's wondering how much he could get as ransom were he to capture you and the king's fiancée."

Joanna paled, but a steely resolve entered her eyes. "Under no circumstances will we go ashore. I'd rather die than allow us to be captured by that ruthless man."

The men withdrew to talk, and Joanna turned to Alix. "We can't leave these men unprotected. I pray that Richard is searching for us, but what if he isn't?" A haunted look filled her eyes. "I'm terrified of what Isaac will do to us. I can't forget how I was treated by Tancred's man. Each day we were imprisoned, I feared for my virtue as well as that of my ladies, but our jailers treated us respectfully, likely on Tancred's orders. Isaac cares nothing for women and should we fall into his hands . . ." Her voice shook. "We'd be violated, of that I'm certain."

Alix's heart raced and coldness slithered down her back. Historically, Richard had rescued Joanna and Berenguela, but what if her presence altered the tapestry of time and events changed? She'd escaped that brutality once, but from what Joanna said about Isaac, she doubted she would again.

The following afternoon, Rob summoned the queens and Alix to the ship's railing to watch as a small boat launched from the port of Limassol and was rowed to within calling distance. A well-dressed man wearing a sword stood in the prow.

"Your Grace and Princess of Navarre, our emperor wishes you would accept his hospitality and come ashore." His French was heavily accented, but understandable.

Berenguela gasped, and her eyes widened. Joanna hesitated, then stepped forward.

"We appreciate the generous offer, but with my apologies, we must remain onboard. My brother, King Richard, of whom I'm sure you've heard, is traveling to meet us and would be wroth if we left the ship. We would accept fresh water if the emperor would be so kind."

Seconds stretched out as anger flashed across the man's face, but then he bowed his head. "I will relay that to the emperor."

The boat turned toward the shore, and Joanna let out a shaky breath. "I fear we haven't seen the last of him. Isaac won't give up that easily."

"By now, the king must be searching for us. We'll keep putting Isaac off, but eventually we might need to take matters into our own hands." Rob tried to hide his emotions, but Alix knew him well enough to sense his fear.

"Let's keep this between ourselves. I don't want to worry the ladies," Joanna said.

The man returned the next day, this time bearing gifts of bread, fine wine, and ram's meat. Joanna thanked him for Isaac's generosity, but once again refused when he entreated them to come ashore. Hatred burned in his eyes. He informed them that no more supplies were to be delivered. If they had need of fresh food and water, they would receive them in the royal palace.

Joanna gave Alix a smile. "We'd best enjoy the food and wine. I've heard Cyprus grapes are some of the finest in the world."

Alix laughed. "Don't let your brother hear that. He swears that no region's wines can rival Aquitaine's."

Worry flooded Joanna's eyes. "Where is Richard? Is he looking for us? I can't let Berenguela know how dire our circumstances might become, but my hope is tested each day that passes."

"All we can do is wait. In the meantime, it might not be a bad idea to start thinking of other options."

*~*~*

The following morning, Alix woke to mist coiled around the ship, encasing the world in a thick, gray cloak. She stepped out of the tent, but was unable to see more than two feet in any direction. Her nails cut into the palms of her hand as distant shouts and yells from unseen men floated to her. Gentle waves lapped against the side of the ship, but there was no wind to disperse the clammy fog. Rob had placed knights along the gunwale to keep an eye out for any unwelcome visitors.

Maud plucked Alix's sleeve. "What's happening out there?"

"I don't know, but let's go back inside the tent. We'll stay there until we know what's going on."

Maud's lips trembled. "I'm afraid. Will that man come back?"

Alix hugged her to hide her own unease and to avoid answering. She should have made Maud return to France with Queen Eleanor.

Hours later, Rob's terse orders filtered into the tent. Alix shoved the tent flap aside and hurried to the rail of the ship. The sun had burned off the mist and five of Isaac's ships bobbed on the sea, bedecked with banners and seething with activity as men positioned themselves on deck.

Citizens had barricaded the beach with barrels, benches, planks, and other obstacles. Her heart lodged in her throat. It appeared as if the city of Limassol had been dismantled to barricade Richard's knights from reaching the shore.

"Jesu protect us," Joanna murmured from behind.

There was no mistaking Isaac's intent of battle. The man in the boat was rowed out again, but this time there were no entreaties—only an ultimatum.

Joanna turned to Rob. "If we go ashore, we'll be imprisoned. If we stay here, could they take us by force?"

"I'm afraid so. We could fight them off for a while, but with their numbers it's likely they would capture this ship."

"We need another option."

Rob's brows drew together. "Alix suggested that we might be able to escape under cover of darkness. I don't know if that would give us enough time to outrun their galleys, but it would give us a chance."

"Then it's decided. Tell Isaac's man that we'd be honored to accept his invitation, but we must prepare to leave. We need one more day."

Rob did and came back, a rueful smile on his lips. "He was none too happy with your answer, but said that he'd return in the morning."

Joanna sighed. "Thank God for that. Speak with the captain and let him know our decision."

Alix stared at the armed galleys floating in the shallows like hounds waiting to be released to hunt down and catch their prey. Their buss was too large and cumbersome to outrun Isaac's sleek ships. With two ships, they might be able to fight off the Greeks, but for how long?

"Joanna said that we're leaving tonight." Elisabetta joined Alix.

"That's the plan. Rob sent word to the other ship. Hopefully, we'll be far enough out to sea by the time Isaac's men realize we're gone."

"Where is the king? What if he doesn't find us in time?"

"Don't give up hope. I know he'll rescue us." Clumps of lead settled in the pit of Alix's stomach. What if Elisabetta was right and Richard didn't arrive?

The sun arced toward the horizon, and the captain gave orders to the sailors to start preparations to depart.

Joanna stood at the railing of the ship, gazing at the empty sea before them. "I thought by now Richard would be here. Something terrible must have happened, for I know he'd never give up on us."

Alix placed her hand on Joanna's arm. "You mustn't think that. There's still time for him to come. Where's Berenguela?"

"Her ladies were upset, and she's comforting them in the tent."

Alix's initial opinion of the Spanish Princess was quickly changing. She'd assumed Berenguela would complain about the spartan accommodations and expect to be coddled, due to her regal upbringing. Instead, she'd shown resolve and determination. Perhaps she would make Richard a better wife than Alix had expected.

"We should go in as well."

"Let's wait a little longer." Joanna gripped the edge of the ship and glanced at Alix. Fear filled her eyes. "We can't allow ourselves to be taken by Isaac. I doubt any of us would survive. I pray this plan will work."

"It will. We have to believe that." Alix turned her attention to the sea. The setting sun lit the clouds in vibrant orange and red. Any other time she would have marveled at the vividness of the sunset. Now she wished they had more hours in the day.

"I never imagined we'd be in this much danger." Joanna's lips trembled and she pressed them together. "Are you regretting your decision to leave France? I'm sure my brother would have left some type of provision for you in his absence."

Alix took a deep breath. She was tired of being accused of trying to exploit Richard. "Your mother asked me to travel to Sicily to be a companion to you until she arrived with Berenguela."

Jianna spun to face her. "I don't believe you. Why would she ask you to be my companion?"

"Messina wasn't the first time I was assaulted. Several years ago, I was attacked by a man who tried to rob me." Alix crossed her arms and leaned against the edge of the ship. "She knew about that, and she worried that . . . well . . . if you had been mistreated, you might feel more comfortable confiding in a woman who'd experienced a similar event."

"My mother asked you to come?" At Alix's nod, confusion flashed in her eyes. "Why wouldn't she tell me? She had the opportunity."

"She hadn't seen you in years. I'm sure spending time with you was more important."

"I'm glad she sent you." Joanna relaxed, smiled, and covered Alix's hand with hers.

From above, a sailor in the crow's nest shouted indistinct words and pointed.

Alix stared in the same direction. In the distance, two specks tossed on frothing waves like tiny white birds. "Is that some of the fleet?"

Joanna shook her head. "I'm not sure . . . wait, there are more. Yes, that must be them!"

Giddiness washed over Alix. The fleet was coming, but was Richard? The sun had almost set when the first of the galleys reached them.

"Whose ship is that?" Berenguela's rushed footsteps approached.

Joanna spun around. "My brother has arrived."

Alix sagged against the gunwale as tension flowed out of her. Richard, in dramatic fashion as usual, had come to their rescue.

Sailors rushed to the edge of the ship to throw over ladders as boats were lowered from Richard's galley.

Joanna and Berenguela were the first to greet Richard as he swung himself on deck. Joanna threw herself in his arms and was lifted off her feet as he hugged her. He then turned to Berenguela and did the same.

His gaze met Alix's over his fiancée's shoulder. His cold indifference fractured. In answer to the worry etched on his face, she nodded and smiled. She assumed he would be content with that, but after releasing Berenguela, he reached Alix in four long strides and clasped her in his arms. The fear and dread of the last several days evaporated as she clung to him, craving the protection she felt from his body against hers.

"Thank God you're safe, Love." His warm breath caressed her cheek.

"I'm so glad you arrived when you did."

Richard shifted his stance and she reluctantly let him go, wishing they could stay in this moment forever. He gave her a smile, and she frowned. His face was drawn and pale. "Have you been ill?"

His lips tightened, and he shook his head imperceptibly. "I'm fine now, just exhausted from searching for you."

Joanna stepped forward, interrupting their moment. "Where have you been and what took you so long to find us?"

"After the storm, we waited in Crete for the rest of my ships to catch up. We traveled to Rhodes and stayed there while scouts were sent to locate your whereabouts. We would've been here sooner, but the winds in the Gulf of Sattalia are some of the trickiest I've experienced. Our ships were pushed backwards to where we entered the gulf."

He walked past the women and stared at the barricaded port and galleys. "Tell me what has happened. Leave nothing out."

Richard gave Rob a grim smile after he'd been apprised of what had been going on. He glanced toward the enemy ships, but they remained anchored in place.

"Isaac has captured my men and put those who are important to me in danger. That was a mistake. Tomorrow I'll deal with him. In the meantime, I'll send some provisions, since I assume you're running low."

"Isaac sent us plenty of food and wine to entice us ashore." Joanna's tone held a hint of sarcasm. "Will you stay and dine with us?"

"Certainly, I will. I want to hear more of this Isaac. I need to know who I'm facing."

## ~ *Chapter 21* ~

ALIX TIGHTENED HER HOLD ON the ship's rail, adrenaline sparking through her. Beyond the enemy ships, Isaac's army gathered along the shore, waiting. It was like nothing she'd ever envisioned. Soldiers rode horses up and down the beach, their armor gleaming in the sun. The wind whipped numerous colorful banners and penoncels into a frenzy. Shouts and yells floated across the water as Richard's men piled into skiffs.

"We're going to war." Joanna bit her lip. "Tell me the truth. Do we have a chance against them?"

"It won't be easy, Your Grace," Rob said. "They have the advantage. We're coming by sea on foot and weighed down by armor and weapons. But the men are experienced," he hastened to reassure her.

"I'm sure you wish you were fighting alongside the men. It must be hard for you to stand by and watch." Alix gave him a small smile.

"Too true, but I'm sure I'll see my share of battle. It might be best if you ladies return to the tent."

Berenguela shook her head. "No, we'll stay. I trust that the Almighty will be on our side."

Although Alix knew what the outcome should be, fear and anticipation surged through her as she watched the battle unfold.

The shouts of the opposing army grew louder as the small skiffs approached the armed galleys. The Greeks sent a barrage of arrows onto the approaching boats. The knights crouched behind their shields, then the crossbowmen sent loose a flurry of their own bolts and arrows. As the first group reloaded, a second one stood and attacked.

Richard's archers always hit their target, but each time an arrow found its mark, another man took his place. Alix's pounding heart threatened to burst out of her chest as the onslaught continued. Arrows from both sides darkened the sky. How much more could the men withstand?

"Look." Rob pointed toward one of the galleys that was surrounded by skiffs. "They're making headway."

The scene reminded Alix of hounds running their prey to ground.

Greeks jumped into the water to escape the arrows, only to be dragged down by the weight of their armor. The few that made it to shore were pulled to safety. Richard's knights boarded the galley and captured the remaining men.

The dead were thrown overboard. Alix swallowed rising bile as the azure sea was tinted red.

The skiffs continued to the shore and stopped a safe distance away to allow the crossbowmen to fire upon Isaac and his men. The Greeks, armed with only lances and staves, fell back, while the archers took cover behind the makeshift defenses that littered the beach. They returned fire upon the skiffs that floundered in the shallows.

"Our men are unable or unwilling to land. They can't withstand this attack for much longer." Rob's gaze was fixed on the battle.

A boat shot forward to take the lead, an unmistakable, armored figure at its bow. Berenguela cried out and covered her face while Joanna clutched Alix's trembling hand. As the boat neared the shore, Richard leapt into the water and marched to the beach, his sword cutting into any Greek who stood in his way.

Alix's heart lodged in her throat. She'd seen battle before, but this was much worse. She watched, helpless to do anything other than pray, as Richard put his life in danger. Knights yelled out as they followed suit.

Rob clenched his fist. "Now the tide will turn in our favor."

"How can you be so certain?" Dread stole through her.

"We might not have the number of men that the Greeks have, but we're more skilled in battle."

Alix forced her attention back toward the beach, hoping Rob wasn't just bolstering their spirits. The burning sun couldn't melt the ice that congealed in her veins as, once again, arrows filled the sky with certain death. The beach was soon littered with dead and wounded men. As much as she wanted to close her eyes to the bloodshed, it felt disloyal to Richard.

The only sounds were the waves slapping against the ship and the distant yells and screams of men engaged in hand-to-hand combat. Swords flashed in the sun and clanged against armor as the soldiers parried and thrust in a macabre dance of death. The fighting was vicious, but at last the enemy began to retreat, Richard's men in pursuit.

"I thought for sure I was going to watch my brother die." Joanna pressed her hand to her mouth.

"Thank God that didn't happen," Alix breathed.

Rob grinned, now that victory was theirs. "Richard is a force unto himself. There's a reason he's earned the name 'Lionheart.'"

"There will be fighting like this in the Holy Land, will there not?" Berenguela asked.

Rob nodded. "I fear so, but we will be victorious. Richard will accept nothing else."

"Alix?" a voice called out.

Alix turned and hurried to the tent. She'd been so focused on the battle, she'd forgotten about the ladies.

"What's happening?" Elisabetta stood at the entrance. "We heard shouting and yelling, but I thought it best to stay here."

Berenguela's attendants huddled together, and Maud sat on the bed, arms wrapped around her knees, tears drying on her cheeks. Alix didn't want to worry them, but they deserved to know.

"The king's men captured the galleys and then headed toward the beach. The boats were yards off the shore, but the knights didn't disembark. The king jumped into the water to take on the Greeks by himself. His men soon followed."

"Is the king . . . alive?" Fear filled Maud's eyes.

"Yes. He fought bravely, not stopping until the enemy took to their heels and fled." Her voice vibrated with pride.

Elisabetta crossed herself. "Thank God for that. When I was working at the palace, I heard the men talk about various battles they'd been in. It must have been terrible to see."

Alix nodded. "I don't want to think about how many were killed."

"Now that it's over, what will happen to us? What if Isaac's men return?"

"I don't know. Once again, we must wait."

It was late afternoon before Joanna and Berenguela entered the tent with news. Richard had sent a messenger to tell them to pack their belongings, for they were to go ashore.

The boatmen who rowed them to Limassol kept as far away from the beach as possible, so they couldn't see the remnants of the battle clearly in the lengthening shadows. Alix breathed a sigh of relief when she clambered off the boat onto solid ground for the first time in weeks.

Richard had ordered a sailor to accompany them who was fluent in Greek and French in case they encountered any townspeople. So far, the port city was devoid of any sign of life and as quiet as a ghost town. Rob led them through twisting, dusty streets lined with small, neat houses.

Although the waves had been gentle, everyone had been sprayed with sea water from the oars. It didn't take long for dust that puffed up from their footsteps to cake the bottoms of their skirts.

Rob stopped in front of an imposing stone structure. "This is Isaac's palace. Richard thought that since the cur abandoned it, it shouldn't go to waste."

"Where is my brother? He's coming, I assume."

Rob's gaze shifted. "I'm not certain, but I'm sure he'll send word."

Joanna raised her brow. "I'll take that to mean he's not."

The hope in Berenguela's eyes faded. Sympathy rushed through Alix. Since leaving Messina a month ago, Berenguela had seen her future husband only twice, once in the thick of battle.

Maud's stomach growled and her cheeks pinked as Joanna laughed.

"Quite right. I think food is in order. There must be a kitchen somewhere. We also need to find rooms to sleep in and somewhere to bathe."

Rob motioned to the sailor. "We'll go and see if any servants are still here and can help."

The ladies explored the sprawling palace until they found the sleeping chambers. After choosing their rooms and putting away their meager possessions, they wandered back to the entrance.

"I hear voices this way." Joanna turned to follow the sounds.

Rob and Georges sat at a table, plates of bread, fruit, meat, and a wine flagon before them.

"There you are. The kitchens were well-stocked, as you can see." Rob waved his hand over the bounty.

Alix smiled at Georges, then sat next to Maud.

"I still can't believe how reckless and brave Richard was," Joanna said.

"You're not the only one." Georges chuckled. "I wasn't sure if we would survive making it to land. Trudging through the waves in armor carrying our weapons and evading arrows isn't easy. Once ashore, arrows and crossbows were useless. From then on, it was hand-to-hand combat." He paused to take a drink of wine.

"Did Richard capture Isaac?" Joanna reached for a piece of bread.

Georges grimaced. "Once it was clear that the enemy and the emperor were retreating, Richard managed to acquire a packhorse and caught up. The poor animal's saddle didn't have stirrups, only cords. Richard challenged the emperor to a joust, but the emperor kept fleeing."

Rob and Georges laughed while Alix and Joanna exchanged unamused looks.

Alix knew it must have galled Richard to have to use a lesser steed and not a warhorse. Issuing a challenge when he was at a disadvantage sent the message that he shouldn't be underestimated. Richard was an accomplished soldier and commander, but seeing him in action today increased her appreciation of the danger he put himself in each time he went to battle.

"I'm certain Isaac would've been captured, but night was falling, and we don't know the paths through the thickets and groves. Richard plans to go after him tomorrow at first light."

Georges took a last bite of meat, drained his cup, then stood. "I wish I could stay longer, but I must return."

"Please tell Richard that we hope to see him soon," Joanna said.

Georges nodded, and Rob walked him out.

Berenguela's eyes shone. "I'd heard tales of Richard's victories and exploits, but I always thought they were exaggerated. I see now that they aren't. I'm honored to marry your brother, Joanna."

A sudden twinge of jealousy and heartache gripped Alix. Their wedding would take place in about two weeks. Richard always viewed this marriage as political, and she'd thought Berenguela had, too, but what if she'd misread her? What if Berenguela was falling in love with Richard? Would it change things so he'd find happiness in a marriage that historically was unhappy?

She was still devastated that she'd had to end their relationship. How would she feel if he moved on while she was unable to?

*~*~*

The horses had been unloaded from the transport galleys and were being exercised on the beach when Georges returned.

Richard ordered his squires to keep them moving, then motioned for Georges to join him.

"I trust the ladies are comfortable in the palace?"

"They are, but disappointed that you didn't visit yourself. I didn't tell them of your illness."

Heat rose in his cheeks at the reminder of his fickle health. "I appreciate that. They had enough to worry about without my adding to it."

Richard returned his gaze to the horses, who were finding their land legs after a month of immobility at sea. When his sister's ship had been blown off course during the storm, he'd sent his scouts to search for their whereabouts. But then a bout of malaria took hold, and he lay on his cot, weak and consumed with fever, helpless to do anything more than envision the worst outcome. At last, the scouts returned with news that the buss was anchored off Limassol.

Although still feeling the effects of the illness, he'd ordered the fleet to set sail. He'd never forgive himself if his sister, Alix, and fiancée were captured, or worse, because of his weakness.

Relief had washed over him when he saw their ship floating at anchor. Once aboard, it wasn't enough to see that Alix was safe. The need to hold her in his arms overwhelmed him and he'd thrown caution to the winds. She'd returned his tight embrace, and for a moment, it felt like nothing had changed and she was still his. But all too soon, he had to release her.

"What's your plan, Sire?"

"To capture Isaac. My spies discovered he's encamped about six miles from here. I'm sure he doesn't know that we have horses, or he would have retreated further inland."

André approached and handed Georges a wineskin. "The horses are warming up and should be ready for tomorrow. When do you wish to leave?"

"Prepare the men to leave before daybreak."

The moon was the sole source of illumination as Richard led forty armed, mounted knights from the beach, the rest of his men following on foot. The jangle of metal, hoofbeats, and the rustle of leaves were loud in the early morning silence.

Away from the cool sea breeze, sweat trickled down his back under his armor as they rode on dusty paths through thick olive groves. Rounding a turn in the path, Richard stopped and raised his hand. André rode up next to him. A group of Cypriots holding banners stood conversing in a grove, apparently unconcerned for their safety.

Richard studied the men before him. "Instead of trying to locate the best route to get to Isaac, I prefer to let his men lead the way."

He spurred his horse forward and burst into the grove. The Cypriots scattered like mice hunted by a cat. Richard and his men trailed them until they reached the emperor's encampment. In the distance was a huge, conical pavilion that Richard assumed was Isaac's. Richard ordered his men to halt to assess the situation. On their arrival, the enemy gathered in groups and hurled insults.

Richard removed his steel helmet and wiped sweat from his brow. His eyes narrowed as the front lines continued to amass, but not in any defined formation. Greek crossbowman lined up and began arcing arrows toward Richard's men, but even that show of force seemed half-hearted at best. He turned to André and Georges, who had joined him.

"Our arrival should have been noted long before now. There appear to be no leaders or sentries." A sardonic smile lifted the corner of his mouth. "If Isaac weren't so corrupt, I might almost feel remorse about destroying his army. Where is that man, anyway? Surely, he's not making his escape."

"There he is." André pointed to a group of soldiers surrounding a man in gleaming armor.

"It's quite difficult to lead your men being so far away from the battle."

An armed clerk rode up. "My Lord King, it seems unwise to engage the opponents at this moment. They already have hordes of people, and more are arriving. I suggest we return to the beach."

Richard's jaw tightened at the implication that he was incapable of defeating this miscreant. He'd been in countless battles and had always emerged victorious. He knew this outcome would be no different.

"I suggest you remain true to your profession. Stick to scripture and leave the fighting to us."

The men laughed as the clerk slunk away, red-faced.

André sighed. "Like it or not, there is some truth to his argument. We don't have the numbers, but look at them. I doubt it would take much to send them fleeing."

Richard put his steel helmet on. "Let's put that to the test, shall we?"

He grasped his lance in his hand and spurred his destrier across the plain, his men behind him. Arrows bounced harmlessly off their armor as they raced into the milling Greeks. A horseman galloped toward him. He tightened his grip and ran his lance through the man's armor. The shattered weapon and the unhorsed man fell to the ground. Richard wheeled his horse and struck another with his sword.

The foot soldiers scrambled to avoid being trampled as Richard's steed reared, sharp hooves flying. Georges yelled a warning, and Richard raised his shield, blocking an attack. His own retaliation was swift and fatal. He had no time to relish his small victory before a group of Cypriots bore down on him. Sweat stung his eyes and drenched his body as he parried and thrust his sword into any man unlucky to be within his reach.

Screams of wounded men and horses filled the air. The Cypriot foot soldiers that were able to had escaped. The few on horseback retreated toward the hill where Isaac was protected by his men. A flash of crimson caught Richard's eye. The emperor's standard-bearer guarded the banner. Richard dispatched him in short order. He tore the banner from the staff and carried it to Georges.

"Keep this safe for me."

"For certes, Sire." He grinned.

André cantered up. "Isaac is still watching, coward that he is."

"Gather some men and follow me."

As soon as Isaac saw them galloping toward him, he turned and fled. They pursued him for about two miles, with Richard in the lead, but Isaac pulled further away. Richard slowed his exhausted, lathered horse and waited for his men.

"I'd hoped to catch him, but his steed is faster than any I'd seen. I can only hope I put the fear of God into him," Richard growled.

The soldiers had started their plunder and had piled treasure in carts when they returned. Dead and wounded men and horses littered the plain. The metallic scent of blood filled the air.

Baldwin de Bethune walked up, shoving a man before him. "Your Grace, this is the emperor's translator. I thought he would be more useful alive than dead."

"Do you speak French?" Richard demanded.

"Yes, Your Grace, as well as Arabic and Turkish," he replied in French.

"You're coming with us then. Take him to the other prisoners."

"I'm surprised that Isaac brought so much treasure with him. I've never seen so many gold and silver plates and silken clothes, not to mention all the oxen, pigs, and sheep." Baldwin chuckled. "I'm not sure we can carry it all back."

Richard grinned and steadied his horse. "At least we can put it to good use. I hope that coward enjoys his last nights of freedom."

*~*~*

Alix sat with Maud in the garden, relaying the story about the legendary Trojan horse when the girl jumped up.

"Your Grace." She curtsied, then turned to Alix. "I'd best go and see if the queens need any assistance."

Alix's heart skittered as she looked up into blue-gray eyes and nodded to Richard. "I hear you sent Isaac running for the hills. I'm sorry you weren't able to catch him."

He grimaced. "I believe the citizens agree with you. That man has ruled this island with an iron fist for too long. I let it be known that whoever desired peace was free to come and go. But if they consider me an enemy, then they'd better not cross me."

"That explains why the town has been busy lately. I heard a commotion earlier. Are you and your men staying here?"

He sat next to her on the bench. She hoped her face didn't betray the surge of electricity that coursed through her at his nearness.

"My vassal, Guy de Lusignan, has arrived from the Holy Land."

Alix raised her brow. "The King of Jerusalem? Shouldn't he be trying to retake his kingdom?"

"He lost his crown when his wife, Sybilla, died. Isabella, Sybilla's half sister, is the heir. She was forced to annul her marriage and marry another man, Conrad de Montferrat. They're the new rulers. Guy is seeking my help to restore him to his throne." He grimaced and rubbed his jaw. "That man has been a thorn in our family's side for years, which is why we banished him."

The breeze blew strands of hair across her cheek. Alix froze as Richard brushed them away, his fingers scorching her skin. She focused on a leaf cartwheeling across the grass. "What happened?"

"The Lusignans didn't agree with the way my father ruled Aquitaine, and they revolted. Father destroyed their lands and seized their castle." He smiled ruefully. "He then left to arrange the marriage between Alys and myself. Before going, he left my mother in the care of the Earl of Salisbury as her military advisor. The Lusignans took the opportunity to reclaim their property, and during a skirmish, the earl was killed."

"I can understand why you are at odds with the family. Are you going to help him?"

"I'm considering it." He paused and cleared his throat. "I didn't come here to talk about Guy."

Her nerves tightened. "What is it?"

He half-turned on the bench to look at her. "The wedding will be on Sunday."

She was prepared for it to happen, but the world tilted and the air was sucked out of her lungs. The sharp edge of the stone bench dug into her clenched hands as his words cut her heart into pieces.

"Berenguela must be very happy. Becoming a wife is quite the occasion," she managed to say.

Richard raised his brow. "I haven't told her yet. I wanted you to be the first to know. I owe you that."

His words brought cold comfort. "Richard, that wasn't necessary, but thank you for thinking of me."

He gave a curt nod, stood, and walked away.

A fresh onslaught of pain overwhelmed her. In forty-eight hours, he would be married. She'd been a fool to think that she was over him. Perhaps the imminent wedding was a blessing. It wouldn't give her time to dwell on her misery.

She took deep breaths and hardened her heart. No one could know how much his announcement had shattered her. By the time she had her emotions and thoughts in check, twilight had cast a purple glow across the sky. Alix returned to the palace and went to Berenguela's room. By now, she would've heard the announcement and might think it strange Alix hadn't made an appearance.

She'd barely knocked on the door when Joanna flung it open. "Thank God, you're back. Richard has been and gone, leaving chaos, as usual."

Berenguela's ladies were digging through trunks, pulling out dresses. Spanish words flew thick as arrows while Berenguela looked on, dazed.

"He told me."

Joanna gave her a wry smile. "How does he expect us to prepare a wedding and coronation in two days? We're not miracle workers. Royal weddings take months of planning. If he weren't my favorite brother, I'd throttle him for this."

"Don't worry. We have plenty of resources. Fortunately, Isaac has luxurious tastes and left everything in the palace. We'll plan a wedding that will rival any."

One of Berenguela's ladies held up a dress for her inspection. She nodded, then turned toward Joanna. "Is your brother always this spontaneous?"

Alix and Joanna looked at each other and grinned.

"We should be grateful he gave us two days," Joanna said.

*~*~*

Alix had tossed and turned for hours before the sun peeked over the horizon, dusting the sky in brilliant oranges and pinks. How could such a beautiful sunrise preface a tortuous day? May 12, 1191, would no longer be a random date in a history book. Instead, it would forever be branded in her mind, for today she'd watch the man she loved marry another. And tonight, she'd use the brooch to return to her own time.

She slipped out of bed and, after getting dressed, roused Maud and Elisabetta.

"Joanna has her hands full with a nervous bride, so the less she has to worry, the better. I need to check with the cooks to see how the feast is coming, but by the aromas coming from the kitchen, I doubt anyone will complain."

"What can we do, dearie?" Elisabetta stifled a yawn.

"I'd like to decorate the hall. I saw linen tablecloths, and we can use the gold and silver plates and cups that Isaac so thoughtfully left behind."

Maud grinned. "This is the first wedding I've been to. It's going to be so exciting."

Elisabetta shook out her blanket and folded it. "What about the marriage chamber?"

A ball of lead clumped in Alix's stomach. "I hadn't thought of that."

"Never you mind. I'll speak to Queen Joanna and see what we can do. Give me a few moments to get ready."

Several hours later, Alix stood at the door to the hall and studied it with a critical eye. The tables were covered with linen tablecloths, napkins, gold and silver plates, and gem-encrusted goblets. Maud had strewn white- and pink cyclamen on the royal table, interspersed with glass vases filled with cut tulips and lilies from the garden.

Elisabetta put her hands on her hips and nodded. "The king should be very pleased."

"I hope so." Alix chewed her lip and glanced around the room, making sure nothing had been forgotten.

"I think we've done all we can. We should see how the bride is doing. I'm sure her stomach is in knots." Elisabetta chuckled.

Berenguela was much calmer than Alix expected her to be. She stood in the middle of the room while her ladies made last-minute adjustments to her dress.

Joanna drew Alix aside. "You're coming to the wedding, aren't you?"

"I thought it would be easier for everyone involved if I didn't."

"I understand, but Berenguela knows nothing of your relationship with my brother. She might wonder why you aren't present."

Joanna had a point. Berenguela thought Alix was merely a kinswoman and, as such, would be expected to attend. Perhaps it was for the best. Seeing him marry would cement the truth in her heart. She loved Richard, but she had no future with him.

Berenguela turned around. Her eyes were huge in her pale face. "Do you think Richard will be satisfied?"

The royal blue silk wedding dress complimented her olive complexion and her glossy dark hair hung loose to her waist. A pearl-studded veil covering her head completed the look.

Joanna clasped her hands together. "You look beautiful. Richard will be more than pleased."

A faint smile crossed her lips. "I hope so. I've waited for this day for so long, I almost can't believe it's here."

"I, as well." Joanna turned toward Alix. "Go and dress and we'll see you at the church."

Alix returned to her room to find her forest-green dress laid out on her bed. She mentally thanked whoever had done it, relieved she didn't have to stress over that choice.

Once dressed, she studied her reflection in her compact. The misery on her face was more suited to a funeral. The hollow smile she pasted on was no better. She took a deep breath and tried again. The second time was passable.

Elisabetta and Maud were outside the palace, waiting for her.

"How are you doing, dearie?" Elisabetta placed her hand on Alix's arm. "As much as you tell yourself it's over between you and the king, this can't be easy."

"I'll be fine. I always knew our time together was limited." If she kept telling herself that, maybe one day her heart would accept it.

Maud's voice rose as she chatted about the wedding, while Alix's dread grew heavier as they walked closer to the church. They found space several rows behind Joanna. Alix gripped her hands, willing herself not to fall apart. After she'd schooled her features into what she hoped was a semblance of happiness, she forced her gaze toward the wedding party.

Richard looked majestic in his crimson tunic with the dark-blue mantle stitched with silver around his shoulders. His eyes widened, then a smile spread across his lips as André escorted Berenguela to where he stood.

The first chink in Alix's armor appeared.

The chaplain began the ceremony. Alix focused on breathing, the meaningless words washing over her until he reached the part where the groom was to plight his troth. Her chest tightened. She forced her chin up and met Richard's unblinking gaze. A second passed, then two, before he turned his attention to the chaplain.

"I promise to have and to hold my bride in bed and at the table," Richard said in a clear voice.

A crevasse snaked through Alix's brittle heart.

"For better or worse, in sickness and in health."

The fissure widened and deepened as Richard spoke each vow. Her eyes burned and her throat tightened. Elisabetta patted Alix's shoulder and gave her a sympathetic smile. A few more words and her world would change forever.

"Til death us depart."

Her heart exploded, and needles of glass lacerated her soul. It was done. Richard was married.

## ~ *Chapter 22* ~

RICHARD STOOD NEXT TO HIS wife-to-be, feeling mere friendship for the woman with whom he would spend the rest of his life. After months of discussions with her father, Sancho, and an arduous journey from France for both of them, the wedding was taking place.

Although they were, in essence, strangers, he liked what he'd seen of Berenguela. The courage she'd shown throughout their ordeals impressed him. He hadn't seen her succumb to tears or hysterics. If they found common ground, he'd be satisfied.

Since leaving France, he'd given little thought to how his wedding would change his life, but when he feared Alix had perished in the storm, he was forced to. After that moment he'd held her in his arms, he'd craved what they'd shared before. He knew her views on adultery. She'd never consent to be his mistress. Marriage was the only way to put an end to the temptation of returning to her. The sooner the better.

He didn't expect Alix to attend, but his gaze scoured the crowd in the hope that she might be there. Pain wrenched his heart as the sun chose that moment to burst from behind a cloud and illuminate the only woman he'd ever love. The one he could never have again. The wind blew strands of dark auburn hair across her cheek, and she brushed them away, her unreadable gaze catching his.

The memorized vows froze on his lips. The chaplain cleared his throat and forced him back to the task at hand. Standing outside the doors to the chapel of St. George, Richard recited his vows, then pushed the gold ring onto Berenguela's finger.

After the ceremony, she was consecrated Queen of England by high-ranking bishops. They returned to the palace, accompanied by cheers and fanfare. Richard smiled and nodded, taking care to protect his new wife from overeager well-wishers.

Berenguela gasped when they entered the dining hall. "Joanna managed all this in two days?"

Richard laughed and put his arm around her shoulders. "I can only imagine what she would have devised if I gave her more time." Surreptitiously, he looked for Alix, but she'd vanished.

"I did have some help." Joanna hugged her new sister-in-law. "I hope you two are very happy." She then stood on tiptoes to hug Richard. "I never thought I'd witness you marry. I'm glad I was able to, although I wish Mother could've been here."

"I too. I fear she'll hold that against me for quite some time."

"As well she should." Joanna grinned.

Guests filed into the hall, and Berenguela smiled and nodded to everyone who congratulated them.

They took their seats at the royal table. Then servants started to bring plates of meat, seafood, and vegetables cooked in aromatic spices. Richard served Berenguela the choicest meats and made sure she lacked for nothing. Although it was a festive occasion, he drank little wine. Berenguela was his wife and he wanted to remain clearheaded and make the wedding night as easy as possible for her.

Joanna leaned toward him. "I know it's customary for guests to accompany the bride and bridegroom to the marriage chamber, but please don't let the bedside revelry last too long."

Richard cocked his brow. "I wasn't planning to. I know she's quite modest."

Joanna frowned. "I'm serious. She's apprehensive about that."

"Don't fear. She's in good hands."

The night wore on, and as men's voices became louder and more raucous as the wine flowed, he turned to his wife. "I think it's time to retire to the bedchamber and continue our wedding night there."

Her eyes widened, but she nodded and gave him a small smile. They made their way out of the hall, followed by his friends, Joanna, and Berenguela's attendants. After the ladies had readied her for bed, the jesting began. True to his word, when his wife's cheeks flamed at the increasingly ribald jokes, Richard ushered everyone out of the bedchamber, including his squires.

"Thank you, Richard." She shifted in the bed and pulled the covers up to her waist. "I appreciate the privacy. I do have a question, however."

He cocked his brow and stifled a smile. Surely, she knew what the night entailed.

"When I was consecrated queen, the bishops called me Berengaria. I assume that's the French version of my name. Am I to be known as Berengaria from now on? The name sounds so foreign to me."

"In public, you'll be known as Berengaria, but in private, I'll call you Berenguela. If that's your preference."

She smiled. "I would like that."

"I daresay you're the only English queen to have been crowned in Cyprus."

"I'm honored to be your queen and wife, Richard."

Searing loss swept through him. He had nothing against marriage, but since meeting Alix, it had become an afterthought. Now, traveling to Outremer, he needed to strengthen his kingdom's boundaries to the south. As king, he needed to secure his lineage. Berenguela could provide both, but his heart ached at what it had cost him.

*~*~*

Alix prowled her room, where she'd sought sanctuary from the gut-wrenching day. Thoughts of returning to Austin had preoccupied her the second Richard was lost to her. The pain in her heart hadn't dulled since the wedding. If anything, it had sharpened.

Maud was in Joanna's service and would be taken care of. The man she loved was married. She needed to return home, to her family and friends. There was no reason for her to stay any longer. She knelt down to rifle through her coffer in search of the pouch that contained her means to escape.

The brooch shone in the lantern light as she turned it in her hand. There was only one choice left. One prick and the life she'd made for herself here would disappear. Forever. She held the sharp end of the pin over her finger, closed her eyes, and pierced her skin. Her breath caught as she waited for the brooch to warm and glow in her hand—the signal it was working.

Distant voices, laughter, and music filtered through the air.

Alix opened her eyes and choked back a cry. She was still in Cyprus, in Richard's time, not in the gardens outside Austin at Nottingham Faire. *I must have done something wrong.* This time she fixed the image of the gardens in her mind. She stabbed the pin into her finger over and over.

The brooch remained cold. Tears of frustration slid down her cheeks. Why was she still in the past?

*~*~*

Alix slumped on her bed as the rising sun illuminated her room. She'd been up for hours, pricking her fingers in the dark, praying for the brooch to work, but as before, nothing changed. She knew extreme emotions triggered the brooch, and when it needed her to do something, like correct history. But what reason could it have to keep her trapped in a time she didn't want to be in?

Hot tears stung her eyes. She'd been depending on the brooch to make her escape. How was she going to bear seeing Richard, knowing they could never be together? She swiped her cheeks, then put the piece of jewelry in the pouch and stowed it in her trunk. Until she could figure out what she needed to do so she could return home, she'd have to make the best of the situation.

"I apologize for missing the festivities last night. I hope the guests enjoyed them." Alix glanced at Joanna as they walked to the hall for breakfast. She was glad Joanna was accompanying her. What type of reception would she receive from Richard's men? She hoped it wasn't pity.

"They did, and Berenguela looked very happy. I'm surprised Richard managed to avoid marriage for so long, but I'm glad I was able to plan it. I know it wasn't easy for you, but thank you for helping."

"I was happy to, especially since you were given so little time." Alix's stomach plummeted as they entered the hall. She wasn't prepared to see Richard and Berenguela sitting at the table with several men. Richard was deep in conversation with the visitors while Berenguela spoke to her ladies.

Joanna's lips twisted. "With Guy at the table, they must be discussing politics. I'd hoped they could put it off, but apparently not."

"Richard told me a little about him, but not much."

"Guy is the man talking to Richard, and that's his brother, Geoffrey." Joanna pointed to the man sitting next to Guy. "Did Richard tell you about Sybilla and Isabella?" Alix nodded and she continued. "The dark-haired man next to Geoffrey is Humphrey de Toron. He was married to Isabella, but the nobles felt that he was unsuitable to rule the kingdom. They preferred Conrad de Montferrat, who was a crusader and had defended the city from Salah-ad-Din. Humphrey was forced to divorce her."

"Richard told me that she married Conrad."

"At the behest of her own mother and stepfather, no less."

Berenguela looked up as they approached and gave Alix a smile. "How are you feeling? Joanna told me that you had a headache last night and retired to your room."

Alix curtsied, mentally thanking Joanna for explaining her absence. "I'm much better today, thank you. I wish you every happiness."

Chairs scraped on the stone floor as the men stood. Richard leaned to whisper in his wife's ear. A smile brightened her face, and she nodded. Alix's heart constricted. He straightened and turned.

Her pulse raced as his gray-blue eyes caught hers. The connection that tied them together flamed in her soul. "Congratulations, Your Grace." She curtsied.

"I'm glad to see your illness was short-lived."

His sardonic smile told her he knew it was an excuse. A strained silence followed until Joanna changed the subject. "Guy looks pleased. I assume you told him you'd back his cause and restore his kingdom to him."

Richard nodded and crossed his arms. "I did. Although we have our differences, he's still my vassal. Conrad de Montferrat is Philippe's cousin and, for certes, has his support."

"After what Philippe did to you, I'm sure you're not concerned with angering him," Alix said."

Richard laughed. "You know me too well."

André hurried up and drew Richard aside. At once, his demeanor changed. "I must leave for my meeting with the emperor."

"You captured Isaac?" Joanna's eyes widened. "Why didn't you tell us?"

"I had more important matters to attend to." He winked at Berenguela, who blushed. "And to answer your question, no, I didn't capture him. After being defeated twice in less than three days, he found that the number of men still loyal to him had thinned greatly. He sent an envoy, offering peace. To tell the truth, I'm glad he did. Following the man across this island was more trouble than it's worth. However, I'm sure he'll regret surrendering when he learns what I will require of him."

*~*~*

The townspeople were gathered in a fig grove situated between the sea and the road next to the city of Limassol when Richard arrived. His horse stamped restlessly as he waited for Isaac.

He'd dressed regally in a tunic of rose samite, a cloak woven with silver half moons and golden suns, and a cap embroidered in gold thread. The hilt of his sword and spurs were gold, and his scabbard was indented with silver, which flashed in the sun.

Isaac arrived with his men and a mediator. His eyes narrowed with hatred as he approached Richard.

Richard greeted Isaac, barely able to contain his own contempt for the man. He specified his demands, the citizens' murmurings growing louder as they were translated into Greek. Isaac was to swear fealty to Richard and accompany him to the Holy Land with one hundred knights, four hundred horsemen, and five hundred soldiers.

He would pay thirty-five hundred marks for the poor treatment of Richard's men while in captivity, and hand over his only daughter and heir as hostage. So that no one could doubt his pledge, he was to give up all his castles and holdings to the English crown, which, if he proved his faithfulness, would be returned to him.

Isaac remained motionless while the terms were being translated, but nodded his head in agreement. Richard and Isaac dismounted, and after Isaac swore his fealty, they exchanged the kiss of peace. As a show of his own good faith, Richard returned Isaac's tent and silver plate, which he'd taken in the battle. Before they'd even left, Isaac instructed his men to set up his tent.

Rob shifted in his saddle to glance back at the conference site. "Those terms were even harsher than the ones you gave Philippe. From the stories I've heard, Isaac's not used to losing. Do you think he'll keep his agreement?"

"In his place, I wouldn't." Richard shrugged. "But we shall see."

*~*~*

Berenguela had entered their room ahead of Richard when staccato footsteps rang out on the stone floor.

"Your Grace," Georges called out. "Isaac has escaped."

Richard gave a short laugh. "I'm surprised it took this long."

Berenguela walked to his side. "You expected this to happen?"

"I'd hoped it would. Now that he's in breach of good faith, I have no qualms about hunting him down and holding him accountable." He glanced at Georges. "How long ago did he leave?"

"Three hours ago. He left before nightfall, taking only his horse."

"He has too much of a lead for us to catch him tonight. Return to camp and prepare the men to leave tomorrow."

"Yes, Sire." Georges nodded and left.

"Isaac is despicable and deserves to be defeated, but how long will that take? He could be anywhere on the island." Berenguela frowned.

"I imagine it shouldn't take too long. A couple of weeks at most."

"Now you're teasing me."

"I never jest about war." Richard raised his brow. "The sooner I'm done with Isaac, the better. Try and get some sleep. It's late."

The next morning, Richard looked up as a rustle from the bed interrupted his low conversation with his pages as they helped him put on his armor.

"I didn't mean to disturb you," he said.

Berenguela rolled over and glanced out the window. "You're going now? It's not yet morning."

"I don't want Isaac to get too much of a head start."

He started to leave, but paused as hurt flashed in her eyes. Defeating Isaac was a priority, but it also provided a target to focus his growing frustration upon. He couldn't be with the woman he loved, but that wasn't Berenguela's fault. He strode to the bed and gave her a quick kiss.

She smiled. "Be safe, Richard."

Stars twinkled in the velvety night sky as he exited the palace. He expected to have to rouse the groom to ready his horse. Instead, his steed was saddled and waiting.

"I thought you might want to get an early start." Rob emerged from the darkness. "I'm still in disbelief that the man managed to flee while under guard."

"A very unfortunate choice for him."

Rob's eyes narrowed. "That's why you allowed him to set up camp where we met. If he were imprisoned in the palace, it would be harder to escape. So, the agreement was for naught."

"Not exactly. If he'd kept faith, I would have more men at my side in the Holy Land, but Cyprus's location is useful in keeping the kingdom supplied with necessary provisions. A ship can sail from the coast at Famagusta to Syria in a day. As of now, supplies to the Holy Land come from Italy. Once he's defeated, Cyprus is mine."

"If we can find him." Rob gave a grim smile. "There are too many places he could hide."

"That might not prove as difficult as one would think. The citizens obviously loathe him and might tell us where he went."

Men were awake and stirring when Richard reached the camp. André and Baldwin de Bethune stood in front of a group of prisoners. A man Richard recognized as Isaac's translator, who was captured in the first skirmish, conversed with them.

"Do his men know where he might have gone?" Richard asked.

"They believe he might have escaped to Famagusta. He has a fortified castle there, but he has others to shelter in," Baldwin replied. "You should also know that he was convinced by one of his knights, Pagan, Lord of Haifa, that you were going to break your part of the agreement and seize him."

"Pagan is known to us," Guy de Lusignan approached the group. "He's Conrad's ally. No doubt sent here to make sure that you are kept busy chasing Isaac while Conrad solidifies his claim to Jerusalem."

Richard's eyes hardened. "Let's not give him the opportunity. Isaac still has allies who are keeping him apprised of our movements. I want you to take some men and head into the interior of the island in case he is hiding out there. In the meantime, the galleys will be divided. We'll sail in opposite directions and reconvene in Famagusta. I mean to put an end to this."

Richard's galleys made good time as they sailed around the coast, capturing ships and castles, but there was no evidence that Isaac had taken refuge in any of them.

Archers held their bows and arrows cocked as they glided into the harbor at Famagusta. Richard gripped his sword, waiting for Isaac's men to burst from their hiding places, but the town was silent.

"Isaac isn't here, or he would've made an appearance by now," Richard said as André joined him.

"He must have gone further inland. Perhaps . . ."

Richard raised his hand to stop him as distant garbled voices grew louder. "Stay alert," he called to his men.

Hs nerves tightened. It wasn't like Isaac to announce his arrival, but he had to be prepared. Men streamed from numerous streets to the port. Relief flowed through him, and he shared a grin with André as Guy's banners snapped in the brisk sea wind.

Once they'd disembarked and set up tents outside of town, Richard sent scouts to find out where Isaac might have gone. Days later, they returned with the news that he'd been sighted in Nicosia.

Richard was bent over the table, studying maps of Cyprus with Guy and Geoffrey to determine which strongholds Isaac might seek shelter in, when Rob burst into the tent.

"Your Grace, a ship has arrived from the Holy Land." He stood aside and two well-dressed men entered the tent, accompanied by soldiers.

An older man with graying hair glared at Guy and Geoffrey before bowing his head deferentially to Richard. "I'm the bishop of Beauvais and this is Dreux de Mello. King Philippe sent us."

Guy sucked in his breath. "The bishop is the man who married Conrad and Isabella. He's Philippe's cousin," he hissed to Richard.

"What news do you have from Acre? Has it fallen?" Richard's hands tensed on the table.

"Hardly. Philippe is waiting for you to arrive before he attacks the city," the bishop replied.

Dreux de Mello crossed his arms. "The king wishes to know why you're tarrying here in Cyprus instead of joining him to conquer Acre."

"Tarrying here?" Heat rushed through Richard's body. "Do you think that we're idling on the beaches, wasting time? If I capture Cyprus, it will be useful as a port to ship provisions to the Holy Land. I'd rather men not die from hunger."

"I think you'd rather chase Greeks than face thousands of Saracens. You're hiding here like a coward while Philippe holds off the infidels."

In four strides, Richard reached Dreux de Mello to tower over him. "We both know that Philippe isn't waiting for me as a courtesy. He needs me to claim victory."

"You put far too much importance on your abilities, Lionheart." The man raised his chin.

"Would you care to find out?"

Richard's men gathered behind him as the atmosphere turned incendiary.

The bishop stepped forward and lifted his hands in supplication. "It was not my intention for this meeting to turn hostile. I don't understand why you and your men are still in Cyprus, but when you are able to, we need you in Acre."

"God's bones," Richard growled after the men had left. "If Philippe were a more competent soldier, Acre would have been his by now."

"What's your plan?" Guy asked.

"I must deal with Isaac. Ready the men. We leave for Nicosia at dawn."

*~*~*

The army moved out, carrying enough water and food to last several days since they had to cross a desolate plain to reach their prey. Told that Isaac planned to ambush them, Richard ordered Guy to take the front while he rode in the rear, expecting the emperor to attack from that direction.

They rode two abreast on a narrow dirt path that wound endlessly through the bleak, arid landscape. There was no relief from the blistering sun. The small villages they passed were deserted, so they couldn't replenish their supplies.

"Where would Isaac plan an attack?" Baldwin gazed at the dry plain that shimmered in the heat. "There's no underbrush or trees for them to take cover."

Richard lifted a wineskin to his lips, grimacing as the warm liquid trickled down his throat. "I'm not sure, but Isaac is canny and knows these lands. Stay vigilant."

Eventually, the landscape changed. They traversed deep riverbeds carved into the barren, windswept terrain, perfect for an army to hide. Richard squinted in the bright sun, searching for any movement.

Battle cries erupted ahead, and hundreds of Greeks burst from their hiding places. The enemy launched arrows toward the front of the army to disperse them, but the men tightened their formation to protect themselves.

A flash of purple caught Richard's eye. Isaac raced along the edge of the gully, then turned toward the rear guard. Richard broke away from the soldiers and rode to face him.

Adrenaline sparked through his veins, and he gripped his lance tighter. At the last moment, Isaac swerved, his horse gracefully arcing away. An arrow flew past Richard's head, followed by a second that bounced off his armor. He spurred his steed after Isaac, but was forced to rein him in as the emperor pulled ahead in a cloud of dust.

Richard returned to his men, furious that once again Isaac had eluded him.

"Sire, are you injured?" Georges demanded.

"No. He missed, although I'm surprised that he fired so accurately while mounted."

"Thank God for that. Apparently, he uses poison-tipped arrows."

"Does he now? This man is becoming tiresome. The next time I see him I will relieve him of his kingdom and his horse. And perhaps even his head."

*~*~*

With no word from Richard for over a week, the mood in the place had shifted to one of apprehension. Alix tried to keep everyone's spirits up by being positive, but history had changed before, she couldn't be sure it wouldn't happen again.

"I feel sorry for the queen," Maud whispered to Alix as they ate supper.

Alix glanced at Joanna and Berenguela. "Which one?"

"Queen Berenguela. She's been married almost two weeks and the king has been gone for most of it."

"I'm sure it must be difficult for her, but at the moment, capturing Isaac is his priority."

Men's voices echoed in the hallway.

"Perhaps that's the king." Maud's voice rose as she stared at the entrance.

"Your Graces, we come with news." Georges hurried to the table, with Rob at his side.

"Has Richard defeated Isaac?" Joanna leaned forward.

"Indeed, he has."

A smile of relief crossed her lips. "Tell us what happened."

"After we arrived in Famagusta and found it deserted, we learned the emperor was in Nicosia. We were prepared to capture the city, but instead the citizens came out to welcome the king." Rob chuckled. "The people of Cyprus were more than willing to rid themselves of Issac and told us that he had fled north. Guy was sent to capture Isaac's castles. The first two fell quickly, but it took several days to take Kyrenia, which was better fortified. We soon discovered the reason. When the garrison surrendered, Guy found Isaac's daughter and wife there as well as the treasury."

"They weren't hurt, were they?" Joanna's tone was sharp.

"No, but they were taken prisoner," Rob replied. "Isaac's daughter means everything to him. Having children myself, I understand. I believe that's his only redeeming quality. He immediately came to the king and submitted on one condition."

"Which was?" Alix's curiosity was piqued.

"That he wasn't placed in iron chains. Instead, Richard used silver ones." Rob chuckled.

"How generous of my brother." Joanna smiled, then furrowed her brow. "But why was Guy in charge of the army? Where was Richard?"

Rob glanced at Georges. "He was feeling unwell, so he stayed in Nicosia."

"How sick was he?"

"He's recovered, but he was feverish for a few days."

"Was it the quartan fever again?" Alix asked.

Rob nodded.

"Why weren't we told? We could have tended to him." Worry filled Berenguela's voice.

"The last thing Richard would want is to be nursed. He's a bear when he's sick. Alix can attest to that."

Alix's stomach lurched as Berenguela's questioning gaze fell upon her. Now she had to come up with a plausible explanation, since a distant cousin likely wouldn't know of this. "I must say Rob's correct. While I was in Poitiers, Richard was stricken with fever. Since I'm familiar with herbal remedies, I treated him.

"I'll pray for his continued recovery," Berenguela murmured, seeming to accept her explanation.

Joanna spun around to face Alix. "This has happened before? Why didn't he, or you, say anything?"

"Richard didn't want to worry you. He contracted the illness years ago. It manifests when he overexerts himself. I didn't think he would get it again so soon."

"He's been ill recently?"

Alix nodded. "In Rhodes, before his fleet found us. I think the battles with Isaac haven't allowed him to fully rest."

Joanna threw her hands up. "He acts like he's invincible, but he's not. I wish he wouldn't take so many risks."

"If you want loyalty, you must lead by example. His men wouldn't respect him if he simply ordered them to fight, then watched from a safe distance. We would follow him to the gates of hell if he asked it of us." Rob shifted his stance.

Joanna sighed. "Let's hope it doesn't come to that. What will happen to Cyprus? Richard doesn't plan to stay and rule it, does he?"

Rob shook his head. "We sail for Acre in two days. He's leaving men in charge who will ship provisions such as wheat, barley, and cattle to be used by the army in Acre. Guy was put in charge of guarding Isaac, a task I wouldn't want. Richard's also entrusting you with the care of Isaac's daughter."

*~*~*

Within moments of their coffers being stowed aboard the buss, they sailed out of the harbor. Alix went out to the deck to escape the stifling warmth of the tent. The light sea breeze stirred her hair, and turquoise waves lapped against the ship. She hoped they would have an uneventful journey, not wanting to go through another storm at sea. Maud stood at the rail next to Isaac's thirteen-year-old daughter, Beatrice.

"Poor child." Berenguela joined Alix. "I can't imagine what she's been through. Her father's been captured, she's with people she doesn't know, and she doesn't understand our language."

"Joanna said Beatrice speaks some French. Her mother was Armenian, but her stepmother is stepsister to Joanna's deceased husband, William."

Berenguela's eyes widened. "So, William knew Isaac? Why didn't she mention that?"

"Isaac's cruelty is well known. I'm sure she wasn't pleased that her husband associated with the man."

"No one can fault her for that. I still can't believe that Richard took Cyprus in fifteen days. When he told me he would, I thought he was being overconfident." Her face glowed with pride.

"He's taken castles that were supposed to be impregnable."

"I wish we were traveling with him. I can't stop thinking about our last journey and what we faced. What will the Holy Land be like? My father made it clear he fears for my safety. Do you think he's right to be so concerned?" Berenguela bit her lip.

"If Richard didn't think he could protect us, he wouldn't have allowed us to come." Her gut wrenched, but she forced a smile. What dangers would Outremer hold for them?

She'd expected to dislike Berenguela, since she was the reason Alix's relationship with Richard was over, but the opposite was proving to be true. Historically, little was known about Richard's wife. Historians had portrayed her as quiet and demure, eclipsed by Richard's charisma. Alix was learning that there was more to Berenguela than she'd initially thought. Here was her chance to get to know her and use her dissertation to bring her out of the shadows.

*~*~*

Richard stood at the bow, his gaze focused on the rocky coast as his galley traveled south from Syria. After months, his destination was drawing near.

André squinted as the sun emerged from a passing cloud. "Imprisoning Isaac in Syria was a shrewd move. Castle Margat is in the hands of the Christians, one of the few that Salah-ad-Din hasn't taken."

"I couldn't leave him in Cyprus, since he still has some loyal followers left. The castle is fortified and easily defended. I thought it would make an ideal prison."

André laughed, then drew his brows together. "I fear the Saracens will prove to be more difficult foes."

"Once we reach Acre and join Philippe, God willing, we'll defeat Salah-ad-Din and reclaim the Holy Land."

Richard's heart pounded and excitement surged in his veins as the ancient biblical city of Tyre appeared in the distance. More than two years after taking the cross and meticulous planning, he'd finally reached Outremer. At times, it had seemed like an intangible dream, but now it was within his reach. If he reclaimed Jerusalem for the Christians, glory would be his. None could doubt he was a great king.

The sinking sun cast a red glow like a beacon over the city, illuminating tall, cylindrical minaret towers unlike the round, squat ones in France, and a large iron chain which barred the port.

Richard motioned to one of his sailors, Peter de Barre, and ordered him to take Baldwin ashore to ask Conrad for admittance into the city. The boat soon returned.

Baldwin climbed the rope ladder and made his way onto the deck. "The garrison refused us entrance. Conrad is in Acre, aiding Philippe, but gave orders to his men that no one was to enter."

Richard cocked his brow and gave a short laugh. "No one, or myself in particular?"

"He did send one of his knights to convince Isaac that you were untrustworthy," André quipped. "He likely believes you're still in Cyprus."

"As much as the Lusignans have rebelled against my family, I'd much rather have Guy on the throne. As my vassal, he can be controlled. We'll anchor here tonight, then make for Acre in the morning."

Richard had invited Guy and his brother Geoffrey to dine with him. Afterward, they studied the rudimentary map of Acre Guy had drawn, showing the gates and towers situated along the city wall. He'd been instrumental in commencing the siege at Acre and knew the city's defenses. They were on the topic of the best placement of siege machines to attack the city when Rob threw the flap of the tent open.

"Your Grace, a ship has been spotted," he announced.

Richard hastened to the deck, followed by the men. The ship was larger than any other he'd ever seen. It was covered by a yellow tarpaulin on one side and a green one on the other and had three tall masts, as opposed to his galley, which only had one.

He frowned and motioned to Peter. "Find out what manner of ship that is."

"Sire, they said it belongs to King Philippe," Peter said after returning to the galley.

Richard noted the lack of flags and banners. "I've never seen a French vessel like that."

"Sire," a sailor called out as he rushed to them. "I believe that's a Saracen ship."

"What makes you say that?"

"I've seen ones like it before. Send a galley after them, but tell the rowers not to greet them. We'll see what their intentions are." Sincerity vibrated in his voice.

Richard narrowed his eyes as suspicion crept through him. If the sailors were misleading them as to who they were allies with, they were on a mission and didn't want to engage in battle.

Another ship was sent to intercept the vessel without greeting them, as the sailor suggested. Richard's hands tightened on the rail, his nerves tingling as he waited for confirmation—friend or foe.

Within moments of drawing near, arrows and bolts rained down on them. Richard immediately gave the order to attack. The ship tried to outrun them, but the light wind died, leaving their sails limp and useless.

The galleys circled the hindered boat, but the soldiers couldn't board. Whenever they tried to move closer, a hail of defenders' arrows forced them back. Their low vantage point also made it impossible for them to toss grappling hooks up and over the ship's tall sides.

Richard prowled the deck, shouting encouragement to his men until his voice was raspy. He wanted to join his men, but had to settle for firing his crossbow whenever a Saracen came into range.

Unable to breach the ship, the galleys pulled back, the sailors muttering to themselves.

"Surely, you're not going to let them escape untouched. Are you turning into cowards? I will hang the lot of you should you let them go!" Richard bellowed.

"That will put the fear of God into them, even though the men know that won't happen." André grinned.

The galleys swung around and approached the enemy. Once they were close enough, several of the oarsmen dove into the water with coils of rope, swam under the ship, and tied up the rudder. The Saracens onboard focused their attack on them to stop their progress, but it was too late. The ship was already floundering. Richard's men threw grappling hooks into the tarpaulins that covered the sides of the ship and clambered up.

The hand-to-hand combat from both sides was vicious. Swords flashed in the sun, and the metallic clangs melded with the screams of men. The deck was soon slick with blood. The Turks flung the English dead and wounded into the water. The English soldiers on board held off the enemy long enough for others to climb over the bulwarks, thirsty for revenge for their fallen comrades.

"Do you think we'll defeat them, Sire?" Jacques inched closer to the gunwale.

"By God, we'd better." Richard's brows drew together. "With the number of soldiers on board, they're likely heading to Acre to lend aid. We can't let that happen."

Cheers from the soldiers on the galleys floated across the sea toward them as the Saracens were driven back into the prow of the ship. It seemed like the tide was shifting in favor of the English army, but the doors to the hold opened and a fresh wave of Saracens burst out. The fighting continued, but Richard's men, already exhausted, fell back until they were forced to retreat to their ships.

Richard's face darkened, and he clenched his fist. "Sink it!" he bellowed.

"Are you sure?" André asked.

"I'd hoped to take the ship, but I won't allow any more of my men to die. Better we destroy it than allow it to reach Acre."

The galleys bore down on the crippled ship and rammed it with their iron-tipped prows. The ship listed as water poured into the gaping wounds that opened in her hull. Within minutes, the waves heaved and engulfed it.

To escape the sinking vessel, the Turks jumped into the sea. Richard ordered his men to spare some so he could question them about their cargo. Thirty-five men were rescued, while the rest drowned or were slain.

Baldwin's skiff approached the galley. A ladder was tossed over the side, and he clambered aboard. He accepted a wineskin that André handed him, drank deeply, then motioned to the wreckage of the Turkish ship that floated on the waves.

"Sire, ten of the prisoners plucked from the sea were put on our ship. One of Guy's men, Humphry de Toron, speaks Arabic and interrogated them. The ship was sailing to Acre with over seven hundred soldiers, and numerous crossbows, bolts, and arrows. They also carried Greek fire."

"I wish we'd been able to take it. The weapons alone would have been useful."

Baldwin gave a short laugh. "The captain evidently thought the same thing. The ship sank so quickly because he'd already given the order to cut holes in the hull before our galleys rammed it."

Richard rubbed his jaw. "I can well understand him not wanting it to fall into our hands. Thank God we came across it when we did. If they'd managed to land, we would have no hope of taking Acre."

## ~ *Chapter 23* ~

NOTHING HAD PREPARED ALIX FOR her first glimpse of Acre as their buss neared the harbor. A tall tower, visible for miles, dominated the city. The besieging crusaders camped outside the high turreted walls, and in the distance, the colored tents and pavilions of Salah-ad-Din's army covered the plains and hills. Richard's red-and-gold banners flew from the galleys anchored near the entrance to the port. Sailors strolled the decks, keeping watch for attacks.

Dread crept through her. She'd read about the adversities the soldiers had faced. Thousands had died from injuries sustained during constant fighting. Death from sickness was rampant. Richard's own health would be impacted by serious illnesses. Acre was also the site of the brutal act that had turned her against Richard during her graduate studies—he'd ordered the deaths of over two thousand prisoners.

In the years she'd known him, her view of him had changed, but now she would have to face the atrocity that would forever scar his reputation. She could accept that killing was a fact of war, but not willful murder. Would her opinion of him change again if she had to experience the horrors herself?

Rob greeted them when they docked. The cool sea breeze dissipated the further they walked, and the sun blazed down from a cloudless sky. Alix wiped her brow and grimaced as her dress stuck to her back.

They passed groups of people, with Italian dialects, such as Genoese and Pisan, mixed with German and French, filling her ears. Alix expected to see soldiers strolling through the camp but was shocked when a group of children ran by, laughing. The inevitable prostitutes were present, but the women purchasing goods in the markets seemed to be soldiers' and merchants' wives.

A true city had been established during the siege. Men stood in line outside of the hospital, and next to a church was a small cemetery. There was even a public bathhouse. This normalcy contrasted with the ever-present war and the enemy who lay in wait, like lions ready to pounce on their unsuspecting prey.

"I had no idea there were so many people here." Maud stared about in awe. "Is that the enemy on the hills?"

Alix nodded, her stomach clenching. "No wonder it's been impossible for the army to capture the city. The soldiers must worry about an attack from that side, as well as from the garrison in Acre."

In the distance, Richard's standard fluttered in the breeze on top of a large tent. Their arrival generated much interest from the soldiers and the women, who watched as they wound their way through the camp. No doubt they'd heard of Richard's Spanish queen and were curious about her.

By the time they reached the tent, Alix was praying for air conditioning. Maud's cheeks were pink from the heat, and Joanna and Berenguela fanned themselves. They approached the squires standing outside the tent, one of whom was Jacques. His eyes brightened and he gave Maud a quick smile. The tent flap was open, and Rob motioned for them to enter.

Richard sat at the table, conversing with a dark-haired man who had his back to the entrance. He stood and walked to Berenguela, gave her a light kiss, then hugged Joanna. Alix's heart quickened as his warm gaze caught hers, but she forced the feeling away and averted her eyes. She'd made her decision.

"At last, you've arrived. I trust you had an easy voyage?"

"Yes, we had no troubles," Berenguela replied. "How long have you been here?"

The other man turned around. "His fleet landed two days ago, with all the fanfare one would expect from Richard."

Richard motioned toward his visitor, who, although not dressed in rich clothes, exuded a commanding presence. "May I present Henri, Count of Champagne? My nephew, and Philippe's, although I don't hold it against him."

Amusement crosses Henri's handsome face. He bowed to Berenguela. "Your Grace, I'm honored."

He hugged Joanna and offered his condolences on the death of her husband and subsequent imprisonment.

"You remember Alix, do you not?" Humor laced Richard's tone.

Alix fought the urge to glare at him and curtsied. Henri had been instrumental in helping grant her an audience with Philippe to sow the seeds that would upend Alys's world.

Henri's eyes widened, and his gaze darted from her to Richard, then back. "Certainly. How have you been?"

"I'm very well, thank you."

If Henri questioned the nature of her relationship with Richard, he was too well-bred to ask.

Joanna raised her brow. "How do you know each other?"

"We met several years ago at a conference between Richard and Philippe," Henri responded.

"You mentioned fanfare as Richard arrived. What exactly happened?" Alix asked.

Richard grinned at her, obviously noting her desire to change the subject. He motioned for them to sit down, taking care to seat Berenguela next to him.

"When Philippe arrived more than a month ago with six ships, the people were excited to see him, but he lacks Richard's flair." Henri grinned. "As soon as the first of Richard's twenty-five ships was spotted on the horizon, the citizens rushed down to the harbor. When the fleet entered, he was standing at the prow of his galley so everyone could see him. The cheers were deafening."

Alix chuckled, remembering his arrival in Messina. "Richard does like to make an entrance."

"He managed that. Philippe was there to meet him, but it was obvious that he wanted to be anywhere else. Although France is the greater of the two kingdoms"—Henri paused and gave a cheeky grin—"Philippe was outshone by his own vassal in wealth and in reputation. The soldiers' celebrations upon Richard's arrival extended well into the night."

Henri took a sip of wine and nodded toward Richard. "You've given renewed hope to the armies. We thought that Philippe's forces would tip victory in our favor, but he's done little to that end."

"Henri arrived a couple of years ago and has since been made commander of the army," Richard explained to Berenguela. He then turned to his nephew. "I need to see exactly what we're up against and what weapons would be best utilized to capture the city in the shortest amount of time."

Henri nodded. "Certainly. We can go now if you wish."

"Good, but first I have something I'd like everyone to see." Richard stood and motioned for them to go out.

Servants were busy raising tents next to his. Berenguela's ladies stood nearby, whispering to each other and glancing around.

"I hope that the accommodations are acceptable. I know they aren't as luxurious as Isaac's palace."

Joanna scanned the tents. "They'll be fine," Joanna said. "What do you want to show us? Surely not our lodging?"

Richard gave her a smile and led them through the camp, acknowledging the cheers and greetings of the French and English soldiers. They stopped at an enclosure next to wooden stables. In the middle, a chestnut dun steed grazed. His coat gleamed like spun gold in the sun, and his muscles rippled under his skin as he moved.

Alix gasped. "He's magnificent. Where did you get him?"

"You remember me telling you that Isaac had a horse that outran mine each time we battled?"

"Is that his horse?"

"It is. His name is Fauvel."

Berenguela frowned. "You stole his horse?"

Richard shrugged. "The man is imprisoned, and I couldn't let Fauvel languish in Cyprus. Not when he's more useful to me."

Alix walked closer to the fence. A small smile crossed her lips. She glanced at Richard, who'd joined her. "I can see why you took him."

On the way back to camp, Richard beckoned to Henri. "I wish to see Philippe's siege engines. In the time he's been here, he should've been able to take Acre. What has he been doing?"

Henri laughed. "According to him, he was waiting until your arrival to share the glory." His smile faded. "In truth, we've had a terrible time. The lack of enough food has led to men weakening and dying from disease. The enemy routinely creeps down from the hill and burns any unwatched siege machines. We're under constant attack, and the men's morale was plummeting. When Philippe arrived, we thought victory was ours, but we've made little headway."

By the time they returned to Richard's camp, the tents for the queens had been erected. Berenguela's ladies rushed out of hers, gesturing and speaking rapidly. She managed to calm them down and ushered them back inside.

Joanna stepped closer to Alix. "I have no idea what they said, but I can read faces. They aren't happy to be here."

"You can't blame them. The journey hasn't been easy, and coming from a palace in Limassol to stay in a tent in the desert isn't what they expected."

"This isn't what any of us expected." Joanna lifted her hands in supplication. "We were almost shipwrecked, imprisoned by a despot, and now we're living like nomads." She sighed and shook her head.

Alix put her hand on Joanna's arm. "The camp is much more habitable than I'd thought it would be. We'll be able to purchase goods from the market, and I saw a church, which should make Berenguela happy."

"Perhaps it won't be too dismal. Since the servants set up only two tents, you and Maud will stay with me." She coiled her thick reddish-blond hair and fanned the back of her neck. "I need to bathe, or I won't be fit company for anyone."

While the pageboys carried their trunks into the tent, they waited outside and watched Richard approach.

"Joanna, Henri is going to show me around. I hope you don't mind if I leave you?"

"Not at all, but please find me a tub before you go."

He laughed and called Jacques over. After a brief conversation, the boy ran off. Richard glanced at Alix.

"I assume Joanna and Berenguela wouldn't want to come, but what about you? Care to be instructed in the art of siege warfare?"

Alix's heart jumped, but she tried to convince herself that it was due to experiencing history firsthand, not the fact that Richard invited her. "I'd like nothing more."

Her cheeks heated at the warning look Joanna gave her. They'd just arrived and already Richard requested her presence over his wife's. She'd told Joanna she wouldn't threaten their marriage and she meant it. Moving forward, she would make sure they spent as little time together as possible.

They left the relative safety of the encampment and walked across the dusty plain toward the imposing walls that encompassed Acre.

Ice slid down Alix's spine as she glanced at the hill covered by countless Saracens. "There are so many."

"We must stay diligent," Henri warned. "The enemy has come close to the ditch that separates us, carrying bows and shooting arrows as if practicing. Unguarded men have been attacked, and tents plundered."

Richard slowed his pace to walk next to Alix. "Considering what happened in Messina, I know you're apprehensive. I'd do anything to change that, but you protected yourself and the others."

Alix's lips thinned. "If Ralph hadn't found us, I doubt the outcome would've been the same."

"Most women wouldn't have fought back. I feel confident in entrusting you with the safety of Joanna and Berenguela."

She nodded, her gaze drawn again to the hill where the enemy waited. Resolve flowed through her. She knew Richard's history, and she wouldn't put them in danger again.

Richard's eyes shone as they approached the siege machines that faced the wall.

"Alix, these are counterweight trebuchets. Instead of manpower to release the long beam, leverage is used. The sling can be lengthened or shortened to change trajectory and distance."

She hid her grin at his excitement. "*Mon Dieu!* I didn't realize they were so immense."

Henri pointed out a siege machine that stood next to a high wall. "That's Philippe's machine. He calls it *Malvoisine.* The Turks have one they call *Mal Cousine,* which they use to destroy Philippe's. I've lost count of how many times they've had to rebuild it."

"When Guy was in Cyprus, I asked about the city—namely, what material the structures were built with. He told me it was limestone. I brought stones from Sicily that are much harder than that. Once my machines are in place, we'll see how long the enemy can hold out." Richard tilted his head and clasped his hands behind his back.

Two soldiers had picked up large stones and were lugging them to the sling. Once they were positioned, one of the men released the hook. The rocks shot through the air with a whine and slammed into the limestone wall in a cloud of dust and debris. Cheers erupted from the men.

Richard led them over to a huge contraption that was being erected a safe distance from the enemies' stone throwers.

Alix craned her neck upward. "Tell me about this machine."

The rectangular wooden tower was built on wheels and had interior stairs leading to the top.

"It's called a belfry and can be moved to different locations. It has multiple levels, so crossbowmen and archers will be protected as they fire on the enemy. The top floor is higher than the city wall so we can lower a drawbridge and storm the battlements. Unlike a siege machine, it will be covered with layers of hides and netting soaked in vinegar which can withstand destruction from Greek fire."

"I've heard of that. Supposedly, it sounds like thunder as it flies through the air." Alix examined the structure closely. "It can't be extinguished with water, so using it is quite effective on land, but in sea battles, it's devastating."

Henri raised his brow. "I'm surprised that you're familiar with Greek fire. I've only experienced it here."

Richard smiled. "Don't underestimate Alix. She's more knowledgeable about politics and war than most men. I'd like to send a message to Salah-ad-Din. If we can enact an agreement that would benefit both of us, then perhaps we can take Acre with no more bloodshed."

Henri cocked his brow. "Very diplomatic of you, Uncle. I'll look into it. You might be interested to know that Philippe has been in talks with the commanders of the city's garrison, although so far, nothing has come of it."

Richard laughed. "Why doesn't that surprise me?"

They walked back to camp, long shadows stretching toward the city walls as the blazing sun sank toward the horizon. The aroma of cooking wafted through the air. Men and women chatted and laughed while children darted around the tents. If it weren't for the numerous campfires on the hill, Alix could almost forget the enemy lurking in the distance.

Acre was dusty, hot, and seethed with activity. Alix and Elisabetta inched their way through the throngs of people in the crowded market. Women waited in lines in front of stalls to purchase fruit, vegetables, and meat. Men stood in groups or paced the perimeter of camp, always keeping watch in case the enemy attempted an attack. Although the siege engines sent rocks smashing into the city walls day and night, Alix never got used to the sound, or the screams of the injured.

She was used to dry, hot Texas summers and was acclimating to the climate. Joanna, Berenguela, and their ladies preferred to remain in their tents during the heat of the day and only emerged in the early morning or as the sun set and the night air cooled.

Alix tanned easily, and her exposed skin had turned a golden brown. Maud, on the other hand, had burned within days of their arrival. A stall selling herbs stood near the hospital, and Alix headed toward it. Many of the dried herbs were unfamiliar to her, but a bundle of thick, fleshy green stalks caught her attention. The merchant spoke a little French, and she managed to convey what she wanted.

"What is that?" Elisabetta picked up a fleshy leaf.

"Aloe vera. The gel inside is used to soothe burns. Maud hasn't said anything, but I know she's miserable."

"I confess I miss the palace in Messina, but I'm getting used to Acre. Queen Berenguela's women, however, complain all the time, if the tone of their voices is any indication. I suppose being of low birth has its uses." Elisabetta chuckled.

"I'm sure the queen is having a hard time getting used to this as well, although I haven't heard a word of complaint from her. This is a harsh place. Men are killed and injured daily from arrows and falling stones. If you don't die in battle, it's likely disease might kill you."

Since her arrival, she'd been busy tending to Richard's men. So far, most of their injuries consisted of lacerations and broken bones from falling rubble. Maud had helped, applying splints, salve, and making herbal teas. On occasion, Alix assisted Ralph with men struck by arrows, but most succumbed to their wounds at the time of injury.

Worry filled Elisabetta's eyes. "I pray that doesn't happen to the king. The queens are trying to be brave, but I can see they're worried about him. As you must be. Have you heard any news?"

It had been barely two weeks since they arrived, and Richard had already fallen ill. It didn't help that Philippe was sick too. News of their illness had spread through the army like wildfire. The excitement that had permeated the camp at Richard's arrival had faded as men waited to hear if the kings would recover.

Alix nodded. "He's being treated by Ralph, and Berenguela is spending as much time with him as she can."

She wished she could see him to put her fears to rest, but Berenguela was his wife, and her place was by his side. Joanna visited often, too, and kept Alix apprised of his progress.

They stopped at a fruit stall, and Alix purchased dates, bananas, and sweet carob beans. Although it was not yet noon, the heat was oppressive, and the stench from the outdoor latrines grew stronger. She swatted at the small flies that swarmed them as they walked back to camp.

Alix was smearing aloe gel on Maud's red, peeling cheeks when Joanna burst into the tent.

"Alix, Richard's getting worse. Ralph believes he has an illness he termed *leonardie*, although he's not very familiar with the sickness or what causes it."

Alix knew of the disease, but centuries later, doctors still didn't know exactly what it was.

"He's delirious with fever. I don't think he even knew I was there. What if he dies?" Joanna's eyes were wide with panic.

"The king is going to die?" Maud's voice trembled.

"No, he's not going to die. He'll recover," Alix soothed.

Joanna wrung her hands. "Would you go to him?"

"I don't want to be in the way, and besides, the doctor probably won't allow me in."

"I'm begging you. While I was with him, he called for you. Your presence might help." Fear and worry were etched on her face.

"Very well. I'll see if Ralph will let me visit him."

Alix walked the short distance to Richard's tent, trying to remember anything about the disease. It was theorized that it was similar to scurvy, but there had been no lack of citrus fruit in Cyprus, so likely that wasn't it. Besides a high fever, patients lost their hair and fingernails. Perhaps it was some sort of bacteria from contaminated water or food, but that was still supposition. This particular malady was unique to the past.

Jacques stood guard outside the tent while Rob spoke to André nearby.

"May I see him?"

"I don't know if the doctor will allow it," Jacques's voice wavered.

"Let her in." André walked over, obviously hearing their conversation. He laid his hand on her arm before she entered the tent. "He's never been this sick before." He rubbed his forehead, tension emanating from him in waves. "Ralph can't break his fever. I fear the worst."

Alix took a shaky breath, then lifted the flap of the tent. She nodded to the doctor as he approached in the dim light.

"Ralph, how is he?"

"There's been no change. He's still feverish and has bouts of deliria." He stepped aside and motioned toward the bed.

Multiple scalpels and small bowls sat on a small table. Alix fought the urge to remove them from the tent. The doctors were convinced that bloodletting helped in the treatment of illnesses by keeping the four humors—black bile, yellow bile, phlegm, and blood—in balance. Alix would've tried to dissuade them, but the pallor of Richard's skin and the knotted cloth around his wrist indicated the procedure had already been performed.

He lay half-covered by a sheet. Chills wracked his body, although the tent was stifling. His lips were pale, but his cheeks were flushed. Her stomach plummeted. This was much worse than when he suffered from quartan fevers. She placed a chair at the side of his bed. A cloth lay across a basin that was on the floor. She dipped it in the tepid water and wiped away the sheen of sweat that covered Richard's brow. He muttered incoherently and shifted restlessly.

"Richard, it's me, Alix."

He stilled, and she grasped his hand in hers. His skin burned to the touch. He lightly pressed her hand—or perhaps she was being hopeful. She caressed his cheek, wishing she knew what caused this disease and how to cure it.

Fear surged through her.

Richard should recover, but history had changed. If she and Maud remained in France, Jacques wouldn't have been injured trying to save them when fighting broke out in Messina.

What if that event had altered the past yet again?

"The queens have visited every day, but this is the calmest he's been," the doctor said from behind her.

"He'll survive, won't he?" Alix tightened her grip on Richard's hand. "I couldn't bear it if I lost him."

Ralph's breath gusted out. "I've done all I know to do for him. I've consulted with physicians in town who are familiar with this illness. It's in God's hands now."

Alix sat next to Richard, holding his hand for hours until his deep, even breathing indicated he was asleep. Unable to do anything more, she forced herself to leave his side. Dusk had fallen, casting long purple shadows across the land. A solitary star twinkled in the velvet sky, and she closed her eyes and made a wish. It was childish, but provided a small measure of comfort.

She'd never seen him so weak and ill. When he had quartan fever, he was irritable, aggravating, and refused many of the treatments. This time he was incapacitated, to the point where he allowed the doctors to do what they wanted. Alix continued the short distance to her tent. She prayed her wish would come true and history wasn't doomed to change, but she couldn't erase the fear that he was close to death.

*~*~*

Richard lounged on the colored cushions that surrounded a low table. Henri had told him that this was customary in Arab lands, and Richard found it to be more comfortable than European seating. The doctors had told him he was on the mend from his near-fatal bout of *leonardie*, but it had been two weeks since he recovered and he still tired easily, although he'd never reveal it. He refused to entertain his men from his bed.

The ladies had arrived earlier and were eating and talking. Berenguela kept her worried gaze on him, but he couldn't fault her for that. He'd had fevers before, but this was much worse. This time he'd feared for his own life.

The times he was lucid, he'd shake with chills. Then his body burned like the fires of Hell. In his deliria, dreams of both the dead and the living consumed him. His brothers, Hal and Geoffrey, mocked him for wasting years planning this journey only for it to end in failure. His mother berated him for dying without an heir and leaving John to rule.

He'd recognized women's voices, but only one had dragged him out of the nightmarish darkness.

Alix sat cross-legged on a cushion nearby, listening to Joanna and Berenguela. She glanced at him. "I'm very glad to see you're feeling better. You gave everyone quite a scare."

"Myself included. I don't remember much. The days and nights blurred together, but I remember you."

Her eyes widened. "I didn't think you knew I was there."

"I knew," he said in a low tone.

She gave him a small smile, her gaze never leaving his.

"Did you hear about Philippe's failed attempt to capture Acre?" Henri asked as he and André joined them.

Richard tore his attention away. "That man is insufferable. I had reinforcements arriving, as well as material to build more siege machines, but they were delayed in Tyre due to the weather. I told him to wait, but he refused."

"I believe the entire camp heard that exchange." Henri picked up a goblet and filled it with wine. "To be fair, his plan was well thought out. While his siege engines continually bombarded the walls and towers, the trench that separates the Turks from us was heavily guarded to prevent an attack from behind." Henri paused to take a sip.

"I'm told the sappers at least made some progress. Is this true?" Richard asked.

Henri nodded. "Yes, they did. Although the wall they were working on didn't collapse, it's perilously close."

"What's a sapper?" Berenguela asked.

Richard turned toward her. "Another way to bring down walls is to tunnel underneath them. Sappers dig the tunnels, prop them up with timber, and then fill them with wood, brush, and anything that will burn. They set it afire, and God willing, the wall collapses."

"Soon after Philippe's army began their attack," Henri continued, "the garrison sent smoke signals to alert Salah-ah-Din's army to come to their aid. They began to fill the ditch behind us with earth, rubble, and all manner of debris to cross it. Although I have little liking for the man, Guy's brother Geoffrey outdid himself. Almost single-handedly, he held off the enemy with an axe. It was a hard-fought battle, but eventually he and his men were able to retake the barricade."

He stared into the depths of his cup. "The fighting near the city was just as brutal. We lost countless men from crossbows and Greek fire. Legions of Turks poured into the city. Between trying to breach the walls and defending ourselves from behind, we were overwhelmed and forced to withdraw. There was one man who displayed courage beyond any."

Richard nodded. "If Philippe's army were made of men like him, Acre would have fallen weeks ago."

Joanna raised her brow. "Who are you talking about?"

"Aubrey Clements. He was a French knight who swore that he'd either enter Acre that day or die trying." A ghost of a smile crossed Henri's lips. "He scaled a ladder, and when he reached the top of the wall, he slew a number of Turks. Men followed him, but the ladder collapsed under their weight. Aubrey was left alone on the wall. He was surrounded and killed. Afterward, the army lost heart and soon abandoned their efforts."

Richard's jaw tightened. "A needless death. If Philippe had waited for my reinforcements, we'd be celebrating tonight."

"You know Philippe. Once he sets his mind on something, he follows through. No matter the consequences," André stated. "You'll be pleased to know that your siege engines are still intact. Philippe's were damaged during the battle."

Richard laughed. "What I offered then was well worth it."

"I doubt my uncle would see it that way." Humor laced Henri's voice.

Alix's gaze shifted to Richard. "What did you do?"

"Philippe was paying his men three bezants a month to guard his siege engines." Richard shrugged. "I offered four to anyone who was willing to join my army, regardless of country."

"I'm sure your army increased rapidly."

"It did. Who could doubt that I'm generous?" Richard grinned.

"Richard also sent a messenger to Salah-ad-Din to ask for a meeting."

Joanna's mouth dropped open. "Is this true?"

Richard nodded. "He refused, albeit courteously. He said that kings don't meet until an agreement has been reached. It's bad form to fight after sharing a meal together."

Alix laughed. "He does have a point."

Eventually, the conversation turned to the best way to attack the city. Richard hid a smile as Alix leaned forward, listening to their planning and strategizing.

Their relationship was over, but he missed their verbal banter and the interest she had in political matters. His wife showed little enthusiasm for such things.

He lost track of time until Joanna stifled a yawn behind her hand.

"Apologies, little sister. I didn't realize we were boring you."

"You're not, but might I have a quick word with you?" She moved closer so that the others wouldn't hear. "You've hardly spent any time with Berenguela since we arrived. She told me that it's been days since you've dined with her, let alone shared her bed."

Richard drew his brows together. "Might I remind you that I've been ill and am recuperating?

"I understand, but before we left Cyprus she spent most nights alone. Why did you even ask Mother to endure an arduous trip and bring Berenguela? I know you wish to have an heir but surely it would have been easier to marry before you left or wait until you returned home. She left everything she knew behind to marry a man who is more interested in—" Her gaze cut to Alix then back to him again. "Someone he can't have. Berenguela is your wife, Richard. She deserves to be treated as such."

Anger swept through him. He didn't need Joanna pointing out what he'd lost or telling him how to conduct his marriage, but she was correct. He'd been neglectful and had relegated Berenguela to the periphery of his inner circle.

"It's quite late," Joanna said in a louder voice. "I'm going to retire to my tent. Alix?"

"I'll take my leave as well." She moved to her knees, then stood.

Berenguela shifted on her cushion. "My lord husband, do you wish for me to stay?"

Although he'd hidden it from the others, exhaustion had set in. He opened his mouth to refuse, but then he met Joanna's warning gaze.

"Yes, I'd like nothing more."

He needed to make more of an effort in this marriage, but for now the relief and happiness that flared in his wife's eyes was enough.

*~*~*

Richard had just finished the cup of foul tea Jacques had brewed for his continued recovery when Georges and André entered the tent.

"Tell me that Philippe hasn't captured Acre," he demanded. "Ralph insists that I remain in my tent to convalesce."

"No cousin, not yet." André sported a sly smile. "But the siege machines continue to batter the walls. It's only a matter of time before they're breached."

"God's bones! I didn't come all this way to allow Philippe to claim victory. I'll lead my men to battle today."

Georges raised his hand in protest. "You're still recovering, Sire. You can't risk putting yourself in danger. Give someone else the command."

"No!" Richard's eyes glittered as he slammed his fist on the table. "By God, I'll be there."

In the short amount of time that his army had been in Acre, they'd made great strides in recovering the city. If he prevailed, this was one step closer to defeating Salah-ad-Din, solidifying his prowess as a battle commander. He wouldn't allow Philippe to usurp his victory.

André cocked his head. "How do you plan on doing that?"

"Come, I'll show you."

The sun blazed down as they walked to where Baldwin de Bethune and a group of archers stood next to a circular hut called a cercleia. Constructed from stiff canes and covered by rawhide, it was large enough for men to stand under, but could easily be moved from one location to another.

"I should have known you wouldn't be content to wait while Philippe made another attempt to capture Acre." André chuckled.

The short walk from his tent had left Richard exhausted, his breath coming in heaving gasps. He tried to hide it from the men, but Baldwin frowned at him.

"Are you still set upon joining the battle?" At Richard's curt nod and steely gaze, he instructed the men to carry the hut to the front lines.

Heat rose in Richard's face as his squires placed a silken litter on the ground. This wasn't the way he'd envisioned capturing Acre—being carried like an invalid. It galled him to have fallen ill so soon after arriving and he feared the men might lose faith in him. He wanted to prove to both the French and English armies he was strong enough to lead them into battle.

"No man here can doubt your courage or leadership." Baldwin handed Richard his crossbow. "On your command."

Adrenaline coursed through Richard's veins as he gripped the crossbow and raised it over his head. "This city has been under siege for far too long," he called out to the men gathered behind him. "Let's accomplish what we came to do. Today, Acre will fall!"

He joined his most skilled crossbowmen in the cercleia that had been moved to the front line and studied the wall that protected Acre.

On the east side of the city, a tower called the Cursed Tower was already weakened along with the nearby wall. To the north, a second major tower was close to collapse. Richard chose these locations as his point of attack. He ordered his men to use the siege engines to batter the tower wall while his sappers dug a passage under the foundation.

As much as Richard wanted to be in the thick of battle, he had to content himself with firing upon any Saracen that tried to attack the siege machines and shouting encouragement to the men.

The sun crept higher in the bleached sky. Sweat slicked his hands and stung his eyes. The screams and yells of men were constant, and the metallic scent of blood filled the air.

Each time a stone smashed into the tower, rubble careened down, weakening it. The sappers lit the wooden debris in the tunnel and thick smoke soon billowed out. The Cursed Tower listed, then collapsed in a plume of dust.

Deafening cheers filled the air. The adjoining walls partially disintegrated, but there was too much debris to mount an effective attack.

Henri hurried to Richard's side, his hauberk blood-stained. "The Turks are a formidable enemy. Now you can see what we've been up against." His gaze was fixed on the battle before them.

"We need to seize the advantage." Richard's voice was hoarse from inhaling the thick dust in the air. "Words of support often fall upon deaf ears. Money, on the other hand, speaks volumes. Send a crier to announce that I'll pay two coins for each stone that is removed from that wall. Once it's demolished, we can storm our way in."

Henri grinned. "I only hope you have enough money in your coffers."

The crier did as ordered and men-at-arms and youths darted forward, the promise of money and glory too strong to ignore. The Turks rushed to defend the wall. Armor and shields provided little to no protection against the darts and arrows that flew into their midst, but the men pressed on.

A strangled cry was torn from Henri's throat. "Damn the brazenness of that cur! That's Aubrey's armor he's wearing."

He pointed to the Turk who stood on a rampart, mocking and jeering the men below.

"Not for long." Richard's muscles ached from exhaustion, but through sheer will, he lifted his crossbow, squinted in the bright sun, and took aim. The bolt whistled through the air and embedded itself in the man's chest.

Within minutes, the enemy swarmed the wall in revenge and sent a renewed onslaught of arrows and bolts raining down. The English army was forced back.

Richard's hand shook as he wiped sweat from his brow. He clenched a fist to hide it, but the frown on Henri's face told him he'd failed.

"Uncle, the fighting is over for the moment. We need to regroup."

Richard nodded, relieved that the decision to stop was made for him. He refused to admit that the heat had sapped the last of his strength. Adrenaline alone was no longer enough to stave off the weariness that flooded through him in waves.

"Acre won't fall today, but it's only a matter of time." He allowed his men to carry him back to his tent.

*~*~*

Alix folded and refolded her dresses to keep busy, but she couldn't concentrate on the task. Joanna paced the tent, her hands knotted, while Berenguela gripped her rosary and murmured prayers. Elisabetta kept Maud and Beatrice busy by having them help her prepare a light meal. Beatrice's French was improving, and she and Maud chatted under their breath.

"Not knowing what's happening is maddening." Alix tossed a half-folded dress on her cot, went to the tent flap, and looked out. Men stood in groups, muttering and casting looks at Richard's tent.

It had been over a week since the last attack on Acre. Days ago, messages had been sent to the kings from Acre asking for a truce. Philippe and his nobles agreed. Richard did not.

His siege engines continued to pummel the walls day and night. He increased the pay for each stone removed from the wall to three bezants, then four. It was sometimes a suicide mission, with men being crushed by falling stones or struck by arrows from archers on the walls, but each day, the breach widened.

To spare Acre from complete destruction and his people almost certain death by the armies, Salah-ad-Din had requested another meeting. The commanders from Acre had arrived earlier that morning for a meeting with the kings.

Maud stood behind Alix. "Will the kings agree to the truce?"

She turned and tried to calm her racing heart. History was on the verge of a momentous event. She'd give anything to witness what was happening. "King Philippe has wanted one for a while and I think King Richard will see the wisdom in it."

Joanna joined them. "My brother doesn't want to lose any more men than necessary. If he can capture Acre without more bloodshed, he will."

Shouts echoed in the distance. Joanna and Alix ran outside, followed by the ladies. Men cheered and clapped each other on the back while women burst into tears and hugged.

Berenguela crossed herself. "Is it over? Acre has been captured?"

"It is done. Acre is ours." Richard strode to them. He focused on Alix, a victorious smile on his face.

Exhilaration swept through her. She moved toward him, then stopped herself. She didn't have that right anymore. A flash of disappointment crossed his face when she hesitated.

"*Gracias a Dios*! I knew you would prevail." Berenguela threw herself into his arms.

"What happens now?" Alix turned toward Henri, who wore a grin as big as Richard's.

"The hostilities have ended and orders given that no one should provoke the enemy or fire upon them or the walls. The garrison will leave the city."

"I assume there were terms?" Joanna asked.

Richard nodded. "The True Cross captured at Hattin will be returned, as well as twelve hundred Christian captives. To ensure these terms, noble Turks in Acre will be given to us as hostages. If, in a month's time, Salah-ad-Din hasn't kept his part of the agreement, they will be at our mercy."

A strange calm descended upon the armies camped outside the crumbling walls as they waited for the enemy to leave. For the first time in months, the sounds of battle and siege engines were absent. After two years of brutal fighting, Acre was captured.

## ~ *Chapter 24* ~

IT HAD BEEN OVER A week since Acre had fallen. Salah-ad-Din had moved his army deeper into the mountains, and the hill lay bereft of brightly colored pavilions. Now that the crusaders occupied the city, the siege machines had been dismantled. Philippe and Richard had kept the agreement they'd made in France and split the spoils, including the captives. Philippe took the Templar's palace while Richard claimed the royal palace for his own.

Richard took Alix and the queens on a tour of the city. She was surprised to be included. Perhaps he felt that remaining civil to each other was in everyone's best interest. The politeness was almost cruel. Being around him reminded her of what she'd given up.

Her first steps inside Acre took her breath away. She was thrilled to see little destruction in the city. The armies had focused attacks from the siege machines on the walls, so many of the interior stone buildings remained intact.

The oppressive tension that had permeated the very air was gone. Although the crusade was far from over, Acre was revitalized. Market stalls and taverns were open, and the soldiers continued to celebrate their victory with wine and the always available women who loitered outside the bathhouses in brightly colored robes.

Richard led them down the narrow streets, pointing out the public baths, the Templars' Hospitaller fortress, and the Pisan and Genoese neighborhoods. In the Genoese market, Alix paused at a stall covered by a canvas awning that sold exotic spices and oils and made a note to return.

"Will the churches be rebuilt?" Berenguela asked as they walked by the desecrated church of St. George.

Richard nodded. "Yes, but first we need to repair the walls. It took years to claim Acre. I don't wish to lose it so soon."

They meandered back to the main wooden gates where Richard's, Philippe's, and the Kingdom of Jerusalem's banners fluttered on the walls.

A satisfied smile crossed Richard's lips.

"What's that smile for?" Joanna asked.

"I'm glad to see that Austrian upstart hasn't replaced his banner."

"Who are you talking about?"

"Duke Leopold of Austria." He grimaced. "The man had the audacity to hang his banner alongside ours."

"And you took offense to that," Joanna stated.

"God's bones!" he exploded. "The man did nothing to capture the city. He didn't have the right to claim it. I had it torn down."

Berenguela gasped at his flash of anger.

"I'm sure he wasn't pleased with your decision," Alix said.

His eyes hardened as he focused on her. "He had but a small army, subsidized by Philippe. The contribution he made to the capture of Acre was minimal. Not to mention he's related to that despot, Isaac."

"Well, that's reason enough," Alix said in a dry tone.

Richard grinned. "Yes, it is. At any rate, it's come to my attention that Leopold's leaving Acre in a few days."

Alix clenched her hands, her nails digging into her palms. That negligible act was to have far-reaching consequences. Historically, Leopold had never forgotten or forgiven Richard's actions. She wished she could tell him that Leopold would take his revenge, but then she'd have to explain how she knew. She'd told Richard she used to dream of future events, but, although he'd accepted that, she wasn't willing to test it. For now, she held her tongue.

Apparently tired of being a guide, Richard ushered them into the palace and took his leave. The queens spent the next few hours exploring the airy rooms and choosing lodgings. Joanna insisted that Berenguela take the chamber closest to Richard's while she chose one further down the hall for her ladies and Alix.

After her belongings were stowed, Alix headed for the baths to wash off the grime and dust from the walk.

In a small reception room, she found folded towels, bath scrapers, and scented oils, obviously left by the previous inhabitants. Alix wandered through the different areas and found one that contained a warm bath. The room was empty, but hearing a distant conversation in Spanish, she assumed it had been prepared by Berenguela's duennas. The water reflected off the mosaic tiled walls and thin tendrils of steam curled upward. She sank into it with a sigh and leaned back against the curved edge.

The palace wasn't as elaborate, with wall hangings and wall sconces like the French ones she'd become accustomed to, but it appeared to be comfortable. However, now that Richard was in closer proximity, that would prove problematic. Her heart splintered into shards each time Richard shared a glance or secret laugh with Berenguela. It was draining to pretend that being near him didn't affect her. She should keep her distance, but not seeing him was worse.

Light footsteps on the stone tiles broke into her thoughts.

"Mind if I join you?" Berenguela asked as she entered with her ladies.

"Of course not, Your Grace," Alix said. She fought to not cover herself with a towel and instead sank lower into the water. She would never get used to the lack of privacy that existed in this time.

"I know Richard tried to make us as comfortable as possible in camp, but I'm glad that we're here now. To think, a week ago, I didn't know if Richard would live or die. Now he has captured Acre." Berenguela said as she splashed warm water over her skin. "I prayed daily that he would succeed."

"No one can doubt his prowess on the battlefield. I can't think of a battle he's lost."

Berenguela bit her lip. "You have a certain camaraderie with him. When you questioned his actions against Leopold, I thought for sure you'd anger him further."

Alix laughed. "He's been vexed with me quite often, but his moods are quick to change."

"I could never speak of this to Joanna, since Richard's her brother, but we've spent little time together since our wedding." Her next words came out in a rush. "I realize he's still recovering, but before he became ill, we spent very little time together and he never stayed in my presence for long. I fear I disappoint him."

Alix stared at the ripples in the water. This wasn't a topic she wanted to weigh in on. "I'm sure it has nothing to do with you. He's been involved in battles since the moment he arrived in Cyprus. Acre had been under siege for two years and still hadn't been taken, even with King Philippe's arrival. Between strategizing, planning, and being ill, Richard's had little time for anything else."

Berenguela nodded, but still didn't look convinced. "I know I shouldn't trouble you with my worries, but I consider you my friend." She took a shaky breath. "I don't think he desires me." Heat rose in her cheeks.

Sympathy swept through Alix. She'd have the same fear if she were in an arranged marriage with a man she hardly knew. Here was her chance to push Berenguela to spend more time with Richard, which might improve their marriage.

"I'm certain that's not the case. When he's fully recovered, perhaps you could plan a private dinner. To start, you might offer to help with his bath and see where things might lead."

Berenguela gaped at her. "I couldn't possibly! He'd think I'm too forward."

"He'd think you're a wife who wants to be with her husband. Like women, men want to be desired. Richard's no different. It's perfectly natural to desire your husband and to find pleasure with each other."

An ache spread through Alix's chest as images of countless nights spent with him played out in her mind. Hollowness filled her soul, and she forced the memories away.

"I've heard women speak of such things. I hope to experience that one day." Berenguela glanced shyly at her.

Alix suggested a few more seduction techniques Richard enjoyed and thought Berenguela would be comfortable performing. Berenguela's eyes widened, but she said she'd try them to please Richard.

"I wouldn't worry." Alix gave her a smile. "It takes time to feel comfortable with a man."

Historically, their marriage had not been a success, and there was even a theory that it had never been consummated, although she'd thought that unlikely. But she liked Berenguela and was truly sorry they were having issues this early. Richard had gone to great lengths to have his wife with him, but they were as mismatched as a dove and a hawk.

*~*~*

Richard leveled his gaze at Conrad de Montferrat and Guy de Lusignan as they entered his palace chambers. His trusted men stood behind him in case they were needed to keep the peace.

"I've met with Philippe, and we've come to a decision which I hope you'll find agreeable."

"Who will be named the rightful ruler of Jerusalem once it's reclaimed?" Conrad glared at Guy. "Hopefully, the one who didn't lose it in the first place."

"It's more of a compromise." Richard hid his smile as Conrad's bluster vanished. He didn't trust Conrad. The more time he spent with the man, the less he liked him. "Although you married Isabella, the heir of Jerusalem, under dubious circumstances, Guy will remain king until his death. In that event, the kingdom will revert to you and your descendants. In the meantime, you will share the royal revenues."

Conrad's face tightened. "What revenues exactly?"

"You'll maintain possession of Tyre. And Beirut and Sidon, if you can recover them. Geoffrey de Lusignan has proven himself a skilled knight during the siege and will be granted Jaffa and Ascalon when they're reconquered."

The de Lusignans were his vassals, and by putting them in charge of critical regions, he could maintain regulation once Salah-ad-Din was defeated and he returned home.

Guy nodded. "Yes, Your Grace. I accept these terms."

"I, as well." Conrad glanced at Richard. "I hope your being denied entrance to Tyre due to my guards being overly protective played no part in your decision."

Richard leaned back in his chair and crossed his arms. "It made it easier."

Knocks echoed on the door, and a squire rushed to open it.

The Bishop of Beauvais and Druon de Mello entered.

Richard raised his brow. "The last time we met in Cyprus, you begged me to come to Acre as soon as possible. Well, Acre has been reclaimed, so why has Philippe sent you this time?"

The bishop stepped forward and bowed his head. "Your Grace, I'm here to inform you that the King of France plans to return home very soon due to his fragile health."

Richard clenched his hand. "What did you say?"

Druon gave a thin smile.

Richard swung around and stared at Conrad. "Did you know of this?"

Conrad's face darkened. "I'd heard. It's already spread throughout the army. If it's any consolation, his men feel the same as you."

"Any chance of making him reconsider?"

"He refused to listen to me and Henri. You're more than welcome to try."

Contempt and fury swept through Richard like wildfire as the men stalked out. He should've expected Philippe would leave the first chance he had.

The success of the crusade hung in the balance. Richard didn't know how many men Salah-ad-Din had at his command, but he needed Philippe's army to help defeat them. If he failed because of Philippe's cowardice, he'd hold him accountable.

*~*~*

Richard stormed into the dining hall and stalked toward the royal table. Philippe's guards trailed behind, but their unwillingness to do more spoke volumes of how they felt about their king.

"Why am I not surprised that you sent your lapdogs to give me the news instead of coming yourself?" Richard stated in a deadly soft voice.

Philippe shifted in his chair and glanced toward Baldwin and André, who flanked Richard. "I've done what I've come to do. Acre has been reclaimed. Now that I've recovered from my grave illness, it's time for me to return to France. I need to return and rule my kingdom as a king should."

Richard clenched his hand. "You coward. I was at death's door but managed to be at the front line, leading my men."

Several of the French soldiers chuckled, and Philippe's cheeks flushed.

"Salah-ad-Din is still free, and the city of Jerusalem remains in his hands." Richard pinpointed Philippe with an icy glare. "You had the opportunity to capture Acre yourself, but you chose to wait for my arrival from Cyprus."

"I was waiting for you so we could share in the victory."

"Then why in God's name are you turning tail when we have the advantage? Surely you can stay until this matter is resolved. If you refuse to continue the war, you're in violation of our agreement."

"Isn't this what you want, Lionheart?" Philippe sneered. "Once I'm gone, you'll have command of the armies. If you can reclaim Jerusalem, then all the glory belongs to you."

If Philippe left with his army, what guarantee did he have that his own kingdom wouldn't be in jeopardy? How like the French snake to try to claim it while he was in Outremer.

"Since you refuse to change your mind, I have one last request of you."

Philippe waved his hand toward his men. "I assume you want to take any of my soldiers who wish to remain into your army. It is done."

"I also want your promise that you won't attack my lands in my absence."

Philippe's eyes narrowed. "Do you have so little faith in me? Your kingdom is safe."

"I want more assurance than merely words. Tomorrow we'll meet with the bishops, and you'll swear that you won't lay a hand on my realm."

Richard spun on his heel and left the room.

"Uncle, wait." Henri caught up to him.

"How long have you been privy to Philippe's plans to leave?" Richard grasped Henri's arm in a vise-like grip.

Henri's face reddened. "I've known for several days. I'd hoped we'd be able to change his mind, but he's as stubborn as you. Do you truly think he'd attempt an attack upon your kingdom?"

"I'd rather sleep in a bed of snakes than accept his word." Richard grimaced. "At the best of times, we've been courteous, but putting aside his sister and keeping the Vexin hasn't done much to foster a closer relationship."

"You should know that many in the French army are willing to stay and fight under you. I am, as well."

Baldwin laughed and clapped Henri on his shoulder. "I have a hard time believing that you're related to that coward, but as long as you fight on our side, I won't hold that against you."

Henri grinned. "Thank you for that."

Richard cocked his brow. "In truth, this might prove to be a boon for me. Now I don't have to split the spoils."

*~*~*

After the ladies and his most trusted men had filed into his chambers, Richard relayed Philippe's news. Baldwin and André exchanged angry glances as stunned silence filled the room.

"I can't believe Philippe is leaving," Joanna said. "Why would he do that?"

"Philippe never wanted to come here. His illness gave him a reason to renounce his vow. Going home to recover is more important than doing God's work," Richard scoffed.

"Without his help, how are you going to reclaim Jerusalem?" Berenguela asked.

Alix held her breath, praying Richard wouldn't lash out.

Richard's lips thinned. "My army is more than capable of defeating the infidels. However, most of the French will remain here under my command."

"And you're going to just allow Philippe to return home? A wolf amongst the sheep?" Alix hoped to divert his annoyance from his wife.

"I made him swear on holy relics that he would leave my lands alone for as long as I'm away." Richard crossed his arms. "When I return, he'll give me a forty-day notice of attack. He's given hostages in exchange for keeping his word—my nephew Henri, and Hugh, the Duke of Burgundy." He shared a grin with Baldwin. "In my opinion, Henri is the only one worth keeping. He's also only taking three galleys and leaving the rest for our use."

Alix furrowed her brow. "How generous of him. But we all know that promises can easily be broken."

"That we do. I admit I've broken pledges, but I'm not the only one to offer empty promises," Richard replied in a neutral tone, as he leveled his cool gaze at her.

The room shrank to just the two of them. He must be referring to her declaration of love for him, followed by her ending their relationship days later. She swallowed convulsively as his blue-gray gaze bored into hers.

"Sometimes they can't be kept, no matter how much you want to." Her face heated at her admittance. She didn't want him to know she still had feelings for him, but his silent accusation stung.

Richard's eyes widened and a faint smile crossed his lips. Her heart jumped. She didn't know what the smile meant but hoped she'd find out.

"I'm not surprised Conrad left with Philippe and returned to Tyre. Besides being unwilling to fight under Guy's flag, he now has Philippe's share of Acre and the prisoners," André said.

Richard turned his gaze toward André. "Philippe expected to get one hundred thousand bezants for the hostages, which would support his army until next year. Messengers have been dispatched once again to Tyre, demanding that Conrad return to Acre with the prisoners so we can negotiate the ransom and give the payment to the French. This time, he'd best not refuse, lest he find me on his doorstep."

The men's talk then turned to strengthening Acre and the looming deadline of Salah-ad-Din returning Christian hostages and the True Cross.

Alix walked to the window that overlooked the courtyard lined with fruit trees and flower beds. Footsteps scuffed behind her.

"Did I misunderstand your words just now?" Richard's baritone voice caressed her like a lover's touch.

Her denial died on her lips. "No. I meant every word I said."

"My feelings haven't changed, either, and aren't likely to. However, stop interfering in my marriage."

She spun around, her gaze faltering under his accusing glare. "What are you talking about? I've done nothing."

Richard moved closer, his body warmth heating her skin through her thin linen dress. He raised a brow. "Giving my wife lessons in seduction?"

"I was trying to help. I thought you'd be amenable to them."

His eyes darkened. "Leave it alone. You, of all people, know exactly what type of marriage this is."

Alix's pulse leapt as he leaned down, his lips inches from hers. She ached to touch him and lose herself in the heat of his kiss.

"There is only one woman whom I truly want in my bed and only one woman to whom I will give my heart, Love."

Richard shaded his eyes from the brilliant sun, pleased with the progress being made repairing the walls. He continued his walk, nodding to the workers and calling out instructions to the masons.

"It's been over a month since you made the treaty with the Turks. The deadline for delivering the hostages has come and gone. They haven't returned the True Cross either," André stated as they skirted two camp dogs wrestling over a bone.

"I'm well aware of that. Salah-ad-Din sends gifts and messengers asking for more time, but I'm growing weary of these games and of being pinned down here. As soon as the terms of the treaty are met, we march south to Ascalon. The city is vital to trade from Egypt to Syria. If we capture it, the Turks' supply chain is cut."

"You're not thinking of bringing the women with us?"

Richard shook his head. "They're much safer here in the palace."

André raised a brow. "How are you enjoying marriage? Your queen seems pleasant and wants to make you happy."

"My marriage is fine," Richard ground out. "I wish everyone would stay out of my affairs."

André laughed. "Has Joanna been giving advice to Berenguela? Most men wouldn't be averse to that."

"No! I wish to God it was her, but it was Alix. She thought it a good idea to instruct my wife in the art of seduction." Richard blew out his breath. "I don't need her meddling."

He'd been surprised when Berenguela had offered to help him bathe. At first, it was pleasant enough, but then her actions reminded him of Alix. He'd become irritated when she told him Alix had suggested them and soon after made an excuse to leave.

After she'd ended their relationship, he'd sensed the woman he desired above all others was slipping further from his reach. Her earlier statement that she still had feelings for him gave him hope that with time, things between them might change. Had he misread her words?

"Your Grace!" Rob jogged toward them. "The Duke of Burgundy and the other two nobles you sent to Tyre have returned."

"Has Conrad brought the hostages?" Richard demanded.

"The hostages are here. Conrad again refused to come."

"Damn that man. At least we can move forward with negotiations now. Hopefully, this will spur Salah-ad-Din to honor the agreement."

"And if it doesn't?"

Richard tightened his jaw. "By God, he will rue the day he crossed me."

*~*~*

Strident voices overlapped each other until Richard raised his hand for silence.

"Your Grace, the deadline expired three weeks ago, and the infidels haven't done what they promised." Baldwin crossed his arms. "They keep asking for more time. How much longer are we going to allow this to continue?"

"Salah-ad-Din has no intention of honoring the terms, so now we're saddled with twenty-seven-hundred hostages." Anger simmered in Richard's voice. The longer they stayed in Acre, the more time Salah-ad-Din had to fortify the cities he'd claimed. "I wish to march south to Ascalon, so a decision needs to be made. Today."

"The simplest thing is to leave them here under guard until our return. Perhaps by then, their ransom will be paid," André said.

"I've already thought of that, but who will stay? I need every man in my army with me. I can't afford to leave any behind."

"We could bring them with us," Guy suggested.

Richard gave a short laugh. "I'd have to guard them to make sure they didn't join the Turks when we cross paths with them. Not to mention I'd have to feed them. I need the provisions for my army. I'd rather not lose men to starvation."

Hugh glanced at Henri, then stood and looked around the room. "It was our hope that we'd negotiate a ransom for the hostages, but it appears that's not to be. If we can't leave them here or bring them with us, I see only one solution."

The room fell as silent as a crypt as his words sunk in.

"You can't mean what I think you're saying," Guy said in a hollow voice. "That's barbaric."

Hugh swung around and glared at him. "Salah-ad-Din himself killed Christian hostages when you lost the battle of Hattin. How wasn't *that* barbaric?"

Guy reddened and sat back in his chair.

Richard frowned. "I'd prefer not to mimic that infidel's actions. If anyone has another solution, speak your mind. I'm willing to listen."

The men glanced at the floor and each other as seconds stretched out. Hugh stepped forward. "It's clear what needs to be done. Give the order and the problem is solved. Or have you lost your penchant for bloodshed, Lionheart?" he sneered.

Richard placed his hands on the table and fixed the man with an icy gaze. "I refuse to make a hasty judgement. I'll think on it tonight and announce my decision in the morning."

"Don't take too long, lest you find the matter has already been resolved."

Audible gasps filled the room.

Anger coursed through Richard's veins. "I suggest you take care in your choice of words," he said in a soft voice. "They almost sound treasonous."

Hugh's face flushed. "That wasn't my intent, Your Grace."

Richard gave a cold smile. "I'm sure it wasn't. This meeting will reconvene in the morning."

Fury consumed him long after the room had emptied. How dare Hugh question, even threaten, to undermine his authority?

But the man had a point. Something must be done with the hostages soon, and if he didn't act, someone else might.

*~*~*

Alix paced in an alcove near Richard's chambers, waiting for him to emerge. This was the act that would change historians' view of Richard forever. His exploits in the Holy Land solidified his legendary status, but this massacre would darken his legacy.

She prayed she wasn't too late, and the decision was already made. The door opened and footsteps echoed on the stone floor.

"Your Grace, please, may I have a word?"

Richard stopped and turned. "What is it? I have pressing matters to deal with."

Alix recoiled from the anger that flashed in his eyes. "Have you made a decision? What will happen to the hostages?"

Her heart plummeted as he looked at her. Nausea churned in her stomach. "You can't kill them! That's cold-blooded murder."

He grabbed her arm and hauled her into his chambers. He ordered the servants out and slammed the door shut.

"Don't ever question my judgement in public. More to the point, how are you even aware of what was discussed in the council meeting?"

"I apologize. But it's true, then? Those men are to be slaughtered."

"We've spent hours debating our options. They can't remain here, and it would complicate matters if we took them south with us. There's no solution that's satisfactory."

"Please don't sign those men's death warrants. There must be other choices."

Richard rested one hip on the table, motioning for her to take a seat. "Tell me what you would do instead."

Alix sat, her mind spinning as she considered plausible scenarios. "I've heard that Salah-ad-Din had sold hostages into slavery—"

"That's not an option," he interrupted her. "No one should be owned by another. Where are your Christian values?"

"I don't agree with slavery, but at least the men would be alive. Surely that's preferable to death."

"I refuse to enslave any man."

"Then have them baptized as Christians and give them their freedom."

A thin smile crossed Richard's lips. "We tried that when we first captured Acre. Men *were* baptized, then fled to Salah-ad-Din's side. I can't release them, only to have to fight them again. Alix, everything you've suggested has been thought of and found to be impractical."

"Those men have families—wives and children. Just because they aren't Christian doesn't mean their lives mean less."

Richard reached out and covered her hand briefly with his. "I can't stay in

Acre while Salah-ad-Din continues to lay claim to Jerusalem. The Duke of Burgundy has been vocal about his choice to put them to death. I can see no other solution."

She'd sworn to herself that she wouldn't do anything to alter history, but if she could repair his reputation, shouldn't she at least try?

She placed her hands on the table and leaned forward. "Remember when I told you that I used to have dreams about events that would come to pass? I had one last night."

Richard stilled. "Tell me."

Alix shifted position under his pinpointed gaze. What could she say to sway his decision?

"In my dream, you're regaled as a brilliant military strategist, a praiseworthy king, set upon reclaiming the Holy Land."

A smile of satisfaction crossed his lips. She then appealed to his hubris.

"But opinions changed. Your decree concerning the prisoners caused historians to malign you. They wrote that you committed this ignoble and bloodthirsty act out of pettiness. You were viewed as cruel and unworthy, which tarnished your reputation forever."

His face darkened and he pounded the table with a clenched fist. The goblets teetered precariously. "Salah-ad-Din put me in this position. He's made no move to pay the ransom for his own men. He thought nothing of killing the Christian prisoners he captured during the battle of Hattin. Yes, I want to prove that we have more scruples, but my hands are tied. I refuse to show weakness to him or to the men I lead."

He paced to the window, then spun to face her. "Was there more to your dream? Is the defeat of the Saracens somehow dependent upon allowing the prisoners to live?"

Alix's breath caught. She knew that he'd do anything to realize his ambition of reclaiming the Holy Land. One word could give him false hope and alter his decision. But then she'd have to live with her deceit. Historically, he'd failed. If she needed to use her "dreams" in the future to protect him, he'd never heed them.

"I don't know. My dream didn't show me that. But you haven't made your choice yet? There's still time to change things? Your act of mercy might encourage Salah-ad-Din to honor the agreement. I know you, Richard. You are not this coldhearted. Yes, in the heat of battle, you've killed men, but this is wrong. This will be a massacre."

She stood, the chair legs scraping on the floor jangling her nerves. "If you go through with this, I don't think I can ever forgive you. I know these men's lives mean nothing to you, but they are important. I beg you to reconsider."

Richard sighed and steepled his hands. "I'm meeting again with my council tomorrow. We'll discuss further options."

Alix nodded. "Thank you for hearing me out. I trust you'll make the right decision."

Chills crept down her back. What if her words managed to change Richard's mind? How would events be rewritten?

*~*~*

The wind whipped Alix's hair around her face and tiny grains of sand stung her skin as she ran to the edge of the city. What had he decided?

Her heart plummeted as the clash of metal and yells grew louder. She burst through a postern gate and stared southeast toward the plain.

Richard hadn't changed his mind.

The fighting was brutal as men lunged and hacked at each other with their swords. The dead littered the ground. Alix covered her screams with her hands and collapsed to her knees. Thick swarms of flies hovered over the soaked ground and the sharp metallic scent of blood tinged the air. Her stomach lurched and bile rose in her throat.

Soldiers milled along the perimeter, keeping watch on the Turkish army in the distance. Richard wanted the enemy to see what he'd done.

"Alix, you shouldn't be here."

She looked up into Rob's worried amber eyes. Streaks of blood stained his hauberk.

"I can't believe Richard allowed this to happen. It didn't have to be this way, even though it is war." Her tone was bitter.

"Yes, it is."

She couldn't bear to hear the answer, but she had to know. "Did he have a hand in putting them to death?"

"No. The Turks attacked after they realized what was happening. As usual, Richard was in the thick of the battle." He grasped her shoulders and pulled her away from the scene. "You need to leave now. It's not safe."

Tears misted her eyes, and she blinked them away. "More senseless death. I thought I could change this. I should've been able to."

"This wasn't up to you. What's done is done. Now go."

Alix walked back to the palace, choking back tears as guilt ripped through her. Interfering with history had devastating consequences, as she well knew, but she'd had to try. She'd failed. How could she forgive him now? Or herself?

Alix entered her room, relieved that it was empty. Her emotions churned. Desperate for clarity and to erase the scent and sight of death, she gathered her toiletries and headed to the baths. She sank into the water and scoured her skin until it reddened but couldn't erase the haunting images on the plain.

Guilt and frustration burrowed deeper into her. With access to books and papers written by historians who'd studied the Crusades, she should've been able to find an alternate solution within the pages.

The bathing room darkened as the sun dipped toward the horizon. She got out of the water to dress before daylight faded, then walked to her chamber.

A deep baritone voice called her name.

Her lungs constricted, and she steeled herself to face him. "Yes, Your Grace?"

His eyes narrowed. "Where have you been? Joanna was worried since she hasn't seen you in hours."

Alix lifted her chin and took a shaky breath. "I went out to the plain. I wanted to see for myself."

"God's bones, Alix. What were you thinking?" He strode to her and gripped her shoulders. "I took no pleasure in this. I hope you know that."

"I'm sure you didn't, but I don't understand how and why you could do this. This will be the one event that will always be remembered. That *I* will always remember."

Anger sparked in his eyes. "If this is an attempt to make me feel guilty, it's not going to work. The army leaves for Ascalon soon. I don't know when we'll return. Perhaps that will give you the time you need to forgive me."

"I'm not the one to give you absolution. Only God can do that."

Richard towered over her. "I care more about your forgiveness than God's."

He pressed a searing kiss on her forehead, then turned away, his footsteps retreating down the corridor.

Alix opened the door to her chambers.

"I went to the church and prayed for the souls of those men." Joanna glanced up from her seat at the table, her face pale and drawn. "I don't envy Berenguela tonight. Richard was in a foul mood earlier, if the raised voices from his room were any indication."

Alix put away her things. "I still don't understand how he could put to death so many with such little thought."

"I'm not pleased with the outcome, but I accept his ruling."

"They didn't deserve their fate." Alix raked a hand through her damp hair.

"Might I remind you that Salah-ad-Din put Christians to death?" Joanna's tone was sharp.

"I believe that was wrong too. I suppose there was no other alternative that was acceptable to him."

"Richard wasn't the only one involved in the decision." Joanna sighed and rubbed her temples. "He met with his council. Sometimes choices aren't based on what's right and what's wrong. There is a middle ground."

Maud and Beatrice entered the room, interrupting their conversation.

Beatrice frowned at Alix. "You made *Melech Ric* quite . . . angry."

This was the name that the Turks had given to Richard. The girls liked the exotic sound of it and had adopted it.

"We were passing his chambers and heard shouting," Maud explained.

"There's no guarantee it's me he's upset with. It's likely another matter that angered him."

"No, we heard your name," Beatrice stated. "You say sorry." Her French was improving, but she still stumbled over words. "He's leaving for war. Don't let him leave angry."

Joanna watched them walk to their beds, then turned back toward Alix. "She's right, you know. If, God forbid"—she crossed herself—"something should happen to Richard, you ought to make your peace with him before he leaves. Not for your sake, but for his."

Alix gave a hollow laugh, remembering her last words to him. "At the moment, I'm sure I'm the last person he wants to see."

"If you believe that, then you're deceiving yourself."

*~*~*

Richard glanced at Georges and Baldwin as they entered his tent. He'd set up his pavilion outside Acre to prepare for the march south, as well as to keep an eye on the enemy still camped on the hill. If Salah-ad-Din decided to attack in retribution, he'd be prepared.

"By the look on your faces, I assume you had little luck in convincing the men to leave the city."

Baldwin grimaced. "Do you think they're going to trade wine and willing women for battle?"

"I need an army if we're to reclaim the Holy Land. Send criers throughout Acre. If the men aren't willing to join us, then bribe them. Money always spurs them to action."

Baldwin chuckled. "That it does."

Richard followed the men out of the tent. André and Rob joined them as he frowned at the sparse number of tents that dotted the plain. His most loyal men had joined without question, but too many remained behind.

"A trickle of men left the city today. How do you propose to encourage the rest?" Rob asked.

"I told Baldwin to bribe them. I don't wish to resort to force, but I will if necessary."

"Let's hope it doesn't come to that," Rob mused. "The ladies will stay here?"

Richard nodded. "It's safer for them to stay behind. The only women allowed will be older washerwomen and cooks." He shrugged at the shocked look on Rob's face. "I don't want the men distracted, and that goes for myself as well."

He turned his gaze to the distant hill, where fires from the enemies' camps would burn throughout the night.

"We'll leave in two days. After the deadline passed, I should've known that Salah-ad-Din wouldn't keep his part of the terms. I refuse to stay any longer."

Anger stole through him as he relived the hour before the council meeting when Georges had burst into the room with news that the prisoners were being forced out of Acre.

He'd raced to the plain to see groups of men led from the city gates. Countless bodies were already piled in heaps. Murmurs and confused glances amongst the soldiers carrying out the killings increased as his presence was noted.

It was too late to stop them. He'd had no choice but to allow it or have his authority questioned. He'd nodded for them to continue, but then a group of women and children were dragged screaming through the gate. One woman tried to run back, a toddler in her arms. A soldier grabbed her and pushed her to the ground. The child shrieked in terror.

His stomach had roiled as he remembered what that bastard had done to

Alix in Messina. He'd motioned to a nearby soldier. "The women and children are not to be touched."

Confusion filled his eyes. "Your Grace, your order was for everyone."

Alix's prophecy came back to haunt him. Although she hadn't seen his victory against the Saracens, the thought of being condemned as a terrible king tore at his pride.

"Noncombatants are to be kept under guard until I decide what to do with them."

The man had hurried to relay his order and, to Richard's relief, the women and children were shepherded back into the city. With eyes upon him, he'd remained to watch the slaughter.

Richard forced the memories away, and after Rob left, beckoned to his cousin. "André, have you discovered who gave the order to kill the prisoners? It had to be someone in the French camp, for no one loyal to me would dare attempt it."

"Not yet, but I will."

"I'd thought Hugh was behind this. It was clear to the council he was in favor of putting the men to death, but he seemed shocked too." Richard rubbed his jaw. "I suspect it's someone in his household who has the influence to deliver Hugh's orders on his behalf. Keep searching for the wretch. I doubt he'll be able to keep his secret for long."

*~*~*

The sun hadn't peeked over the horizon yet, but Richard had been up for hours. Men stirred and nodded to him as he made his way through the camp to where the horses were stabled. The grooms were busy feeding and watering the destriers. Richard greeted them, then checked on Fauvel. The steed whinnied at his approach. He murmured to him and ran his hand down the horse's muscular neck.

"Have the horses saddled within the hour," he ordered.

"Yes, Sire."

Baldwin and André were waiting outside his tent when he returned and followed him in.

"I assume there are soldiers still loitering in Acre?" Richard asked.

André grimaced and glanced at Baldwin. "We offered money, but some still refused. Hopefully, guilt sets in, and they decide to honor the vows they swore."

"Today's march will be short. We'll cross the river and then camp close by. If any men change their mind about joining, they'll be able to catch up." He motioned to the table laden with bread, cheese, and wine. "Help yourself. I don't wish to stop too often to eat and rest. I'd rather not be easy prey."

Jacques brought him his armor and two pages hovered nearby to help him dress.

"Have the ships been ordered to travel south?"

Baldwin nodded. "They set sail this morning."

In times of battle, towns and nearby fields of crops were commonly burned, so the attacking army was forced to move on and forage for what little food they could find. He couldn't afford to have his men and horses starve. His transport ships would be stocked with the bulk of the provisions. While the army marched south along the coast, the galleys would follow them. Smaller, more lightly stocked ships could rendezvous with the army at scheduled stops along the way.

Richard grinned. "At least we don't have to deal with dangerous weather. I'm told this is the dry season, so storms won't slow us down."

Rob entered the tent. "Your Grace, the army is ready on your command."

Richard strode outside to where men stood in groups, waiting for his orders. The sun streaked the cloudless sky in shades of pink and orange, promising a warm day ahead.

A light breeze stirred his thinning hair. The doctors had told him that fingernail and hair loss was a side-effect of *leonardie*. After almost dying from the illness, losing his hair was adding insult to injury.

He knit his brows as he glanced at the vacated hill, where hundreds of the enemies' dampened campfires remained, smoke curling in the air.

"Salah-ad-Din's army has been on the move since early this morning. I've no doubt the Turks will follow us."

André crossed his arms. "Although they're mounted, they travel light with bows and arrows."

"If previous battles are any indication, then their manner of attack will be to launch arrows from a safe distance in an attempt to disperse us. They have speed and agility on their side. If we break formation, our men will be at their mercy. I'll lead the army in the rearguard and watch for attacks from behind."

A commotion amongst the men interrupted him.

"I hope you weren't planning to leave without saying farewell." A lilting voice called out.

His knights left to deliver the orders to the army and to give him time to say his goodbyes.

Richard turned toward Joanna. "It was getting late. I thought you'd decided to sleep in this morning." He grinned.

"I'm sure we got as little sleep as you did."

Berenguela stood next to Joanna, worry etched on her face, but his gaze was drawn to the woman standing behind them.

His wife rushed to him and threw herself into his arms. "I know God is on our side, but please be careful."

He gave her a quick kiss, tasting the salt of her tears on her lips. "I'll be fine. The next time I see you, we'll be victorious."

She moved aside to let Joanna say her goodbyes.

"Be safe, Richard. I'm already worried and you haven't even left."

He hugged her and stared over her shoulder at Alix. Joanna pushed away and gave him a small smile.

Alix hesitated, then stepped forward and held out a pouch. "Here are some herbs and salves that might be useful on the march."

His pulse leapt as her sandalwood perfume mixed with her intoxicating scent enveloped him. He opened the pouch, pulled out an unfamiliar fleshy plant, and cocked his brow.

"It won't sicken you, I promise." A small grin lifted the corners of her lips. "It's called 'aloe.' The gel inside can be used on sunburns and wounds. Take care of yourself."

"You won't be rid of me that easily."

Warmth and something deeper flashed in her eyes. "I pray that is so." She retreated to where Joanna stood.

Richard's heart jumped. He knew she was still angry with him, but her words renewed his hope that her feelings toward him were changing.

The queens' ladies had come as well to see them off. Jacques and Maud whispered to each other. Beatrice stood nearby as a groom led Fauvel to them.

"You will defeat the enemy, *Melech Ric*, no?"

"I plan to."

"Take care of Fauvel. He was my father's favorite horse."

Richard chuckled. "I will, lass."

"The men are ready, Sire," Baldwin said.

Joanna and Berenguela once again said their goodbyes. Richard shared a last glance with Alix, then mounted Fauvel. His mind was already turning to the march ahead of them as Baldwin led the army out of the camp.

Richard fell in with the rearguard and kept a watchful eye on the hills. As he'd expected, the Turks paralleled their movement but kept their distance. As the army marched, Salah-ad-Din sent bands of skirmishers to harass them in hopes of breaking their rank, but the men held firm. They crossed the Acre River without incident and pitched their tents between the river and the sea.

*~*~*

The following day, they began the long march to Jaffa, Richard leading his men along the sandy beach. The moment they began their journey, the enemy shadowed their course like a plague. Like before, the main body of Salah-ad-Din's troops maintained their distance while small groups of twenty or thirty rode along the undulating sand dunes. Intent on harassment, they sent barrages of arrows toward the army, then darted away. The missiles fell short, embedding in the ground yards from the soldiers' feet, the puffs of sand dissipating in the breeze.

Richard had divided the soldiers into three divisions. He took the vanguard, the middle part was made up of English and Norman soldiers, and the Duke of Burgundy and the French made up the rearguard. The supply train of wagons and carts traveled in the back.

Multitudes of pennants and banners attached to lances waved in the brisk coastal wind. In the middle of the army, men pulled a large cart. Richard's standard was attached to a tall mast so that it was easily visible. He ordered it to be guarded at all times. It would be used as a refuge point for the wounded, and, as long as the banner flew, the men knew the king still lived.

The scorching sun crept higher in the cloudless pale-blue sky. Conversations were replaced by the mournful cries of seabirds, the clink of armor, and the constant bloodcurdling yells of the enemy.

Richard fell back to ride next to Rob. He narrowed his eyes as an arrow fell twenty feet from the infantry line. "They're growing bolder."

The men's pace slowed, and they cast glances at the enemy, who hovered tantalizingly out of reach.

"The men are fearful, Your Grace," Rob said.

"I'm aware of that. In Acre, we had better protection. But out here, we're at their mercy. However, they don't seem interested in mounting a full-scale attack. Yet."

Rob nodded.

"Don't break formation," Richard called out. "Ignore all provocation. Maintain the pace."

Sweat dripped down Richard's face, but he dared not remove his helmet. He lifted his wine pouch to his lips, the trickle of warm liquid down his parched throat doing nothing to quench his thirst.

The winding path they traveled narrowed as the shifting dunes encroached upon the coast. Light fog gathered on the sea and rolled inland, limiting visibility. Richard's muscles tensed. If the curling fog thickened, it could be disastrous for them. He raised his hand to slow the men.

"Rob, we'll go two abreast and keep watch for ambushes. If I planned to attack, this would be the place to do it."

"They'd have the element of surprise, but the dunes don't provide enough protection for them."

"They're not the ones that need it. We're going to be forced to spread out the line to traverse the path. Our protection is what's lacking."

Richard scoured the dunes for signs of the enemy as his division split into two lines and continued the trek. As the last men passed, he followed, his grip tensed on his lance. Visibility had dropped to a mere five feet around him. He strained to hear the pounding hooves of an attacking army, but the only sound was the keening wind and the crash of waves upon the beach. The path gradually widened, and the fog thinned, but he remained alert.

"Your Grace, Your Grace!" a man yelled as he careened toward them. He reined in his winded steed. "The rearguard is under attack."

Adrenaline sang through Richard's blood. "Rob, gather some men and follow me."

He wheeled Fauvel in a tight circle and galloped toward the rear of the army. The soldiers had broken formation and battled in small groups. The Turks had the advantage of agility. They used arrows to force the men to shield themselves, cut them down with the swords, then galloped out of distance.

Richard raced into the fray, his sword flashing as he wielded it, the enemy falling before him. Fauvel's nostrils flared as the metallic scent of blood maddened him. Arrows hissed from a bow, striking Richard and penetrating his blood-spattered armor. With a violent twist, he spun Fauvel toward his opponent, but Rob had driven his lance into the man's chest, unhorsing him. A couple of infantrymen leapt forward and ended his life in a lethal flash of steel.

The rearguard managed to regroup, and losing their advantage, the Turks retreated. Richard and a handful of knights chased them and managed to slay a few before they disappeared into the dunes.

Richard returned to the soldiers, trying to keep his simmering anger in check. "Where's the duke?"

Hugh rode up, his hauberk bloodied and riddled with arrows.

"I ordered you to stay in formation. What in God's name happened?"

"Sire, the wagons slowed where the path narrowed and only two at a time could pass. We couldn't see anything in the fog. The enemy was on us before we knew what had happened. They killed the men in the wagons, as well as their horses. They also stole supplies."

Richard's fury ebbed. The men transporting the wagons weren't soldiers, and being overburdened, they'd had no chance.

"Get the men back in formation. I feel the enemy is done with us today, but we'll stay with you until we rejoin the army."

Once they reconvened with the other divisions, Richard returned to the front.

André raised his brow. "Jesu, I'm glad none were fatal."

Richard glanced at the arrows that stuck like quills in his hauberk. "I'd rather look like a porcupine than have my reign end here." He pulled one out and grinned. "Now we have more ammunition."

"How many men were lost?"

"Only one soldier, but many noncombatants. We'll find a suitable site to camp and rest. I won't have a repeat of this fiasco."

The sun was arcing toward the horizon when they reached the Kishon River. After checking that the water in the cisterns was safe to drink, Richard gave the order to camp on the spacious plain.

"You look pensive, Uncle." Henri joined Richard and André while they waited for their tents to be pitched. "We had a narrow escape, I admit, but we held the Turks off. Do you think they'll return tonight?"

"No, I'm sure we'll have a quiet night." He lifted his chin toward the terrain in front of him. "Look at the plain and tell me what you see."

Henri studied the landscape and frowned. "Salah-ad-Din camped here. The area that's been trampled is immense. His army is much larger than we thought."

"Exactly. We need to rethink our strategy. Now that we're in the open, he's much more dangerous."

"How long are we planning to stay here, Uncle?" Henri asked.

"A couple of days at the most. That will give men time to join us from Acre. We also need to decide what's essential and what's not. The footmen are overburdened with supplies and arms."

Henri crossed his arms and nodded in the direction of the French army, who camped some distance away from the English. "I assume Hugh won't be in charge of the rearguard."

Richard narrowed his eyes. "I have half a mind to send *him* back to France, but I need the man. The Hospitallers will take the rear. I refuse to be surprised like that again."

*~*~*

A rabbit emerged from the thick grass and startled Fauvel, who shied into Rob's steed.

"Easy there," Richard soothed as he fought to keep Fauvel from bolting.

"As much as I was tired of the constant wind and sand, I prefer the beach path to this one," Rob said.

The road they'd traveled on for days was little more than an animal trail, dense with thorny bushes and tall grass which slowed down the foot soldiers and the wagons.

"I agree. Henri said there's a village not too far ahead. We'll stop and rest there."

It was early afternoon when they reached the small village, which had been razed to the ground. After dismounting and watering the horses, they made their way to a group of trees. André joined them, and Richard tossed him a skin filled with lukewarm water. He drank deeply before handing it back.

"I hope we're not staying here tonight. There's barely enough space for the men, let alone the horses and wagons."

Richard sat and pulled some dried meat from his pouch. He took a bite and grimaced at the slightly rancid taste. "No, we'll let the army catch up and rest, then continue to Le Destroit. The Templar fortress there should offer better protection."

Several hours later, Richard gave the order to move. The enemy lurked in the distance and the last thing he wanted was an ambush in darkness.

The sun had almost set by the time they reached their destination, and pages hurried to set up Richard's tent. He gazed out at the broad plain that merged into distant hills until the two were indistinguishable in the deepening twilight. His thoughts spun. The Turks knew this land, giving them the clear advantage. When and where would Salah-ad-Din plan his attack?

Jacques approached and cleared his throat. "Sire, your tent is ready. Can I help with your armor?"

Richard nodded and entered his tent. Jacques pulled off his hauberk, and Richard gasped as the mail scraped against his sunburned forearm. After dressing, he went to a trunk where the maps were stored and rifled through them until he found the one he wanted. The pouch Alix had given him lay at the bottom. He picked up both and carried them to the table.

Henri entered unannounced. "That looks painful." He motioned to Richard's arm as he sat down at the table.

"It is." Richard pulled out the fleshy green plant and tossed it in his hand. "Are you familiar with this?"

"Yes. Did the doctor give it to you?"

"Alix did. I had my doubts about using it." He gave Henri a wry grin.

"Speaking of Alix, things seem tense between you two. I don't mean to pry, but . . ."

"Then don't." Richard's tone was neutral, but his jaw tightened.

Henri leaned back in his chair and raised his hands. "I apologize for asking, Uncle."

Richard sighed. "It's been complicated for a while."

"It must be difficult when the woman you love isn't your wife."

Richard smiled slightly and nodded. He'd hoped that eventually Alix would accept his marriage for what it was—political—and they could restart what they once had. But although she had come to see them off, there was a distance in her that hadn't been there before the massacre. It was clear she hadn't forgiven him. One day, he'd tell her the truth concerning the prisoners.

Henri spread the map out on the table, anchoring the edges with candles, while Richard cut open the aloe and spread the sticky gel on his arm. He closed his eyes in relief as the pain lessened.

"Arsuf is quite some distance away." Richard joined Henri and pointed to the coastal city. "Every town and village we've passed through has been burned to the ground. We'll need more supplies soon." Richard traced a path south from their location to Caesarea. "We'll march here, then reconvene with the galleys."

"What about the men still in Acre? We're traveling at a slow enough pace for any to catch up, but since we left, the number of men who continue to join has dwindled."

Richard frowned. "I'm aware of that. When the galleys return to Acre for more supplies, I'll issue an edict that everyone who pledged their vow will keep it."

"I pray they do. You've seen evidence of the size of the enemy army. We need every man available if we wish to defeat Salah-ad-Din."

*~*~*

Alix and Elisabetta wandered through the market, stopping to purchase fruits and vegetables. Although the town bustled with activity, there was an underlying current of wariness in case the Saracens chose to attack the lightly defended city and reclaim it.

Elisabetta narrowed her eyes at the loitering soldiers they passed in the narrow streets. "How dare these men stay while the army travels south? They didn't leave their homes in France to take up with whores and drink their days away. They should be fighting alongside the king."

A couple of soldiers stumbled by, their arms slung around two prostitutes.

Alix shook her head. "Perhaps the king is better off with them remaining here."

The mention of Richard pierced her heart. Brutal, sickening images from the massacre continued to dominate her dreams. She'd wake at night, her stomach twisting with nausea and guilt for not being able to stop it. Rationally, she understood the reasoning behind his decision, but she struggled to move past it. It was a senseless killing that she and history would never forget.

The light breeze carried the sweet scent of flowers and spices from a small stall. "Do you mind if we stop?" she asked. "I want to see if I can find sandalwood oil."

Alix studied the small bottles of scented oils until she found the one she wanted. She pulled out the glass stopper and inhaled the exotic, spicy scent.

Elisabetta smiled knowingly. "Isn't that one of the king's favorites?"

Alix dug through her pouch to find some coins to avoid answering and handed them to the young girl minding the shop.

Elisabetta waited until they'd walked away. "Dearie, it's obvious he still loves you. I can see you feel the same about him, even though you deny it."

"It doesn't matter." Alix shrugged. "We can never be together again."

"As I told you a long time ago, there's no shame in being with him."

Alix stopped and faced Elisabetta. "I'd feel ashamed. Besides, I couldn't do that to Berenguela."

"I do feel for the queen." Elisabetta sighed. "She cares for him more than she lets on."

Guilt rippled through Alix. She loved Richard, but Berenguela was her friend. She couldn't bring more unhappiness to the marriage than was already there.

Beatrice rushed to them as soon as they entered the palace hall. She grabbed their hands and pulled them after her. "The king's galleys arrived, and his men are here. They have news."

They hurried to the dining hall to see Berenguela and Joanna were deep in conversation with André and Humphrey de Toron. Jacques sat some distance away with Maud, his hand covering hers.

"Alix," Joanna called and waved her hand for them to join her. "Richard sent André and Humphrey to get more supplies and to order the remaining soldiers to join the army. They're telling us about the march south."

André smiled and nodded to Alix, then continued with his story. "It's been challenging, to say the least. The enemy always follows, but keeps their distance." He took a deep drink from his goblet.

Joanna frowned. "Has there been much fighting?"

André and Humphrey exchanged glances.

"There are daily skirmishes, Your Grace, but we've been able to fend them off. The king is constantly in the thick of the battles and has forced the Turks to retreat numerous times," Humphrey said.

Berenguela's eyes shone with pride, but Alix glanced at Joanna and saw the same fear she felt must be reflected in her own eyes. Of course, Richard would be in the middle of the fight.

"How many men have been lost?" Joanna asked.

André shook his head. "The march from La Destroit to Caesarea was very difficult, due to the distance as well as the heat. Men dropped from heat exhaustion and hunger. Those who were ill and fatigued were taken to ships and transported to our destination." He paused. "The ones who died were immediately buried."

Humphrey hastened to reassure them. "The last couple of days, we've stayed in Caesarea and the men have been able to recuperate."

While servants placed dishes of meats and vegetables on the table, Alix leaned close to André. "Why did Richard send you here? Surely, he'd want you by his side."

He turned so the others wouldn't see and pulled back his sleeve. His hand and wrist were swollen and discolored.

"It's a tarantula bite. I've never felt such pain. It was as if a hot poker pierced my skin, then it immediately swelled. This happened four days ago, and I still can't hold a sword. I'd be useless in a fight."

Alix raised a brow. "Not to point out the obvious, but tarantulas are large, are they not? How did you not see it?"

He shrugged. "They come out at night. I was moving rocks to make room for supplies when it darted out. I saw the doctor and he said its bite, fortunately, isn't fatal."

During dinner, the men recounted stories of the journey, but as soon as the plates had been cleared, André turned to Joanna.

"I regret that we can't stay longer, but we must return early in the morning."

"Has my brother mentioned when we will join him?"

André shook his head. "That I don't know. Once we arrive in Ascalon, I'm sure he'll send word."

"Please tell my lord husband I'll pray for him and the men. I have faith they will prevail," Berenguela said.

"Certainly, I will, Your Grace."

"Let Richard know my thoughts and prayers are with him too," Joanna said.

"Send my prayers as well," Alix added as Joanna nudged her.

The men took their leave, Jacques trailing behind. The sadness on Maud's face tugged at Alix's heart. "Go and say your goodbyes properly."

Maud's eyes widened, and then she rushed after him.

Joanna shook her head and grinned. "Perhaps I'd best have a discussion with my brother concerning those two."

"That might be a good idea."

Joanna lowered her voice. "Speaking of Richard, have you forgiven him?"

Alix blew out her breath and stared into the distance. "I'm still trying to accept how he could commit such a barbaric act. I'm very glad he released the women and children, since they posed little threat, but thousands of men lost their lives."

"He met with his counsel, and they were in agreement."

"I'm aware that others echoed the decision, but it doesn't make it right."

Joanna put her hand on Alix's arm. "I, too, was horrified by what happened, but he had his reasons. Being king isn't easy."

Alix gave a small smile. "With great power comes great responsibility."

"Exactly. Sometimes the choices he makes won't be popular, but they're for the good of the people. Richard values your opinion of him. Don't judge him too harshly." Joanna gave her a sympathetic look, then left.

"The queen's right," Elisabetta murmured.

Alix spun around. "I simply can't forget that thousands of men died because of his choice. I just wanted a different outcome that would change things for the better."

"How do you know it would be better? You can't predict the future, dearie."

"The men would be alive. Isn't that enough?"

Elisabetta shrugged. "I'm sure it wasn't an easy decision for him to make. If the men had been released, with the king and the army gone, no one would stop them if they chose to attack Acre. I doubt they would treat us well if we were captured."

Elisabetta left, and Alix headed toward her room. Logically, she knew she was being unfair to Richard. He wasn't the only one who'd considered the idea, but none of the council had arrived at an alternative solution.

"Alix, might I have a word?"

She turned in surprise to see André striding toward her. He grasped her shoulder and led her to an alcove.

"I take it you're still upset with Richard concerning the deaths of the hostages?"

Alix's lips tightened and she gave a short nod.

"What I'm about to tell you might change your mind. Richard didn't make the decision. He was trying to find an alternative, but never had the chance. The council hadn't even met when we received word the hostages were being brought out of Acre."

"Someone else gave the order?" She crushed the glimmer of hope that bubbled through her. As much as she wanted it to be true, it was impossible. "No one would have the audacity to authorize it, not without his knowledge."

"There's only one man who has almost as much sway as Richard. Hugh, the Duke of Burgundy. One of Hugh's men announced to the French army that

Richard had given the order to kill the prisoners, and the duke sent him to do the deed. Coming from someone in Hugh's camp, none would question it."

He held out a piece of parchment. "This is a letter from Richard to Hugh, stating that he will find who was behind the massacre and he will be punished."

Alix took it and read it. "Is this true?" She hardly dared to believe it. "Why didn't Richard tell anyone? Everyone believes he was responsible."

"He can't let anyone know that he wasn't in control of the situation. How would the men react if they knew his authority had been challenged?"

She frowned. "Why would the man do this? Surely, he knew he'd be discovered."

André nodded. "Apparently, he'd nursed a personal grudge against Hugh for years and this was a way for him to retaliate. Everyone knows Richard can have a quick temper and he would've assumed Hugh had given the command. The man was betting that Richard's immediate reaction would have been to discipline Hugh, or worse, and consider the consequences later."

The man couldn't have been allowed to live. Dread welled inside her as she imagined what had been done to him.

She pressed her lips together. "What punishment did Richard exact?"

"None, for the culprit had already been dealt with. I learned from the French soldiers who remained here that he suffered an accident several days after the prisoners' deaths. Hugh's life had been put at risk, and he wasn't going to accept that." He nodded toward the letter. "Richard wanted you to know the truth."

Footsteps scuffed behind them. Alix gripped the parchment in her hands and clasped them behind her back.

"You're still here, André?" Joanna asked as she approached.

"I was just leaving, Your Grace."

"I'll walk you out."

Alix said her goodbye, then hurried to her room, clutching her prize. This was irrefutable proof he hadn't given the order. Excitement welled through her as she unrolled the parchment and ran her finger over Richard's familiar seal stamped at the bottom of the letter.

Her pleas must have changed his mind. Historically, it was believed that as the leader of both armies, Richard had the final word. This letter would turn history's view of Richard around and perhaps restore his reputation. She needed to keep it safe until she could find a way to allow it to come to light.

## ~ *Chapter 25* ~

THE GALLEYS RETURNED TO CAESAREA, transporting much needed supplies and, after Richard's decree, most of the men who'd remained in Acre. The army continued south at a measured pace to the Dead River, the flotilla of ships following. After a particularly brutal day of being harassed by the enemy, Richard chose to remain near the river for a couple of days, careful not to push his men past their endurance.

Once the men were well rested, he ordered the army to amass in groups for another day's march. He put the Templars in charge of the rearguard, and he'd lead the front.

The wide coastal road passed through a flat desolate wasteland, but the path gradually narrowed as tall dense grass encroached. The horses were able to push through the thick reeds at first, but soon they were laboring.

Scouts were sent ahead to see if the path improved but returned with grim news that they needed to find a different route.

Richard studied the impenetrable foliage, then glanced toward the mountains. Ancient rivers had carved deep wadis in the shaly plain. During the summer months, they were dry and presented an ideal place for the enemy to hide and wait.

"God's bones." Richard sighed. "I don't wish to head inland, but we have no choice." He turned to André. "Tell the men to keep in formation. If we stay close, hopefully, we can mitigate potential casualties."

André left to deliver the message to the troops. By the time he returned, Richard was leading the way, keeping a safe distance from a deep riverbed embedded with rocks and debris. The wadi narrowed ahead of them, and the banks steepened into precipitous cliffs.

Movement flashed on Richard's left. He raised his hand to halt their progress. A group of Turks burst from the dense brush, sent a volley of arrows at the men, then raced away.

He grasped his sword as they advanced. "Stay together and continue slowly!" he called out.

In the distance, three troops of Turks galloped toward the rear of the army. Richard's heart pounded with adrenaline. "They're planning to attack the rearguard. Follow me," he ordered.

Without hesitation, he turned and sprinted toward the enemy. Screams from men and horses grew louder as they neared. Arrows and darts rained so thickly upon the Templars that all they could do was deflect them with their shields. Horses lay dead and wounded on the ground. Richard rode into the melee, cutting down any Turk within distance of his blade. His knights joined him, and under the fresh onslaught, they forced the enemy to draw back.

The Templars took advantage of the change in circumstance and charged. Richard sliced at the foes with his sword, then wheeled Fauvel in a tight circle to avoid a fallen horse. A spear pierced his hauberk. Pain coursed through him. Unbalanced, he pitched sideways, the weight of his armor dragging him down. The ground rushed to meet him.

An image of Alix filled his mind. He would return to her. At the last moment, he gripped his saddle tightly with his thighs and pushed himself upright. Cold sweat poured down his back. Shaken by the almost disastrous outcome, he took several deep breaths to gather himself.

The Turks were relentless as they continued to shoot arrows to disperse and weaken the formation. Georges charged past Richard to attack a handful of men who surrounded several defenseless foot soldiers. He forced them back, then drove his lance into one of the Turks, who lay wounded on the ground. Defeated for the time being, the enemy retreated to a safe distance, allowing the foot soldiers to rejoin the army.

Richard nodded to Georges, grateful he'd taken the offense. He refocused on the battle. The men couldn't know he was wounded, for fear of them losing heart. The blistering heat intensified. Stinging sweat burned his eyes and slickened his grip on his sword, but with the vicious fighting on both sides, he couldn't let his guard down.

Dusk was falling when the enemy finally withdrew into the foothills. Richard praised his men for their prowess and bravery, and returned to the vanguard. Sharp pain radiated through his body as the adrenaline faded. By the time he reached camp, his side was on fire. He dismounted and stumbled as dizziness washed over him. He held on to the saddle until his head cleared.

André looked at him, and frowned. "Richard! Are you injured?"

Richard raised his hand. "I'm fine. A Saracen got lucky with his spear, but I don't think it penetrated too deeply."

"We'll see about that. Jacques, go find the doctor, and tell him to come as soon as he's able."

Richard staggered into his tent, then slumped onto his cot.

"I'll help with your armor," André said. He slowly pulled the hauberk off and removed the thick padding underneath it.

Richard gasped as the material was pulled away. A small puncture wound was surrounded by a large purple-bluish bruise that marred his skin from his ribs to his hip.

André's breath whistled through his teeth. "Jesu, you're lucky. If the spear had had more force behind it . . ."

"Let me see the wound, Your Grace." Ralph entered the tent, with Jacques following behind.

Richard grit his teeth while the doctor prodded the wound.

"The spear didn't pierce too deeply. You'll be bruised and sore for a while. I'll give you some salve and herbs to ease the pain."

He opened his bag and found the items he was looking for. He handed them to Jacques, who took the herbs and went to heat water to boil them in.

"You likely won't follow my orders, but try and rest for a couple of days."

André waited until the doctor left, then turned toward Richard. "You need to be more careful. What if you'd been seriously injured, or worse? What would happen to your wife and sister?

Richard shifted gingerly on the cot. He'd been closer to death than he wanted to admit to himself, but at the time, his only thought had been of Alix. Not Joanna, and not his wife.

Jacques returned with the steaming brew. "Can I get you anything else, Sire?"

"No, this will do." He took a sip and grimaced at the bitter taste.

If he hadn't been at the front of the counterattack, his army's resistance might have failed. But, if he'd fallen, the war could very well have ended. Perhaps there was a way to put a halt to this constant conflict without more battles.

"Cousin, come here tomorrow morning and bring Henri. I think a meeting with Salah-ad-Din is in order." Richard grinned at the shocked expression on André's face. "Now, the both of you, leave me."

*~*~*

"Your Grace, is it true what the men are saying? Humphrey de Toron acted as translator at a meeting you requested with Salah-ad-Din?" Rob asked as the army marched toward the thick forest of Arsuf, leaving the relative safety of the river.

Richard grinned. "He did, indeed. We met with Safadin, Salah-ad-Din's brother. I asked him to return the Holy Land."

"Obviously, he didn't, or we wouldn't be marching south." Rob narrowed his eyes. "I can't believe you expected him to agree to that, so what was your real reason behind the meeting?"

"I hoped to find out what their plans were and how prepared his army is. I also wanted to mislead them as to my own intentions."

"Receiving orders last night that we were leaving this morning was a surprise to everyone, especially since you're still recovering."

Richard nodded at the distant hills. "As you can see, his army was caught off guard, and we're not being followed. The last thing Salah-ad-Din expected after our brief and decidedly uncordial meeting this morning was for us to march."

The flat plain gained in elevation and narrowed as stands of trees thickened. Richard's nerves were strung tight. Branches creaked overhead in the breeze and the undergrowth rustled with what sounded like small animals, but which could be enemy footsteps. What if he'd miscalculated and was leading his men into a trap? There were countless places to hide, and they would be at Salah-ad-Din's mercy.

At last, the trees began to thin, and the men exited the forest onto a plain where the Rochetaille River carved its way to the sea. Richard kept close watch on his army until the rearguard emerged unscathed from the forest. While the tents were being set up, scouts were sent to locate Salah-ad-Din's camp. They'd had a much needed respite from skirmishes, but Richard was sure that by now the Turks were shadowing them again.

He half-listened to Henri and Rob's banter, his attention wavering each time voices sounded outside his tent. At last, Jacques announced the scouts' arrival and he hurried outside to meet them. After a brief discussion, he returned.

His breath gusted out as he sat down and pulled his goblet toward him. "The enemy isn't camped too far away, but the scouts report the army is massive. There are easily thirty thousand Turks. Now I know the reason we were left alone on the march. Salah-ad-Din spent the day drawing up his army. He's done with skirmishes. He wants a battle."

"We have less than half that number of men. There's almost none left in Acre to recall." Rob sagged back in his chair.

Richard drummed his fingers on the table. "I hope to reach Arsuf without a battle and that might still happen, but if not, we need to be prepared."

Henri gave a cold smile. "This war has gone on far too long. If there's anyone to end it, it's you."

Richard lifted his goblet. "May it be God's will."

*~*~*

By dawn, Richard had met with his nobles and most-experienced knights to plan who would take charge of the battalions. The Templars took the lead, followed by the Angevins and Bretons. Guy de Lusignan led the third battalion of Poitevins, while the Norman and English marched behind, guarding Richard's standard. Henri commanded the left inland flank, while the Hospitallers oversaw the rear.

Richard, Hugh of Burgundy, André, and other handpicked knights were free to ride up and down the line to reinforce any weakness if necessary. The carts and wagons traveled between the army and the sea so they wouldn't be attacked and become liabilities.

The soldiers marched so close to each other that it was impossible to throw a stone without hitting a man or horse. Along the wooded hills that sloped down to the plain, Salah-ad-Din's army was lined up as thick as hedges.

An eerie silence blanketed the army as they faced the full strength of the Muslims. The enemy outnumbered them two-to-one.

It was midmorning when Salah-ad-Din sent the first wave of about two thousand skirmishers racing toward them. The shouts and screams, mixed with the Saracens' trumpets, horns, and drums, were deafening.

Both sides suffered casualties from arrows and spears, but as hours passed under the blistering sun, the relentless barrage wore on the Frankish army. Weighed down with armor, exhaustion began to take as much of a toll as the fighting.

Pale-red dust roiled by the hooves of thousands of horses thickened the air, hiding the enemy until they appeared from the dimness within striking distance. In between fighting off constant waves of Turks, Richard kept vigil over the lines of men. If any section of the formation broke, the enemy would have the advantage.

A group of Turks bore down on the foot soldiers, who stumbled backwards.

"Hold tight! Stay your ground!" Richard bellowed, his words all but lost in the din of the battle.

The line of men closest to the attackers dropped their weapons and fled toward the safety of the sea. The remaining soldiers hesitated, their nerves wavering. Richard galloped forward to fend off the enemy, Baldwin de Bethune close behind him. They sliced their way through, giving the men enough time to regroup. More knights arrived to bolster the line, and the Turks wheeled their mounts and vanished into the thick dust.

Baldwin glanced at the soldiers, who'd returned to their positions. "The line held—this time—but how much more can the men take?"

"We stay together and keep marching. Once we reach Arsuf, we'll have protection. I don't want to lose more men than necessary by forcing a battle."

The men were bone-weary from deflecting the constant barrage of arrows and darts that hummed through the air, but they pressed on. Richard was drenched with sweat from the heat radiating from the baked earth as well as the brutal sun.

"Sire!" a man called out.

The messenger reached Richard's side, his mail streaked with blood and dust. "Sire, the enemy is attacking all sides of the rearguard. We're losing too many horses and men to hold them back. Please give us leave to retaliate."

"No! Return to your position and tell the men to stay in formation." Richard's voice was gravelly from the dust and shouting orders and words of confidence to the men.

The vanguard had reached the orchards that bordered Arsuf when the master of the Hospitallers rode forward and pleaded with Richard to allow the rearguard to attack the enemy. Once again, Richard refused.

The first battalion was setting up camp when loud cries captured Richard's attention. In the distance, a small band of Hospitallers had broken loose and charged the Turks. Within minutes, thousands of soldiers followed. Richard's chest tightened as he watched Henri and the Earl of Leicester lead the left flank and the center of the army to join the others.

War wasn't what Richard wanted, but it was too late to recall the troops. Without a second thought, Richard shouted to the remaining army to follow him, then galloped toward the battle.

Carnage lay before him. The Hospitallers' shift from defense to offense had surprised the Turks. Men and horses littered the ground from the bloodbath, but the enemy had quickly reorganized. Richard was aware of the danger his army potentially faced. If he overcommitted the lines, the enemy would surround them, and, being separated from the rest of the battalions, they would be cut down.

Richard held Fauvel in check, the steed chafing at the bit to join the fray.

"Baldwin, guard the standard and maintain formation. If the men have a rallying point, we can fall back and regroup if necessary."

"Yes, Sire." He smiled grimly. "Let's put the fear the God into the infidels."

Richard raised his arm, his sword flashing in the sun, then galloped toward the battle, his knights close behind. Hours passed while the battle raged. The billowing dust was so thick, it was impossible to tell friend from foe. The Franks pushed the enemy back, but Salah-ad-Din's men managed to counterattack. At last, the Turks were forced to retreat under the nonstop onslaught. As the men slowed their advance and turned back to reconvene at the standard, Salah-ad-Din launched another charge.

The Turks who had retreated turned back and joined the fresh onslaught, smashing the cavalry with heavy cudgels and swords. The men staggered and wavered. Henri burst out of the line with his men and charged the enemy. Any who didn't die from his blade fled for safety.

Richard and his knights chased the Turks toward the mountains, where they disappeared into the forest. Furious he'd lost his prey, Richard reined in Fauvel and returned to his men, whose horses couldn't keep up.

"I think we can say that this day belongs to us, but I'll feel better once we reach Arsuf."

André was covered with blood and dust and his armor dented where a cudgel had caught him by surprise, but he managed a twisted grin. "I hope we've seen the last of them, but I doubt it."

"I'm sure we'll battle again, but for today, victory is ours." Richard leveled his gaze at Henri, who had joined them. "I gave the order to stay in formation."

"Once our men attacked, I couldn't stand by and watch." Henri's jaw clenched and he shifted in his saddle.

Richard sighed. He would have done the same. "From now on follow my orders. I'd hoped to avoid a clash, but if it hadn't been for your quick reaction, the outcome could have been quite different."

Henri's dark eyes crinkled at the edges, and relief flashed across his face.

They rode back to where the army had regrouped around the standard, then the battle-weary men limped into Arsuf.

# ~ *Chapter 26* ~

ALIX STARED AT HER DARK-BLUE dress laid out on the bed and tried to calm her jangling nerves. Days after the battle, messengers from Arsuf had arrived at the palace with the news that Richard had forced Salah-ad-Din to retreat, although the Holy War continued.

However, in the last month, communication from Jaffa, where the army was now encamped, had ceased. Everyone was on edge, hoping for some word from Richard and dreading the worst. At last, a courier arrived, sending a frenzy through the palace.

Richard was returning to Acre.

She hoped it wasn't because he'd fallen ill or been injured, but she kept her fears to herself. Joanna and Berenguela were thrilled, and she didn't want to worry them.

She'd helped them plan a festive dinner for him, but as the hour drew nearer, Alix's dread about attending grew.

In the two months Richard had been gone, her feelings for him had shifted. When she'd believed he was behind the massacre, it was easier to turn off her emotions. Now that she knew the truth, that because of her he'd changed his mind, her love for him had resurfaced.

Unable to delay any longer, Alix dressed, then brushed her auburn hair until it shone like silk in the sun. A knock echoed on the door, and Maud peeked in.

"Are you ready? The men are gathering in the dining hall."

Alix nodded, took a deep breath, and followed Maud.

Voices grew louder as they neared the hall and butterflies erupted like mini volcanoes in her stomach. Her steps faltered as she entered. Joanna sat at the high table, but Berenguela and Richard were absent. Relief turned into disappointment, but she told herself it was only because she wanted to see if he was uninjured.

Maud left to sit with Beatrice, who was surrounded by the younger knights, likely starving for attention, even from young, innocent females.

Joanna motioned for Alix to join her. "I'm glad you're here. This was supposed to be a dinner for Richard, but as you can see, he hasn't put in an appearance yet."

"You can't blame him. I'm sure he and Berenguela are reconnecting."

Joanna laughed. "That's a polite way to put it. I understand, but I'm still a bit annoyed. We planned this, and he can't be bothered to show up on time."

Alix raised her chin toward a table where Guy de Lusignan, his brother Geoffrey, and Humphrey de Toron sat with a group of men. "At least the men seem to enjoy it."

A commotion at the entrance sent her pulse racing. Richard approached the table, his arm around Berenguela's shoulders, nodding at something she said, then his gaze fixed on Alix. Warmth spread through her heart and a lightness filled her soul at the sight of him.

He escorted Berenguela to her seat, then sat beside her. Alix took a closer look at him. He was even more handsome, if that was possible. After spending weeks in the sun, his fair skin had bronzed, and his blue-gray eyes were startling in his tanned face. His normally chin-length red-gold hair was short and sun bleached.

Richard rubbed his hand over his head as his gaze met hers. "I decided to shave it since I was losing my hair, anyway. At least I'm still not as bald as a newborn babe."

"I quite like it, Your Grace."

He grinned, then lifted his goblet and took a drink.

"We've received very little news since you defeated Salah-ad-Din. What's happening?" Joanna asked.

"As you know, he was defeated on the field, but he and his army managed to retreat. Since that day, he hasn't dared to engage with us again. Instead, he lies in wait like a lion ready to pounce on his prey. After a brief stop in Arsuf, we continued to Jaffa." He paused to eat a bite of chicken. "The Turks destroyed the city, so the only place we could camp was in an olive grove."

Joanna frowned. "Is the army returning to Acre? Is that the reason you're here?"

Richard's brows drew together. "You're aware that my galleys have been traveling from here to Jaffa with supplies?" At Joanna's nod, he continued. "Many of the wounded and ill were sent by ship to recover, but very few have returned. Most prefer to stay here."

"So, you've come personally to convince them to return," Alix said.

"Yes, and to escort everyone to Jaffa."

Alix sucked in her breath. Berenguela's and Joanna's words tumbled over each other. Obviously, this was the first time either of them had heard the news.

Richard laughed and lifted his hands to slow them down. "Acre was the safest place for you to remain while we traveled, but I'd feel better if you joined me."

Joanna frowned. "Didn't you say that the city is in ruins, and you are camping amongst trees?"

"We've rebuilt much of the city and repaired the walls. Besides, the grove is quite comfortable." Richard's lips twitched.

"Why are you still in Jaffa? When you left Acre, you were traveling to Ascalon. Has that changed?" Joanna asked.

"We received word that the Turks were destroying Ascalon. Geoffrey de Lusignan, who was appointed titular count of the region, and others were sent to assess the situation and found it to be true," André explained as he approached, evidently hearing her question.

Richard's hand tightened on his goblet. "Salah-ad-Din destroyed the city to stop us from gaining access to Jerusalem and the Nile region. I wish to continue south to retake Ascalon, but first Jaffa must be rebuilt."

Berenguela gasped. "What about Jerusalem? You vowed to reclaim it for the Christians."

"I will." Richard's tone hardened. "But I believe that laying siege to Ascalon will profit us more. Once we take it, then we turn our sights to the Holy City."

"After Geoffrey's return, the army council met. The French wanted to remain in Jaffa, rebuild the city, then attack Jerusalem, where Salah-ad-Din and his army are. Richard opposed that." André shrugged. "In the end, the majority prevailed, and we stayed in Jaffa."

Relief suffused Berenguela's face. "Thank God. Now you can fulfill your vow and go to Jerusalem. I'm certain that this decision is for the best."

Richard's eyes narrowed and he took a deep drink from his goblet.

Alix recognized his rising anger and changed the topic. "When do we leave for Jaffa? I do hope you'll give us time to pack."

He glanced at her, amusement flashing in his eyes. "I plan to stay several days, so that *should* give you enough time."

Now that the tension had eased, Richard and André discussed the best way to encourage the men to leave Acre and return to Jaffa. The candles were almost burned out when Richard leaned over to whisper in his wife's ear and laughed when she blushed.

"It's growing late, so we'll take our leave." He stood and pulled Berenguela to her feet, but his last glance was directed at Alix as they walked away.

Joanna raised her brow. "You've kept your word about ending your relationship with my brother, and I appreciate that. I'd hoped they would have a satisfying, if not a happy, marriage, but they are mismatched. I know she wants to give him an heir. If he stays in Jaffa long enough, perhaps she will, and their marriage will strengthen."

Alix focused on the burgundy liquid in her cup. "I hope for that too."

Before Richard had left Acre, trying to keep her feelings for him hidden had been grueling. Seeing him again had undone her efforts. No one, especially Richard, could know that she was regretting her decision.

*~*~*

Aided by a strong rear wind, the galley plowed through the undulating deep blue waves. Sea spray sparkled like diamonds and created small rainbows in the morning sun. Alix stood by the rail and watched the sandy coast slide by, imagining the Frankish army traversing the narrow beach while the Saracens observed like hawks from the dunes. A shadow fell over her. Richard approached to lean on the gunwale.

"I thought ladies loathed to hear about the brutality of war, but Maud and Beatrice have been pressing me to give a thorough account of how Salah-ad-Din was defeated at Arsuf." He laughed.

"I hope you didn't go into too much detail, but I'm not surprised. Both think highly of you. Of course, in Beatrice's case, when your father is a cruel despot, that's not too difficult to achieve," Alix teased.

"Minx." He grinned at her, then cocked his brow. "Are you still vexed with me?"

Alix brushed strands of hair out of her eyes and tilted her head up. "André showed me your letter. Although I wish the prisoners had been saved, I'm relieved that you weren't behind it."

He folded his arms on the ship's rail. "The council likely would have chosen the same outcome, but what you said to me about your dream changed my mind. You couldn't tell me definitively, but if saving the men bolstered my chance of defeating the infidels, then I would've come up with another option. I don't wish to be reviled as king for centuries to come, but now . . ." He gave her a lopsided smile. "Unfortunately, I wasn't given that choice."

"True, but knowing it wasn't upon your order changes how I feel about it. And you."

"You don't know how glad I am to hear that."

He glanced at her, and her heart leapt at the relief and affection in his eyes. This wasn't helping to keep her own feelings detached.

"I don't wish to pry, but have you mended things with Berenguela?" Alix knew the question would steer them into strained, but for her, emotionally safer, waters.

The civility between Richard and his wife had lasted a mere two days before tension concerning his apparent reluctance to reclaim the Holy Land resurfaced. From the little information she'd gleaned from Joanna, there were deeper marital issues too. Richard had made himself scarce while Berenguela sought comfort in prayer.

He stared at the sea, his hands clenched on the rail. "You heard the arguments."

"It was hard not to."

"We need to focus on Ascalon, but she, and everyone else, wants me to reclaim Jerusalem."

"Richard, you must consider what the men have given up. The majority of the soldiers have been here for years, away from their homes and families."

"I'm aware of that." He glared at her.

"They're tired of fighting. Their goal of retaking Jerusalem and fulfilling their vows is within reach." Alix gave him a smile and placed her hand on his arm. "I understand that Ascalon is strategically important, but as persuasive as you can be, I'm not surprised the men are against your decision."

Electric shocks shot through her as Richard covered her hand with his. She tried to pull away, but his grip tightened. Her breath quickened as she looked up into his blue-gray eyes.

"You're one of the few who understands where my mind lies. I value your insight and your loyalty more than you know, Love."

The term of endearment lit her soul and warmth filled her heart. "You have my loyalty always."

Richard squeezed her hand, then looked at the sandy coast that skimmed by. "You'd best tell the ladies we're nearing our destination."

"That's not necessary," Joanna said in a quiet voice from behind. "I can't tell you how glad I'll be glad to stand on solid ground."

Although the sea had been relatively calm, she'd become sick the instant they left the sheltered harbor. Alix had given her ginger syrup to keep the queasiness at bay, but she hadn't been able to keep it down.

Richard freed her hand and Alix shifted away from him, the breeze cooling her heated cheeks. He gave her a small smile, obviously as flustered as she was, and moved to allow Berenguela and Joanna space at the rail.

"I know this voyage is miserable for you, but it's much faster and safer than traveling on land," Richard said.

"Where's the city?" Berenguela stood on tiptoes to see better.

"You'll be able to see it when we round this bend."

Jaffa came into view. Alix stared, shocked at the scene before her. Berenguela's ladies joined them, burst into a torrent of Spanish, and gestured rapidly to each other until she ordered them to be silent.

The city was almost destroyed. The few standing walls in view of the port were surrounded by mounds of rubble. Acre had been damaged when they'd arrived, but it was habitable.

They disembarked in silence. Richard led them half a mile to an olive grove where the soldiers had set up their camp under the shade of the trees. His tent was marked by his lion banner that fluttered in the coastal wind. Two smaller tents stood to the left.

"This is the best we could do, considering the circumstances," Richard said.

His queen pasted on a smile and nodded, but it was obvious that she had no desire to be there.

"Berenguela, yours will be the one next to Richard. We'll take the other tent," Joanna said.

The light coastal breeze rustled the leaves on the trees and created intricate patterns on the sun-dappled ground. In the distance, women laughed.

Joanna raised her brow. "So, the women *did* travel from Acre. No doubt the soldiers are enjoying the entertainment."

Richard sighed and crossed his arms. "They began arriving a few weeks after we did. It takes time to rebuild the walls, and in the interim, the men have grown lax."

"Your Graces, how was your journey?" Henri joined them.

"Fortunately, it was uneventful," Joanna replied.

He smiled, then drew Richard aside and spoke in a low voice to him.

"I need to see to some matters. If you ladies require anything, just ask." Richard gestured toward his squires, who'd arrived with their trunks, then left with Henri.

Joanna assumed charge and pointed out which ones belonged in their respective tents.

Berenguela sighed and dragged her hand through her hair. "This isn't what I expected. It's hardly livable. Why did he bring us here? I was thrilled when Richard said we were to join him, but perhaps we should have stayed in Acre."

Sympathy for the younger woman surged within Alix. Being separated from Richard didn't help to strengthen the marriage. Alix had expected that they'd be left behind for weeks or even months a time until Richard wanted them to join him, but she doubted Berenguela had.

"You've been apart for weeks. I'm sure he wants you by his side."

Hope flared in Berenguela's eyes. "I want to believe that. His mood has been unpredictable the last several days."

"I know there's been tension between you since he arrived in Acre." Alix stepped aside to allow a couple of pages to carry trunks into Joanna's tent. "This could be a chance to make up."

"I could arrange for us to dine privately." Berenguela's cheeks pinked. "I'd like nothing more than to be able to announce I'm carrying his son in a couple of months."

Alix managed a weak smile. The thought of it tore at her soul. Historically, Richard never had a child with Berenguela, but since his history was changing, that might too.

*~*~*

The palace in Acre was pure luxury compared to camping in an olive grove, but for Alix, this was an excellent opportunity. She was living history. Historians had written detailed accounts of Richard's capture of Acre, but little was known of Joanna and Berenguela's stay in Jaffa. Every night Alix sat on her cot and jotted down the day's events. She wished she could include every detail, no matter how insignificant, but she'd have multiple tomes by the time she returned home.

She missed the bustle and sights and smells of the markets, not to mention the palace baths, but Jaffa, for all its simplicity, had its own charm. There was plenty of fresh fish and game, and pomegranates, figs, almonds, and citrus fruits grew in abundance.

"That should be enough." Elisabetta added three more large pomegranates to the basket.

The constant wind, heavy with the scent of ripe citrus, mingled with the briny aroma of the sea as it sang through the groves. Alix's hair whipped around her face, and she brushed away strands that clung to her forehead and cheeks.

"When we return, I hope Maud is there to help with breakfast. I swear since we've arrived, she's been absent more often than not."

Elisabetta's infectious laugh echoed among the trees. "She's in love—something you still know about."

Alix picked up the basket and began the walk back to camp. "I have no idea what you mean."

"Come now, dearie. A blind man could see that you love the king, and he, you. If a man looked at me that way . . ." Elisabetta fanned her face and grinned.

"There's nothing between us. Not anymore." Alix hoped it sounded convincing, since it definitely wasn't true on her part.

Distant hoofbeats and men's voices grew louder. Richard and his soldiers rode into sight, and she darted off the dirt path to avoid being run over. He reined in Fauvel about ten feet from her. At least fifteen men accompanied him, but she only recognized Rob and Baldwin.

"Alix, this is a pleasant surprise. What brings you out here?"

She shifted the basket on her hip and managed to curtsy, albeit a bit off-balance. "We're gathering breakfast. What of you and your men?"

"You've never been hawking before, have you?" Richard asked.

"No, Your Grace." The idea of a hawk killing another bird for sport was distasteful to her, even though that was their natural hunting manner.

"I think we should remedy that at once. Join us."

Excitement strummed through her, but she forced it down. She didn't know most of the men, and she obviously wasn't Richard's queen. He didn't need unwelcome gossip.

"Thank you, but I must return to camp. Queen Joanna needs help with breakfast."

"My sister is very capable of handling things herself."

"Go. I'll take the fruit back to camp." Elisabetta took the basket.

Alix narrowed her eyes at Elisabetta, but couldn't refuse the king's request in front of his men. She bit back her sigh, then turned and looked up at Richard.

"I'd be happy to accompany you, but, as you can see, I'm not dressed for riding, nor do I have a horse."

Richard dismounted and beckoned to Alix. "You'll ride with me. I'm sure you can manage your skirts."

Fauvel pawed the ground, and Alix's heart jumped into her throat. The horse she'd ridden in France was smaller and more placid than the destriers Richard had brought. She'd seen men trampled under the sharp hooves of warhorses. She walked slowly to Fauvel. Richard put his hands around her waist. Heat rushed through her body and her nerves tingled.

"Place your foot in the stirrup and I'll lift you."

She scrambled into the saddle, then focused on tucking her skirts under her legs to avoid the curious stares of the soldiers. Richard swung up behind her and put his arm around her. The unyielding steel links of his mail bit into her back. She inched forward to put space between the thin cloth of her dress and his hauberk. Richard's armor-clad arm tightened, drawing her against his chest. Heat rushed through her as she felt the muscles in his thighs flex against hers.

"You have nothing to fear, Love. As you keep reminding me, I'm a married man and my interests *should* lie elsewhere."

Giddiness washed over her as his warm breath caressed her ear. "I'm glad to hear that. Why do you need so many soldiers accompanying you if this is only a hawking expedition?"

"We're also looking for Salah-ad-Din's men. My scouts have reported they've been seen in the vicinity."

She twisted to look at him. "The enemy is nearby? I thought they were further inland. Are we not safe here?"

"For certes, you're safe. Do you doubt that I can protect you?"

"I know you wouldn't put us in danger." Trepidation crept through her. When Richard left them in Acre, soldiers guarded the city, and the palace offered protection. Camping out in the open, she felt defenseless.

They rode in silence until Richard pulled Fauvel to a stop and raised his hand. He motioned for Rob to ride forth with the hawk. He gave the order for the hood to be removed, then Rob released the bird. A flock of sparrows burst from a distant copse of trees, and the hawk picked his prey. Like an arrow, it flew straight toward the hapless bird. In seconds, it was over, and the hawk circled victorious before returning to Rob.

"What did you think?" Richard asked.

"It was quite impressive. Your bird is very well trained."

"Indeed, she is." Pride echoed in his voice.

Richard settled back in the saddle and pulled her close again. Her pulse raced as his warmth enveloped her. As much as she was discomforted by his closeness, she also craved it. The sooner they reached their destination, the better.

He spurred Fauvel forward and led the men to the grove. "We'll rest the horses here."

Richard helped Alix dismount, then busied himself watering and tending to his horse. Several large rocks were strewn on the ground, and she chose one to sit on.

"How are you settling in?" Rob leaned against a nearby tree. "We've rebuilt much of the city walls, but it takes time."

"To be honest, as soon as I saw Jaffa, I wished we were back in Acre, but I quite like it now. However, I do miss the markets and the baths."

He gave her a half grin. "Jaffa doesn't offer much entertainment. I hope we can reclaim Jerusalem soon and return home."

"I wish for that as well."

"Rob," Richard called out as he approached. "Go with Will and scout the perimeter. We must remain vigilant."

"Yes, Your Grace."

"Who's Will? I don't think I've seen him before," Alix said.

"William de Préaux. He and his brothers served my father and made the wise decision to serve me."

That name was familiar to her, but the hazy memory hovered tantalizingly out of reach. Richard sat on the ground and leaned against the tree that Rob had vacated. He handed Alix a waterskin.

She took a sip, welcoming the water that trickled down her throat, and handed it back. "Thank you."

He took a deep drink and waved in the direction of Jaffa. "I do apologize for the state of the city. I'd hoped to have more of the walls repaired by now."

Alix shifted on the rock. He must have overheard her and Rob's conversation. "I understand that it was in worse condition when you arrived. Would it have been easier for us stay in Acre?"

"Are you beginning to regret that I brought you here?"

"You must be more specific. Do you mean Outremer or Jaffa?"

Richard glared at her.

Alix laughed and leaned forward to put her hand on his arm. "Richard, I had no idea what to expect when we arrived in Acre, but experiencing this has been more exhilarating than I ever could have imagined. I know it can't be easy to keep the peace between your men and Philippe's, and fight the enemy as well. I think you're doing a commendable job."

"I wish everyone was as easy to please," he murmured.

Alix suspected he was referring to his wife. Berenguela tried to make do with what they had but grew more unhappy each day. She missed the bustle of Acre, where she could buy different foods and necessities. The palace had afforded her more privacy than the tent which she shared with her ladies. She also hadn't spent as much time with Richard as she'd wanted.

Maud and Beatrice, on the other hand, were thrilled to be in Jaffa. The squires and the younger soldiers were very attentive, now that they weren't fighting constant battles. Maud and Jacques had been spending more time together, which was a bit worrisome. Young love and little supervision weren't a good combination. This could be the perfect time to broach the question of Maud's prospects.

"Richard, forgive me if I'm being too forward, but I'd like to discuss something with you. I'm sure you've noticed that Maud and Jacques are becoming quite close. I worry about her future, since her parents are deceased and she has no dowry. Might you be amenable to arranging something between them?"

He shifted position and stretched his legs out. "I've grown fond of the lass, and I'm quite willing to consider it."

Relief and a tinge of jealousy coursed through her. She wanted what Maud would have, a future with the man of her dreams.

Richard stifled a yawn, fatigue etched on his face. Rebuilding the city and worrying about potential attacks were taking their toll. His eyes fluttered closed and soon he was breathing deeply. A smile crossed her lips. He looked younger in sleep, with the tension melted away.

The stand of trees offered a peaceful oasis in the midst of battle. The horrors of war faded. She closed her eyes and tilted her face to the sun, the light breeze like gossamer on her skin. She wished she could freeze time and stay locked in this moment.

Yells and shrieks shattered the calm. Her blood curdled. A group of Turks burst into the grove and bore down on them.

"Richard! Wake up!"

He'd already leapt to his feet and raced to mount Fauvel. Seconds later, he wheeled his steed to face the enemy.

Alix cowered behind a boulder as the clang of metal rang out. Richard's men joined the fray, and the Turks fled with Richard in pursuit.

"Alix, come with me now!" Rob shouted as he rode to her. "We need to leave."

As much as she wanted to see what happened to Richard, Rob was right. Alix clambered onto the tallest rock, and he hauled her onto his horse.

The fighting grew louder. Another group of Turks rushed out from their hiding place and surrounded Richard and a handful of his men. The enemy shouted, but the only word she understood was *Melech* repeated over and over.

Alix turned in the saddle to see what was happening. "Rob, wait. I beg of you. I need to know Richard is safe."

Once they were a safe distance away, Rob reined in his horse. Richard was in the middle of the skirmish, slashing his sword at any enemy within reach. Her chest constricted and she couldn't draw breath. Once again, the Turks shouted out *Melech*. Richard paused and began to raise his sword.

A soldier pushed forward. "I'm the king. I'm *Melech*."

The Turks seized him at sword point, then retreated. Richard started after them, but his men blocked his way, forcing him back the way they'd come.

Garbled angry voices became clearer as the men neared.

"Richard, you must return to camp. It won't take long before they realize Will isn't the king," Baldwin stated.

Richard had a shocked expression on his face. "We can't leave him to his fate. He put his life in danger for me. I won't abandon him."

"If they'd captured you, this war would be over."

Alix's head swam, and she clutched the pommel of the saddle with white fingers as the enormity of the situation sank in. Thank God the enemy hadn't recognized Richard. After the massacre in Acre, Salah-ad-Din might have him executed in retaliation.

Richard glared at him. "I'm well aware of that, but if they kill him . . ."

"Let's pray that doesn't happen," Baldwin said. "Now, we must leave."

Richard threw one more glance in the direction the enemy had gone, then took the lead and galloped back to camp.

*~*~*

Henri stormed out of Richard's tent, narrowly missing Alix and Joanna as they approached. "My apologies, but Richard doesn't seem to understand the magnitude of what happened today. Would one of you try to talk some sense into him? My words have fallen on deaf ears." He stormed off.

Joanna glanced at Alix. "I feel the same. What if Richard had been captured?"

Alix's nerves tightened each time she relived the moment Richard had prepared to give himself up. "This time he was fortunate, but next time he might not be."

Jacques opened the tent flap, and they entered. Richard sat at the table next to Berenguela, a mutinous look in his eyes, while Baldwin and André stood across from him.

"This must stop, cousin. As Henri said, you're taking too many chances with your safety. You can't be so reckless," André argued.

"If you insist on going on reconnaissance outings, bring more men with you," Baldwin added.

Joanna rushed to Richard and gave him a quick hug. "They're right, Richard. What if it were you in the hands of the enemy? At best, you would be imprisoned for God knows how long."

"I should have done something." Richard raked his hand through his hair. "If Will is put to death, I'll never forgive myself."

On the return to camp, Alix had finally remembered why William's name was familiar. She'd read in one of her history books that after Will pretended to be the king, he was held captive. Eventually, he'd be ransomed, but not for many months.

"They won't kill him," she burst out.

"How do you know that?" Richard demanded.

"He put his life in danger to save you. Surely Salah-ad-Din would respect that type of courage and allow him to live." She hoped Will's fate wouldn't change.

"I pray that's true. To put your minds at ease, I'll be more careful in the future."

"Make certain that you do." Baldwin nodded, then took his leave.

Richard motioned to the servants, who hovered in the shadows, to pour wine and bring the dinner dishes in.

André sat next to Alix. "I heard you were with Richard on his hawking excursion. I'm aware he was also looking for signs that the enemy was nearby. Which they were. It was irresponsible of him to put you in danger."

"Rob made sure that I was protected." Alix sipped her wine.

"I don't have to tell you what would happen to you if you'd been taken?"

Ice ran down her spine. She would have been sold into slavery, or worse.

"If you came to harm, Richard would blame himself."

After the dinner dishes were cleared, Richard and André pored over maps of the region, choosing which route would be best to travel to Jerusalem.

Alix sank down next to Joanna and Berenguela to sit cross-legged on one of the cushions that littered the floor.

"It must have been terrifying when the enemy attacked," Berenguela said.

"I admit I was afraid, but Rob made sure I was out of harm's way." Alix neglected to tell her that a couple of Richard's men had been injured during the skirmish and later died from their wounds.

"I told him he should have been more mindful." Berenguela glanced at him and shook her head. "If he'd been captured, the Holy War would be over. We'd never reclaim Jerusalem."

"I'm thankful for Will's bravery and I do fear for him, but Berenguela's correct," Joanna said. "If Richard had fallen into Salah-ad-Din's hands, all would be lost."

"I honestly think this was a genuine mistake and one he won't make again," Alix stated.

Berenguela gave her a half smile. "I also learned that he's been meeting with Salah-ad-Din's brother. They've even exchanged gifts. Why is he consorting with the enemy?"

Alix shrugged. "I've no idea. Unless it's a plan to find out what's going on behind the enemy line."

"They met soon after the Turks were defeated at Arsuf. If we had the advantage, why meet at all?" Berenguela asked.

Joanna frowned. "Richard isn't foolish. He has his reasons, whether they make sense or not."

"Thank you for that show of faith," Richard said dryly as he and André joined them. "I do have my reasons. It's come to my attention that Conrad de Montferrat has held his own discussions with Salah-ad-Din. I've learned that Conrad has offered his help in exchange for lands he considers beneficial to him." Richard reclined on a cushion, propping his head up with his hand. "Since our arrival, he's made no effort to support us in our fight. I'm certain he still resents the fact that I returned the kingdom of Jerusalem to Guy."

Alix furrowed her brow. "Surely Salah-ad-Din isn't considering an alliance with him?"

Richard's lips tightened. "From the few interactions I've had with Conrad, Salah-ad-Din would be naive to trust him, and that he's not. I've only conferred with Safadin, but I hope to remedy that soon. I believe there's dissension within Salah-ad-Din's ranks and an opportunity to foment it."

"What makes you think that?" Joanna asked.

"I have spies in the enemy camp, although the information isn't always accurate. If I can create mistrust between Conrad and Salah-ad-Din, perhaps he'll be more willing to negotiate with me in person."

André glanced at Richard. "Your latest proposition might sway him."

Richard shook his head slightly, but it was too late.

"What do you mean by that?" Berenguela asked.

André shrugged. "Several weeks ago, we met with Safadin, and Richard asked for the city of Jerusalem to be returned. As expected, he was denied."

"Why am I not surprised? But that can't be the proposition you suggested," Joanna said.

Richard grinned. "I proposed an alliance between us by offering you as wife to Safadin."

The only sound was Berenguela's sharp inhale.

"You can't be serious." Joanna glanced at André. "Surely, my brother jests."

André focused his gaze on a point in the corner of the tent.

Joanna's jaw clenched. "Under no circumstance will I marry him."

"The agreement was in our best interest," Richard stated. "If Salah-ad-Din granted Palestine to his brother, for your dowry, I would generously give all the coastal cities from Acre to Ascalon. You and your new husband could live in Jerusalem and Christians would be allowed to visit at will."

"You've given this quite some thought, but it will never happen," Joanna scoffed. "You'd best tell him it was a misunderstanding. I refuse to marry a non-Christian and our enemy."

She stood and stalked out of the tent.

Berenguela stared at him. "Richard, how could you possibly consider marrying your sister to an infidel as a chance to retake Jerusalem? Where are your Christian values?"

Alix's mind spun. This abrupt change in negotiation tactic with the Turks on Richard's part confounded historians to the present. What would he gain from offering his sister in marriage? Here was a chance to learn something that historians were still in the dark about.

"What's your reasoning behind this?" she asked. "You had to know that Joanna was never going to agree to the marriage and if you forced her, you'd risk alienating her."

Richard raised his brow. "Come now, Alix. Why do you think I made the offer?"

Alix frowned as she mulled it over. "As a younger brother, Safadin can only watch as Salah-ad-Din grows more powerful. Perhaps he feels resentment and jealousy. If he's given Jerusalem and the coastal cities, he could become a ruler in his own right."

Admiration flashed in his eyes. "That's part of it."

"They must suspect that you're not serious. You'd never allow Joanna to marry one of the enemies, so what do you get out of it?"

"I hope to widen the cracks that already exist in the Turkish army. The less united they are, the more beneficial to me." He sat up and held out his cup for a servant to refill. "I'm preparing for my army to march to Jerusalem, but I need to plan my supply route. By meeting with Safadin, I hope to keep his attention on me and keep him in the dark as to our plans."

"Once we begin our journey to the Holy City, our supply chain is put at risk. While we followed the coast, the enemy couldn't attack our supply ships, but once we turn inland, we're at their mercy," André explained. "There are many cities between Jaffa and Jerusalem that the Turks have destroyed, but if we can repair them, they can be used for supplies."

"I'm glad to hear that you weren't seriously considering the marriage, but you said nothing about leaving," Berenguela said.

Richard shrugged and took a sip from his cup. "I don't relish the idea of heading further inland, but we have no choice. In the next few days, I'll take some men and travel to Yasur to rebuild the fortress there. I'm aware it will take time, but I can't risk more battles without reinforcements or supplies coming from Jaffa."

Exhaustion from the day's events caught up to Alix. "It's been quite a day. May I take my leave?"

Richard stood, gave her his hand, and pulled her to her feet. "I do apologize for putting you in that situation. I couldn't bear it if anything had happened to you."

"You were in more danger than I was. I thank God Will had the courage to pretend to be you." Alix drew in a shaky breath. "I don't want to think of the alternative."

A shadow crossed his face. "I owe him much."

"We all do," André said as he walked to them.

Alix nodded to Richard and Berenguela, then left. André followed close behind. She paused, then fell in step with him.

The moon was a sliver in the sky, and Alix was glad of André's company in the dark, although she doubted it was coincidental. After the ambush that morning, every rustle in the bushes put her frayed nerves on edge. She kept envisioning the enemy encroaching on the camp, preparing for an attack.

They reached her tent, where she bid André goodnight and ducked inside.

Joanna sat at the table, her hands clenched around a wine goblet. "Did my brother say anything more about this . . . arrangement?" Her voice was brittle.

"I'm sure he'll tell you eventually, but he has no intention of marrying you to Safadin."

Joanna's eyes widened and she pressed her hand to her chest. "I prayed Richard was jesting but sometimes I can't tell when he is or not."

Alix laughed. "That's what makes him a good negotiator. You're never quite sure where you stand."

Joanna shook her head. "My brother is many things, but I trust his judgement. I just wish he'd leave me out of his schemes."

Alix sympathized with her. Even though she knew his history, often she felt as if they were chess pieces on a board, playing a game of Richard's making, and he was the only one who knew the endgame.

*~*~*

Richard turned from the maps spread on the table as Berenguela stirred in their bed, rustling the sheets.

He lifted the curtain that separated the sleeping quarters from the outer room. "I didn't mean to wake you."

She raised herself on her elbows. "It's not even light yet. You were going to say goodbye, were you not?" Her voice was drowsy.

"For certes. I'm not leaving for several hours."

"Come back to bed, then?" She glanced up at him through her lashes.

A shiver of guilt ran down his spine. Several days had passed since he'd asked Alix to ride with him, but the feel of her soft curves pressed against him was burned into his memory. Raw need for her had smoldered and flamed until the only one way to dampen the fire was with copious amounts of wine.

"I have much to do . . ."

Her cheeks reddened, and she gripped the blanket with trembling fingers. "I understand."

Richard rubbed his chin and sighed. He liked Berenguela, but his heart belonged to another. He sat on the bed and took her hands in his.

"As much as I would like to spend all morning in bed, I must see to my army." He brushed her sleep-tousled hair from her face and placed a chaste kiss on her lips.

"How long do you think you'll be gone this time?"

He shrugged and stood. "I've no idea."

Richard walked to the tent flap and called for Jacques. Moments later, the boy entered. "Bring me my armor."

The curtain shifted as Berenguela emerged. "Jacques, that will be all. I'll tend to my husband."

Richard raised his brow but motioned to the boy to leave. Berenguela took his hauberk, the rings clinking melodically as she helped put it on, struggling a bit with the unwieldiness of it.

Her hands lingered on his chest, then she caressed his cheek. "Are you certain you can't put off leaving for a little while longer?"

"Unfortunately, no."

Disappointment and hurt flashed in her eyes.

Once again, a flash of guilt gripped him. "I'll return before we depart."

The sun illuminated the low-lying clouds with burnt orange as it edged above the horizon. The camp was empty except for the men who remained behind to rebuild the walls and to keep a sharp eye on the gates, allowing only merchants carrying food and supplies to leave. Richard walked the short distance to the edge of the grove, where his army gathered in the dawn, to ensure the men were preparing for the day's travel.

André turned and lifted his chin toward the men. "They'll be ready on your orders, Sire."

"Good. We'll leave within the hour. I don't anticipate a long march today, so there's no need to rush."

André nodded, then looked back at the camp. "I hope we've left enough soldiers to guard the women. In our absence, I fear Salah-ad-Din might take advantage and attack."

"I've no doubt they'll be well protected. Rob and Georges have been appointed to look out for them. They've sworn on their lives no harm will come to the ladies." Richard's tone held a hint of amusement, but he didn't want to admit he was still worried. With the large number of men Salah-ad-Din had at his disposal, he could well afford to send several groups to attack Jaffa while engaging Richard's army elsewhere.

"Hopefully, the enemy's attention will be aimed at us." He gripped Richard's shoulder. "Go say your farewells. I have a feeling we'll be gone some time."

Sensing that Berenguela needed more reassurance than Joanna, Richard went to his sister's tent first and was ushered inside by Elisabetta.

"I assume you're here to say goodbye," Joanna said. "I wish you weren't leaving."

"You'll be well protected. You have nothing to fear."

Joanna hurried to him, and he caught her tightly in his arms.

"I'm more worried about you. After that disastrous hawking excursion of yours, I dread something worse occurring."

Her reminder of what had nearly happened to him rekindled the ever-present guilt and fear that consumed him. There was no way to know if Will was alive or not. He'd sent spies to see if they could discover any information, but they'd failed.

"I won't," he said. "I do have some good news, at least for you."

"News concerning what?"

A sly grin crossed Richard's lips. "I regretfully informed Safadin that you were unable to accept the marriage proposal on account of him being a non-Christian."

"Truly, you told him that?" At his nod, she crossed her arms. "Alix told me you weren't seriously considering it."

He chuckled. "That explains why you haven't been furious with me."

She laid her hand on his chest. "Take your time saying goodbye to Berenguela. You still haven't spent as much time with her as you should."

His brows drew together. Trying to maintain an equal balance between waging war and his marriage was impossible, especially when his crusade took precedence. But Joanna was correct. He needed to pay more attention to his wife, especially since he needed heirs.

"Point taken, little sister."

"I'm glad Alix traveled with us, but wouldn't it have been simpler for everyone if she'd stayed in France? I think she is the main reason for trouble in your marriage." Joanna paused and bit her lip. "She told me Mother wanted her to be my companion, but I don't understand why she agreed. Especially if she was planning to end the relationship. Does she have other intentions?"

Richard's eyes glittered. The pain that pierced his heart was as fresh as the day Alix had ended things. "She has no ulterior motives. Mother asked her to come on *my* orders."

"I thought Alix . . . wanted something more from you."

He gave her a thin smile. "She wanted me to allow her to stay in France."

Joanna stood on her tiptoes and gave him a hug. "I'm so sorry. I had no idea. I know that you love her, and if it's any comfort, she still cares for you." She stepped back.

Richard nodded and left the tent, annoyed that his sister thought Alix was devious and taking him for a fool.

"Your Grace," a familiar voice called out and stopped him in his tracks.

He turned and walked toward Alix until he could smell the spicy scent of sandalwood that clung to her skin. She moved closer, and his pulse raced.

"I should be used to watching you leave," she said. "But it never gets any easier."

"Hopefully, this will be the last time."

He reached out and brushed strands of coppery hair that had caught on her full lower lip, his fingers lingering longer than necessary. She shifted her stance and a flush crept up her cheeks. Joanna's words echoed in his ears. Did she still have feelings for him?

She hesitated, then moved forward to hug him. "Please take care. I do worry about you."

He tightened his arms around her. "I appreciate your concern, but I'll be fine," he murmured.

Alix leaned into him for a moment, then moved back. "Try not to put yourself in unnecessary danger. Although with you, that might be an impossible request."

Richard grinned. Alix's lips pressed together, and he relented. "I'll be careful and return safely."

"See that you do." She nodded to him and turned away.

He continued the short distance to his tent. Berenguela sat at the table, but hurried to him when he entered.

"I apologize if I was being selfish earlier. Although I don't wish for you to leave, reclaiming Jerusalem takes priority."

Richard put his hands on her shoulders. "When we return victorious, I'll make it up to you."

Her face glowed. "I have faith that you'll prevail."

"How could you have any doubt?"

The army camped for several weeks between two fortresses that Salah-ad-Din had ordered destroyed. Richard appointed his men the task of repairing Casal Maen while the Templars restored the Casal of the Plains. Salah-ad-Din had withdrawn to the safety of Jerusalem, but continually sent soldiers to harass the lines of communication from Jaffa, as well as foraging parties that weren't properly guarded.

Richard had ridden out to inspect the rubble around the perimeter of the destroyed town with his masons when distant cries of help mingled with screams and metallic clangs from swords hitting shields sent chills down his spine.

He galloped back to the encampment and ordered the Earl of Leicester and Baldwin to take soldiers and lend aid. He armed himself quickly and, with a handful of men, followed. When he arrived, the armies were in a heated battle. The Turks surrounded the Templars, who stood back-to-back, warding them off. André and his small retinue of knights were in the thick of the fray, charging through the ranks of the enemy and sending them fleeing, but their numbers continued to grow.

"Your Grace, we have too few men to help the cause," one of Philippe's French knights called out. He gestured toward the Templars, who struggled to keep the Turks at bay. "They have no chance of rescue. I think it's better to leave them to their fate than to put your life at risk and endanger the crusade."

Rage rushed through Richard's veins and his face darkened. "How dare you suggest that I abandon the men that I sent here to fight? If they should die while I watch safely from afar, then I don't deserve to be called king."

He leveled a searing gaze at the man, spurred Fauvel forward, and crashed into the Turkish force, scattering them. His knights followed him into the melee, and although they were few, their arrival gave new life to the Templars and André's men. Under a fresh onslaught, they were able to rout the enemy.

Richard led the men in pursuit of the Turks for miles until their camp could be seen in the distance. They captured as many as they could, then returned to where the battle began. He joined Baldwin and André, who were overseeing the squires who attended to the injured and dead.

André made the cross with his left hand over a mortally injured knight and grimaced with the movement. He cradled his right arm and rivulets of dried blood streaked his hauberk.

Richard's face blanched. "God's bones . . . how bad is the injury?"

"I'll survive, cousin. It looks worse than it is. I was a bit unlucky and was pierced by a lance. However, the Turk that wielded it was more unfortunate than I."

"Tell me how this carelessness happened." Richard nodded toward the body-littered plain as they began their slow ride back to camp.

"The squires were foraging for grass for the horses and strayed from the protection of the Templars. The Turks saw an advantage and took it. My men and I were within shouting distance and joined the fight," André explained.

"Thank God you reached them in time."

André gasped as his horse stumbled.

Worry crossed Richard's face. "As soon as we return, I'll summon the physician."

"I won't argue with you."

When they reached Richard's tent, he sent Jacques to find the doctor. André sank into a chair, his face gray with pain. Richard handed him a cup of wine, then paced the breadth of the tent. André had fought by his side for years and was one of most trusted comrades. He'd lay down his life for him and knew André would do the same. Renewed fury at the French coward's suggestion that he watch while his men were slaughtered coursed through him.

The tent flap opened, and Ralph entered. "Let's see what we have."

With Jacques's help, he carefully pulled off André's hauberk. His right arm was discolored and swollen, the bones offset. Jacques paled and stumbled backward.

Ralph waved the boy away and glanced at Richard. "Sire, I think I need your help with this."

He instructed Richard to hold André's upper arm. "Keep steady while I put the bones back in alignment."

Ralph gripped André's wrist, then twisted.

"Jesu!" André sucked in his breath. "I wished you'd left it as it was."

"You'll thank me in time." Ralph splinted the arm, wrapped it in flannel strips, then fashioned a sling. "Try to keep from exerting yourself or joining any battles for at least a month. To make certain you'll follow my orders, I think you ought to return to Jaffa to recover."

He turned, dug through his bag, and handed Richard a small vial of opium. "If the pain becomes too great, make a tea with this, but use it sparingly. Let me know if he takes a turn for the worse." Ralph bowed, then left.

"I'm not leaving. The fortresses still need to be repaired, not to mention, the closer you march to Jerusalem, the more dangerous it will be." André shifted in his chair and winced.

Richard nodded and raked his hand through his hair. "I assumed you wouldn't, but you're useless to me if you can't fight." Amusement colored his tone, but concern flashed in his eyes. "Until you fully recover, you'll oversee the rebuilding of the walls."

"Very well, although you'd best not retake Jerusalem without me. I want to be there when we defeat Salah-ad-Din."

Richard grinned and lifted his wine goblet. "I wouldn't have it any other way."

*~*~*

The wind gusted across the plains, carrying a chill that heralded the coming of winter. Having spent the better part of the afternoon ordering final adjustments to the rebuilding of the city walls, Richard entered his tent, relieved to be out of the constant gale. He'd barely removed his hauberk when André burst in.

"Cousin, is it true that you're planning to march to Jerusalem in two days? It's been almost two months since my injury. Why haven't I been put in charge of a battalion?"

Richard motioned for André to take a seat, and a servant hurried to pour some wine. "I need you elsewhere. I've been told that winters here are miserable. With Jaffa being in the condition it is, I'd rather the ladies return to

Acre, where they'll be more comfortable." He paused to take a sip of wine. "I'd like you to escort them. Knowing the women are in the palace will ease my mind."

Although André's arm had healed, Richard worried that his lack of preparedness for battle might result in another injury. One that was fatal.

André stared into his wine cup as moments passed. "Very well, I'll take them to Acre." He glanced up. "You do realize that I'm aware of what you're doing. I'm more than able to ride and fight by your side."

"I want to make certain of that before we face another battle. I've already sent word to Acre and a galley should be on its way. Tomorrow, you'll leave for Jaffa. That's an order from your king."

André chuckled. "I must admit, returning to Acre is an improvement over the conditions here. I assume Rob and Georges will accompany me?"

Richard nodded. "I'm also sending a small retinue of soldiers. Once you reach Acre and the ladies are protected, we'll discuss your return."

The Frankish army left the area and moved forward to a position between the strongholds of Lydda and Ramla, which had been razed to the ground on Salah-ad-Din's orders. He wanted to ensure that Richard's army would have little in the way of protection and sustenance.

Richard began to repair Ramla, but now he encountered a new adversary— the elements. The weather deteriorated, and the army faced constant rain and hail. They spent six weeks in freezing, wet weather, gathering food and weapons that arrived from Jaffa. Biscuits crumbled in the soggy conditions and salt pork rotted and became inedible. The tenuous line of communication with Jaffa was under almost daily attacks, which lessened their supplies.

Religious fervor was increasing, but the winter weather had taken a huge toll on the army. It had taken over two months to travel thirty miles. Countless men had sickened and were now buried in unmarked graves far from their families and homes.

Richard's army had inched forward until they reached a small, ruined fortress at the foot of the Judean hills. They were closer to their goal of reaching Jerusalem than they'd ever been.

But waging war in these conditions was an insurmountable undertaking, and Richard wasn't prepared to jeopardize the crusade.

He summoned the council to gather in his tent to announce his intent. The men shifted in their seats, their gazes darting back and forth to each other. Richard drummed his fingers in time with the rain that beat a constant tattoo on the cloth material as they put forth their arguments.

There were two schools of thought in opposition—the men who were military strategists and the others who were warriors, who believed the war had to be fought with might, sword, and God on their side.

"I'm aware that we're getting close to Salah-ad-Din, but attempting to take Jerusalem in this weather is madness. Even if were we able to defeat the garrison, could we hold it?" Richard sat back and crossed his arms. "I'm not willing to put the army in a position of almost certain defeat."

Guy de Lusignan narrowed his eyes. "For years we've fought the Turks and now we're hovering on their doorstep. Yes, our army has suffered great losses, but so has theirs." He pounded the table with his fist. "This is the time to strike."

Murmurs of agreement rumbled through the council, but voices of denial rang out.

"The king is correct," Baldwin stated. "Salah-ad-Din has a larger army and can call on reinforcements at will. We might be able to take Jerusalem, but what then? How long could we hold it?"

"What are you suggesting? That we turn our back and retreat?" Guy scoffed.

Richard nodded. "As much as I abhor the idea, I believe our best course of action is to march to Ascalon. If we can cut Salah-ad-Din's supply line from Egypt, then we can take advantage and mount an attack."

Hugh of Burgundy narrowed his eyes. "So, you'll get what you've wanted all along. I'm not ready to concede defeat, and neither are my men. I'll wager Philippe wouldn't agree with you, either."

"That coward turned tail and fled back to the comforts of France. I doubt he cares what happens to Jerusalem or his army." Richard placed his hands on the table and leaned forward. "I'm not willing to mount a siege that we have little hope of winning. Now, let's put this to a vote."

Hugh bolted to his feet. "I'll never agree to this."

"I must side with Hugh," Guy said. "For too long, we've fought. I refuse to give up now."

"Sire, you know my mind. I'll march with you to Ascalon." Baldwin gave a short nod.

Each man stated his decision and, when the last had voted, Richard looked around the room. "It is decided. We'll go to Ascalon."

Amidst murmurs and looks of hatred thrown by the French, the men filed out. The tent seemed cavernous now that it was empty.

Richard took a deep drink from his goblet, turmoil churning within. The vote had been much closer than he'd wished. Retreat wasn't in his nature, but waging a war where the likely outcome was defeat was foolhardy. Many of the soldiers were there for religious reasons. Even if they were able to take Jerusalem, the men might feel that they'd fulfilled their vows and makes plans to return home. How would they be able to keep the city against a horde of Saracens?

He had no doubt that his decision was in the best interest of the crusade, but once it was announced to the men, could he keep the army intact?

*~*~*

Several days later, battered by the inclement weather and discouraged that they were turning their back on the city they'd come to reclaim, the army limped back to Ramla. Once there, Richard's fear was realized. Many of the French, including Hugh of Burgundy, returned to Jaffa. Others went to Acre and even Tyre to join Conrad.

Richard led a much smaller army toward Ascalon with his nephew, Henri. Icy rain poured on them as they trudged along the muddy, churned-up road. The soldiers and horses were exhausted from the weight of their armor. The carts clogged in the mud, which had become like quicksand. Food supplies were lost in the mud or rotted in the damp

When they reached the destroyed city, murmurs of discontent swept through the army. Not a single wall stood. Barren skeletal trees offered little protection. Trickles of doubt flowed through Richard. What had he led his men into?

Within a week of their arrival, Richard had thrown himself into the momentous task of repairing the walls and towers. Couriers were sent to Jaffa and Acre to entreat the French to return and lend aid. They did so on the condition that they would only stay until Easter. If any decided to leave before then, they would be free to do so. Determined to make some progress after a dismal campaign, Richard accepted the offer.

*~*~*

Alix laid her wrist across the soldier's forehead, then stood. He was feverish, like the other men. Ralph had left with Richard, so she'd been nursing the soldiers, who were suffering from some unknown malady.

"I'll give you some feverfew." She motioned to the servant who hovered behind her.

She walked to the table and bent down to pick up her pouch. Her head swam, and she closed her eyes and took deep breaths until the dizziness passed. Since she was the only healer in the palace, the last thing she needed was to fall ill.

"Make him some tea. It should help bring his fever down. I'll come by in the morning to see how's feeling."

After giving him more instructions on how to make the tisane, she left. The soldiers were staying in the barracks not far from the palace, but by the time she'd walked the quarter mile, she was out of breath and shaking with cold.

Voices echoed from the dining hall and the smell of food reminded her that she hadn't eaten since breakfast. Maud and Elisabetta were eating at one of the trestle tables, so Alix made her way to them.

Elisabetta moved over to allow Alix room to sit. "How are your patients? It seems like every day, more men are becoming sick."

"There's been some improvement, but they're still ill."

She reached for a plate filled with chicken, but her stomach roiled when she inhaled the aroma. Instead, she settled for a chunk of bread. Alix tried to focus on the conversation, but her head spun. Sweat beaded on her upper lip as the room became unbearably hot.

"Are you feeling well?" Elisabetta's voice echoed like she was underwater.

Alix looked at her through a haze of swirling black spots. "I need some air."

She staggered to her feet and swayed. Her head pounded and her stomach churned like the sea in a storm.

Maud stood, and she waved her away. "I'm going to lie down. I'm certain I'll feel better in the morning."

Alix managed to walk a couple of feet before blackness filled her vision. Her knees turned to water, and she collapsed on the floor.

*~*~*

Voices floated around her like ghostly whispers, piercing the fogginess that enveloped her. She tried to open her eyes, but the brightness of the sun stabbed like daggers of light.

Hands supported her back, and cups holding vile-smelling liquids were lifted to her lips. Each time she drank, her stomach revolted, and she was turned over just in time to retch into a basin. Her body burned with fire, and then chills shook her entire frame until she thought she'd never get warm again.

Images of war and shouting haunted her tortured dreams. She kept seeing Richard's death at the hands of the enemy—his mutilated body lying on the battlefield. She'd wake, drenched in sweat. Her reprieves were short-lived as she was given more sleeping draughts and soon was back in the throes of her darkest fears. At last, the nightmares faded, and she was able to sleep through the night.

The early morning light that peeked through the high slit windows barely illuminated the room. She peered through heavy-lidded eyes, expecting to feel the sharp pain in her head, but it had subsided to merely a dull ache.

Hazily, she took in her surroundings. She must be dreaming. This wasn't any room that she recognized, and Richard was slumped in a chair at the table. He stared into the empty space before him, his face drawn and gray with exhaustion. She tried to focus on the vision, but the room spun back into darkness.

*~*~*

When she opened her eyes again, the sun's rays had lengthened across the floor. It wasn't her imagination. Richard slept in a chair next to her. His arms were folded on the cot, his head cradled between them.

Warmth and love filled her heart. She reached out, ran her hand over his hair, then caressed his cheek and jaw, stubbled from not shaving. He stirred, and she snatched her hand back. Richard sat up and stretched.

His eyes widened. "You're awake. How are you feeling?" His voice was husky with sleep.

"Much better."

He brushed his lips against her forehead. "Thank God your fever has broken. I'm summoning the doctor."

He hurried to the door and, after a brief conversation with an unseen person, returned. Richard sat on the bed and took her hand in his. "I was so afraid I was going to lose you."

Fear flashed in his eyes and dread coursed through her. She must have been sicker than she'd thought.

The door opened, and Ralph entered. "Your Grace, I must respectfully ask you to move."

His lips twitched as Richard stood but only stepped back three feet. The doctor felt her brow, then tested her pulse.

Relief crossed his face, and he smiled at her. "You're very lucky. For a while, we weren't sure if you'd make it."

"Was it *leonardie*?" She prayed it wasn't.

Ralph shook his head. "It doesn't appear to be. You could have been sickened by contaminated water or food. I believe you're on the mend, but you need rest." He raised his brow at Richard. "I assume asking you to leave is out of the question."

Richard gave a curt nod.

"Very well. Send for me in case her fever spikes again." The door shut behind him.

"May I have some water, please?" Her throat was as dry as a desert.

Richard poured some into a goblet, helped her sit up, and lifted the cup to her lips. She put her hands on his to steady it. The tepid water was like heaven as it trickled down her throat.

She leaned back against the pillow and held the cup on her lap. "You're here. I thought I was dreaming."

He pulled the chair closer. "I arrived five days ago, but you were already ill. I immediately sent for the doctor."

"That explains why he's not with the army." She looked around the chamber. "I don't recognize this room."

"Joanna thought it best that you were separated from the ladies since they didn't know what ailed you."

Richard stood and refreshed the water in her goblet.

She narrowed her eyes when he returned. "You didn't add a sleeping draught, did you?"

He laughed. "No, Love, I prefer that you're awake."

Alix took a deep drink from the cup, relieved to be able to keep it down. "Why are you here? When André returned to Jaffa to escort us to Acre, he informed us that the army was traveling to Ramla. Since then, we've had sparse communications, but we know that you turned back from Jerusalem and marched to Ascalon."

The announcement hadn't surprised her, but Berenguela had been beside herself when she heard the army was within reach of the Holy City, but retreated without any attempt to capture it.

Richard sighed and rubbed his jaw. "I suppose you hold me responsible as well for not reclaiming the city. My wife certainly does."

She shook her head, regretting it as her vision swam.

"The weather was dismal. I lost men and horses daily. I know my decision wasn't welcome, but I believe it to be the right one." He paused. "Are you sure you feel well enough for me to continue?"

Alix smiled. "Yes, I want to hear more. I've missed discussing politics and strategies with you."

His gaze caught hers and her heart jumped at the tenderness in his eyes.

"I've missed it as well, more than you know. Once I made it known we were heading south, the French scattered like rats from a sinking ship. I was able to recall Hugh and his men to Ascalon to help rebuild the city, but soon he ran out of money and asked me to compensate them. It was already costing me a fortune to pay the men to repair it. I refused, and he fled back to Acre."

"You came here to convince the French to change their minds?"

A questioning look entered his eyes. "Are you aware of the uprising between the Genoese and the Pisans?"

She tilted her head, then nodded as vague memories of shouting flooded back. "I thought that was part of my nightmares."

"Unfortunately, it wasn't. The Pisans remained loyal to me and held them off. They sent for my help. I believe Conrad of Montferrat was behind it, and Hugh was all too willing to lend his aid. Conrad hoped the Genoese could capture the city, then deliver it to him." A storm of emotions filled his eyes. "When I learned that you were sick ... God's bones, Alix, if I'd lost you ..."

He leaned forward until his breath caressed her face. Her heart stopped. The brush of his warm lips on hers was as light as butterfly wings, but electric shocks shot through her.

The door creaked open, and Joanna entered with Maud. Richard sat back, irritation crossing his face. Alix, on the other hand, was glad about the interruption. Richard was off-limits. So far, she'd managed to stand by her vow, but her resolve was crumbling. Each time she was with him, a spark of life ignited within her, and in his absence, a gaping abyss filled her soul.

Maud carried a tray with dishes and began to prepare a plate for Alix. Tendrils of steam twisted upward, and Alix's stomach growled as she inhaled the aroma of cooked meat and lentils.

"Why didn't you tell us Alix's fever had broken? We heard it from Ralph," Joanna scolded.

Richard grinned at her. "I apologize for being remiss." He turned to Alix. "Now that you're in capable hands, I must attend to some things, but I'll return this evening."

He left, and Joanna sat in his recently vacated chair. "How are you feeling?"

"Much better than I was."

Maud carried the plate to the bed, and Alix propped pillows behind her to lean against. She hadn't eaten in days and took a small taste of boiled lentils to see how they settled. Satisfied the food would stay down, she took a larger bite.

"When the king arrived, he was furious that he wasn't told earlier that you were ill. He's been at your bedside for days." Maud grinned impishly. "I hope we didn't interrupt anything between you."

"He was making sure that I'm still recovering," Alix stated. "Nothing more."

A knowing smile crossed Joanna's lips. "Well, he's not the only one. Everyone's been worried about you."

Alix took another bite of lentils and swallowed quickly. "I forgot to ask. The men I was tending to . . . have they recovered? I hope more haven't fallen ill."

Joanna's gaze slid away.

A sick feeling filled Alix's stomach. "Did they recover?"

"Most of them did, but a few didn't survive." Joanna took a shaky breath. "Ralph didn't give us much hope."

Chills ran down Alix's spine. Richard hadn't told her that she'd been that close to death.

Joanna glanced at Maud, who'd taken Alix's empty cup to refill it. "In Messina, I told you that I mistrusted your intentions toward Richard," she said in a low voice.

"I remember."

Joanna leaned a bit closer. "I must apologize to you. I told Richard about my suspicions. Needless to say, he wasn't happy to hear them. He said you didn't even want to come to Sicily." Misery filled her eyes. "I wish I'd known. I've misjudged you. I hope you can forgive me."

"Of course, I forgive you. You're protective of him. I understand that."

Joanna placed her hand on Alix's arm and smiled.

Maud returned with the cup and handed it to her. They stayed until Alix finished her meal, then took their leave to let her rest.

Once the door shut behind them, Alix's thoughts spun. What if she had died? Up until this point, she'd been so focused on living in Richard's world that she'd given little thought to her own life in Austin. A surge of homesickness washed over her. Her eyes pricked at the thought of never seeing her parents or her friends, Cara and Thomas, again.

There also were so many things left unsaid between her and Richard, at least on her side. This wasn't her time, and he was married to a woman she considered a close friend. But as much as she tried to deny it, the truth was, she still loved him.

When he'd kissed her, she hadn't been assailed by guilt. Instead, it felt comforting and right. She'd ended their relationship, but her confidence in that decision wavered.

*~*~*

Hours later, a light knock on the door roused her. Richard walked in, followed by Ralph.

"Joanna said that you were feeling better, but I thought it best to have you examined again to make certain," Richard said.

Alix shook her head. "I don't think it's necessary."

"It's not your choice."

Ralph performed a quick checkup, then patted her shoulder. "I see no lingering effects, but rest for another day or so to make sure."

Alix smiled. "I appreciate your coming here to tend to me. I hope it wasn't too much of an inconvenience."

"Not at all. Besides, the accommodations are much better than at Ascalon." He chuckled and took his leave.

Richard sat in the chair next to the bed. "That puts my mind at ease, considering I need to leave in two days."

Heaviness once again filled Alix's heart. "You're returning to Ascalon already?"

Richard shook his head. "I'm meeting with Conrad tomorrow. For months, I've asked him to support our cause, and each time, he's refused. His attempt to capture Acre with the aid of Hugh and his men and unite it with Tyre is an act of betrayal. I'm done with his insubordination."

"What do you mean to do?" Alix raised the pillow higher behind her and settled back.

"I hope we can come to an agreement. Although I named Guy de Lusignan King of Jerusalem, Conrad's marriage to Isabella gives him a claim to the throne. He has powerful allies and is a stronger leader than Guy. I wouldn't put it past him to attempt another uprising." His jaw clenched. "Jesu, I wish I could rid myself of the man."

Coldness stole through Alix. "Richard, don't make light of that. Especially in regard to Conrad."

"Love, it was merely a jest. Now, I'm famished. I ordered some food if you care to join me."

"Richard, you've spent more time with me than you ought to have. I'm sure you'd like to dine with the others."

"I prefer to be here. That is, unless my presence is unwanted."

She laughed. "No, I've enjoyed you being here, although I'm sure I haven't been lively company for most of the time."

He took her hand in his and caressed it with his thumb. "As I've said, I'd rather be with you."

A tapping on the door echoed in the room. Richard opened it to allow a couple of servants to enter with trays and flagons. After they put the items on the table, he motioned for them to leave.

"Do you feel up to joining me?"

"I think I can manage that."

Alix sat on the edge of the bed and took deep breaths as she waited for the lightheadedness to fade. She was feeling stronger, but being confined to bed for days had taken its toll. She was as weak as a kitten.

"Allow me."

Richard scooped her up, and she wrapped her arms around his shoulders. She swallowed convulsively as she felt the play of his muscles through her shift. His body heat enveloped her, and tingles cascaded down her spine. Her willpower was crumbling.

He hooked his foot around the leg of a chair and pulled it out, the legs screeching against the floor. He set her down and began filling the plates. She picked up a flagon and poured dark burgundy liquid in a cup for him. The other flagon held water.

Alix filled her cup, then gazed at him. His red-gold hair was longer, the ends still bleached blond by the sun, but the tan he'd developed in the summer had faded. Between skirmishes and helping rebuild the fortresses himself, he'd maintained his muscled physique.

He handed her a plate. She smiled. "This reminds me of our private dinners in Poitiers."

"I remember. Love, I know you wish things were different, but you're being here means more to me than you'll ever know."

"I'm glad I'm here too, but each time you leave and put your life at risk, I fear for your safety." She stared at her plate. "I don't want to regret that I left things unsaid."

His cup stilled as he was lifting it. "What things exactly?"

Her feelings for him were carved into her heart, but what of his for her? Her stomach knotted. What if she'd read too much into his words, or worse, put him in a position he didn't want to be in? *I need to know.*

Alix took a deep breath and steeled herself. "Although our relationship is over, I want you to know that I still love you."

# ~ *Chapter 27* ~

ALIX HELD HER BREATH AS the seconds stretched out.

"I never expected to hear those words from you again." He reached out and covered her hand with his. "My feelings for you haven't changed."

Warmth flowed through her veins, melting away the fear. "I don't know what *our* future holds, but I wanted you to know how I feel. I hope this doesn't affect our friendship."

He cocked his brow. "How can it not?"

"This doesn't change anything between us, Richard. It can't. I refuse to be the cause of any infidelity on your part."

Richard took a deep drink of wine. "I know your feelings on this, and I respect them. I don't have to like them, however." He grinned at her.

She finished her meal, then yawned behind her hand. "I hope I start feeling stronger soon. I'm not used to being ill."

"It takes time to recover. I know that all too well." He stood and pulled her to her feet.

Richard left to summon the servants, and by the time they returned, Alix had climbed into bed and pulled the blanket up to her shoulders.

The servants cleared the table in record time, then shut the door behind them.

She folded the top of the blanket down and looked up at Richard. "Will I see you before you return to Ascalon?"

"For certes. I want to make sure that you're completely recovered before I leave."

He extinguished all the lanterns, save one. The flickering light highlighted the angles of his face, throwing his high cheekbones into relief and accentuated his physicality. Memories of countless nights she'd spent in his arms overwhelmed her. He walked toward her, his eyes fixed on hers. Tense silence stretched between them. He leaned down.

Her heart slammed against her ribcage. She wanted his lips on hers, his hands traveling down her body and the weight of him pressed against her. He hesitated, but merely dropped a kiss on the top of her head.

"Get some sleep. I'll see you tomorrow."

He strode toward the door. Frustration gripped her in iron bands. Alix dug her nails into her palms to keep from calling him back. As much as she needed and wanted him to return, she couldn't go back on her decision. She didn't regret telling him how she felt, but he was correct. Now that they'd admitted their feelings for each other, how could their relationship remain the same?

*~*~*

Richard entered Conrad's tent, followed by Baldwin, André, and the rest of his council.

"Care for some wine?" Conrad asked as he motioned to a servant.

Richard nodded and took a seat at the table. His continued exasperation with the marquis's actions had increased over the course of the last several days, but he forced himself to remain civil.

"I assume you're here because you objected to my attempt to take Acre," Conrad said.

Richard caught André's warning glance and sipped his wine to rein in his growing anger. "That was a blatant act of betrayal. I've implored you countless times since we arrived in Acre to join my army so we can defeat Salah-ad-Din. Yet, each time, you refuse. Now, you've recalled the French army to Tyre. I need men to defeat the infidels."

Hugh of Burgundy, who sat next to Conrad, leaned forward. "Must I remind you that Conrad is Philippe's cousin? In the king's absence, he will uphold his oath to support him in any manner he can."

"Must I remind you that after Philippe fled Acre and returned home, it was I who paid your men when your money ran out?" Richard replied in a silky tone.

Hugh reddened and sat back in his chair.

Conrad steepled his hands. "Tyre is an important coastal city. Should Salah-ad-Din capture it, I could lose everything that I've spent years fighting for. Although you named Guy King of Jerusalem, my wife, Isabel, has a claim to the throne, and she's carrying my heir. Richard, I wish I could help, but I need to protect my interests and those of my cousin."

Richard kept his retort to himself. If he lashed out, Conrad would never agree to lend his aid. "If we fight together, we can reclaim Jerusalem."

Conrad shrugged. "And what then? You take your army and return home while I remain here to try and defend it against the Saracens? I prefer to protect what I have rather than fight for the unattainable."

Anger seared Richard's blood, but he knew Conrad wouldn't change his mind. He stood and stalked from the tent before he completely lost his temper. He mounted Fauvel and waited for Baldwin, André, and the rest of his men to join him.

"That went as expected," André stated.

"The further I get from Conrad, the longer his life is safe," Richard growled. "I'm surprised he's still supporting Philippe, considering how little he helped once he arrived. Even in France, Philippe has a long reach and continues to be a thorn in my side. I can only hope he's keeping his word and not attacking my lands."

During their return to Acre, more pressing matters consumed his thoughts. He needed to rebuild Ascalon. The French had given their word they would stay until Easter to lend their aid, but the deadline was fast approaching. He also didn't trust Conrad to not attempt another attack.

It was late afternoon when the walls of Acre appeared in the distance. Fresh tension congealed in his muscles, but it had nothing to do with Philippe or Conrad. With copious amounts of wine and sheer willpower, he should be able to manage a few more nights here.

A pageboy ran forward, and Richard dismounted and tossed him the reins. He headed to his chambers, but Joanna intercepted him.

"What is it?" he asked testily.

She gripped her hands as her words tumbled over each other. "Alix has taken a turn for the worse."

Cold fingers clutched his heart. "Has she seen the doctor?"

Joanna nodded, her eyes focused on the ground. "Yes, of course, but you should go to her."

Worst-case scenarios flashed through his mind as he rushed to Alix's sickroom. He flung open the door and barged in.

She jumped up from the window seat, her eyes wide. "What the—what are you doing here? Has something happened?"

"I heard you relapsed." Relief coursed through him as he stared at her. "Obviously, that was untrue."

"I did feel a bit more tired than usual this morning, but as you can see"— she lifted her hands—"I'm fine. Who told you that?"

"Someone with whom I'm going to have a serious talk."

"It must have been Joanna." Alix shrugged. "She left here an hour or so ago, but I have no idea why she'd tell you that."

Now that his fear had subsided, he took in her appearance. She wore a thin linen shift, her hair still damp from a bath. The lantern backlit the curves of her hips and the swell of her breasts, leaving little to the imagination. Sexual frustration crescendoed to another level as aching need centered in his groin. Richard swallowed thickly and willed his thoughts to turn to safer waters.

"I'm glad to see you're the picture of health, but I should go. It's been a long day." He spun on his heel and strode toward the door.

"Richard, please wait."

He stopped and turned, his mouth drying as she walked toward him. Her shift clung to her body as she moved. Desire burned in his blood as he remembered the taste and feel of her in his arms. He needed to leave now, while he still had his wits about him.

"What is it, Alix?" His tone was sharper than he intended.

Her cheeks flushed. "N-nothing. Good night."

Richard nodded stiffly and left. He wanted her more than he thought possible, but he'd honor her wishes, however much they tested him.

Needing to vent his emotions on the person who had been instrumental in causing them, he stalked to his sister's room and pounded on the door. Elisabetta opened it and darted to the side as he strode in.

"Leave us," he said, barely glancing at her.

Joanna sat at the table, reading a book by candlelight. The door snicked shut and he took a deep breath. "What are you playing at?"

"I've no idea what you mean."

"Telling me that Alix relapsed, all the while knowing she's fine? Why would you worry me needlessly?"

She closed the book and lifted her chin. "I'd hoped your marriage would improve, but it hasn't. I misjudged Alix and the depth of your feelings for each other. I wanted to make amends." She gave a small smile. "The other day it was clear we interrupted something between you two. I thought that if you had another chance alone—

"That what?" He walked to the table, slammed his hands on it and leaned toward her. "She'd change her mind?"

Alarm flooded her eyes, and she recoiled in her chair.

"You have no idea what it costs me to be around her and not be able to be with her."

"Richard, I'm sorry. I was only trying to help. I want to see you happy, and I have no idea why Alix continues to deny you."

"This is not helping. From now on stop interfering in my private life!"

Frustration morphed into a rush of hot anger. Richard swung away from her and left before he said something he might regret. He opened the door to his chambers with enough force to send it crashing into the wall. Jacques jumped and tipped over a flagon of wine.

"Be more careful! Clean this mess up at once!"

Jacques blanched and backed up. "I . . . I'm sorry Your Grace. It won't happen again."

"Whatever is going on?" Berenguela asked as she entered the room. "I heard shouting as I came down the hall." She glanced at the liquid that dripped from the table like drops of blood into the burgundy pool below. "All that for spilled wine?"

Richard narrowed his eyes at his wife. He turned on his heel and stalked past Jacques.

Berenguela waited several minutes before she followed him into the sleeping chamber. "You're in a mood this evening."

"It matters not." He raked his hand through his hair.

"Something is troubling you, or you wouldn't have berated the poor boy. What is it?"

"If it were important, I'd tell you."

"Would you?" she asked in a soft voice. "You rarely confide in me. I'm your wife, Richard. You *can* talk to me should you to choose to."

There were few women whom he felt comfortable confiding in, and none were his wife. He remained silent.

Hurt filled her eyes. "I'm going to see to the cleanup." Her light footsteps faded.

He stalked to the window and stared at the stone guard towers on Acre's wall until they became indistinguishable from the night.

It was excruciating to be around Alix. He ached to hold her in his arms, caress her, and watch the play of expressions on her face as he pleasured her.

God's bones, he wanted her in his bed, but he knew her too well. She'd made her decision.

*~*~*

The following morning, Alix returned to her own room. Although she still had bouts of fatigue, her wayward feelings toward Richard were the deciding factor.

Being sequestered had allowed her to spend time alone with him. For a few blissful hours, it was the two of them in their own private world. She could ignore the fact he was married and live in a fairytale of her own making.

Last night she was going to ask him to stay a while longer, but from his response, it was obvious he'd rather be elsewhere. Hot shame washed through her as she remembered the sharpness in his tone and coldness in his eyes. Had he merely been giving lip service when he said he loved her as well?

She rapped on the door, then cracked it open. Maud glanced up from where she sat at the table, brushing her hair. She threw down her brush, which fell off the table and clattered on the floor, and ran to hug her.

"Are you staying here now?"

"Yes, I feel perfectly fine. Where are Queen Joanna and the ladies? Have they gone into town?"

Maud shrugged and bent down to pick up the brush. "I'm not sure where they went. For now, the king has forbidden us to go to the market, in case fighting breaks out once more. After what happened in Messina—I couldn't go through that again."

Moments later, a knock sounded on the door, and Maud went to answer it. Beatrice and Elisabetta entered.

"We went to your sickroom, but you were gone. You're better now, yes?" Beatrice asked.

Alix nodded.

"Good. The king would have been very angry with you if you'd died." She grinned.

Beatrice and Maud went to the table to chat, and Elisabetta shook her head and turned to Alix.

"That one notices everything, but she's correct. Your king didn't leave your side for days."

Alix glanced at the girls, but they were laughing and paying no mind. "He's not *my* king," she said in a low tone. "At least not in the way you're suggesting."

Elisabetta raised her brow. "Are you so certain about that? Kings rarely spend days and nights in sickrooms of women who aren't their wives."

Heat crept up Alix's cheeks, and she glanced away. "He was merely concerned."

"Hmm, I'm sure that's the case. Come now, I'll help you ready for supper, if you'd like. After eating practically nothing for a week, you must be starving."

Alix's footsteps echoed on the stone floor as she walked to the dining hall. Her breath hitched at the thought of seeing Richard, and she wiped her slick hands on her skirt. She inhaled deeply and willed her vibrating nerves to still. Was she holding a torch for someone who no longer cared for her?

Entering the hall, she forced herself to look straight ahead instead of searching for him. By the time she reached the table where Berenguela and Joanna sat, her emotions churned like a storm-tossed ocean.

Berenguela stood and hugged her. "I prayed daily for your recovery."

"Thank you, Your Grace."

"Richard was just as concerned." She raised her brow. "Considering he knows nothing of medicine, I daresay he spent more time with you than the doctor did."

Alix was saved from answering as Berenguela turned toward a commotion at the doorway. Richard, his household men, and his council strode in. Alix kept her gaze on the ground as he approached, then ventured a glance after she curtsied. His gaze lingered on her for a few seconds, his expression unreadable.

He stopped behind Joanna and bent down to whisper something in her ear. She smiled in relief and nodded.

Once he was seated, Alix sank into the chair next to Joanna's. Conversation immediately turned to what the council had decided.

"What is going to be done about Conrad?" Joanna asked.

"I've deprived him of his portion of the revenues from the Kingdom of Jerusalem."

"He already has Tyre and the support of Philippe, who gave him his shares of everything gained in the Holy Land. How does that punish him?"

Richard drummed his fingers on the table. "I understand putting this into effect is nigh impossible, but I have very little recourse. Many of the French are already in Tyre, and the ones that are in Ascalon to help rebuild are only staying until Easter. Afterward, I'm certain they'll join Conrad. I'd thought to leave tomorrow morning, but with the situation unresolved, I'm staying for the time being."

Alix choked on her wine while Joanna and Berenguela peppered Richard with questions about how long he expected to stay.

She had planned to use his absence to contemplate her feelings about him. God knows she could think more rationally when he was out of sight. Lost in her thoughts, the conversation flowed around her until she was nudged by Joanna.

"That's good news, don't you think Alix? I worried that when Richard left, there could be another uprising. Now that he's staying for several more weeks, my mind is eased."

"Yes, yes, of course it is."

Joanna knit her brow. "I shouldn't have told Richard that you had relapsed. It was a mistake. You've hardly said a word all evening. I hope I didn't cause more tension between you."

There was already so much strain between her and Richard, she doubted Joanna's actions had exacerbated it. Alix forced a small smile and shook her head. "I am still feeling a bit tired."

"That's understandable. It took Richard about a month to regain his strength after his bout with *leonardie*." Joanna glanced at her brother. "By the look of things, he and Berenguela are preparing to retire for the evening."

Alix peered around Joanna and met Richard's intense gaze. Butterflies erupted in her stomach. *He still makes me feel like a flustered teenager.*

He and Berenguela stood, and he motioned for her to precede him. Alix curtsied as they passed, her breath gusting out as she straightened.

How was she going to manage with him always being nearby?

*~*~*

A couple of weeks had passed since Richard announced he was staying in Acre, but in the past few days, intermittent storms had moved in from the sea. Torrential rain mixed with cold weather, forcing everyone to stay inside the palace. Seeing Richard more often was a constant reminder to Alix of what she couldn't have. Since that night when he'd abruptly left her room, he'd kept his distance.

Her feelings were still unresolved, and she wanted someone to talk to. In Austin, she could always confide in her best friend, Cara, but here she couldn't breathe a word of this to anyone.

At last, the rain stopped, and Alix took advantage of the break in the weather to escape the confining palace walls. The dark storm clouds had parted as if God waved his hand and replaced them with a brilliant blue sky. The garden was lush and green, and warmer weather had moved in.

She wandered amongst the fruit trees until she found a small, secluded bench and sank down on it. Honeybees buzzed as they zigzagged from flower to flower and various birds filled the air with song.

"I thought if I searched long enough, I'd find you here." A deep voice broke the silence.

Alix's heart took flight like a bird beating its wings against the air. She started to rise to curtsy, but he shook his head. "We're alone for now."

"You were looking for me?"

"Yes. There's something I'd like to discuss." Richard sat next to her, filling the space with his presence.

"I haven't forgotten your concern about Maud's future, so I've spoken to Jacques. He is, indeed, quite taken with her. Since she has no dowry, I'm willing to provide what's necessary to secure a union between them."

Alix gasped. "Truly?"

He nodded, and Alix fought the urge to fling her arms around him.

"Thank you. You have no idea what a relief this is. I was starting to think I'd been selfish and should have allowed her to stay in Poitiers, where your mother could make provisions for her."

"As I've said before, I'm quite fond of the lass. I'm happy to do this." He sighed and ran his hand through his hair. "Jesu, Alix, do I have to tell you how difficult this is?"

Happiness drained from her, replaced by regret. Alix put her hands on the bench and shifted her position. She never should have told him she still loved him. She'd only thought of herself, not the ramifications it could have for him.

Richard moved his hand, so his fingers brushed hers. She gasped as electric shocks raced through her. He grazed her lower lip with his thumb, then cupped her face in his hands and leaned down, his lips inches from hers. She stared at his mouth, desperate for him to kiss her.

At last, his lips captured hers. Lust sparked in her veins. Her head swam as his kiss deepened and his tongue touched hers. She swayed into him and placed her hand on his upper thigh to steady herself. His muscle contracted, and he pushed her hand lower.

"Be careful where you touch, Love. You might put me in a very compromising situation, although I'm willing to chance it," he murmured.

She stared into the depths of his eyes, losing herself in gray-blue pools filled with desire. He tangled his hands in her hair and kissed her again, slowly exploring her mouth. Heat flooded her belly as she imagined his lips elsewhere on her body.

Distant voices carried to them, and they jumped apart. By the time Joanna and Berenguela appeared, Alix's breathing was almost back to normal, but aching desire lingered.

Berenguela's gaze pierced Alix, then shifted to her husband. "Richard, what are you doing here?"

"I was telling Alix I'm providing a dowry for Maud, but her marriage to young Jacques will have to wait until after Easter."

Of course. Marriage in this time was forbidden during Lent, which gave them over a month to prepare. Alix dropped her gaze and smoothed her skirt, still not trusting herself to speak without revealing her emotional state.

Joanna grinned. "We'll have time to plan it, then. Unlike the three days you gave us for your own wedding."

Richard shrugged. "I didn't see any point in waiting any longer than necessary." He winked at Berenguela, who blushed. "You managed the feat in a short amount of time. I'm certain you could again. Now I have some business to address. Send Maud to my chambers this evening so I can announce the news myself."

Berenguela watched him leave, an unreadable expression in her eyes, then turned to Alix. "When the subject was broached, he said you'd already mentioned it, but"—she nodded toward Joanna—"Joanna was also very convincing."

"You spoke to Richard about this matter too?" Alix asked.

Joanna nodded. "They're obviously growing closer, and I worried things might go too far. I think this is one marriage that will be a love match."

"I'm sure they'll be very happy." A shadow crossed Berenguela's face, then vanished.

Alix glanced at Joanna and raised her brow, but Joanna shook her head imperceptibly. Berenguela stayed and chatted a bit longer about the wedding before taking her leave.

"Did something happen between her and Richard?" Alix asked.

"This is the first time in months they've been together for longer than a week. Although he's been in a better mood and they haven't argued at all, he hasn't spent much time with her. More than anything, she longs to give Richard a child, but I'm beginning to fear that might not happen."

A twinge gripped Alix's heart. Queens were expected to provide heirs, and if they were unable to, the fault fell upon them. "She's young. There's plenty of time for children."

Joanna arched her brow. "Now, care to tell me what's going on between you and Richard?"

Alix's stomach clenched. "I've no idea what you mean."

"Come now, I'm not blind. Anytime you two are in a room together, you pretend like the other doesn't exist. Yet today, you seemed quite close."

Alix smoothed her skirt again as she fought to come up with a plausible explanation. "We did have an earlier disagreement concerning Conrad. I thought Richard should have given him a harsher punishment. But we've since made amends."

Joanna crossed her arms. "I suppose I shouldn't expect you to tell me the truth. Not after my being suspicious of you. But one day, maybe you'll confide in me."

The wind picked up, dropping the temperature several degrees. The scent of rain permeated the air.

Alix looked up at the darkening sky. "We'd best get back before it begins to storm."

They reached the palace ahead of the afternoon shower and stood in the hallway to catch their breath.

"Since Maud is to meet with Richard this evening, I'm going to help her get ready," Alix said and made her escape before Joanna could question her further.

Maud sat at the table, bent over a dress as she mended it.

"The king has requested for you to meet with him before supper."

The garment slipped out of Maud's lax fingers. "Whatever for? Have I done something to displease him?"

"No, you've done nothing wrong," Alix soothed. "He merely wishes to speak with you. I'll help you dress if you like."

An hour later, Maud was wearing her best dress, and Alix had brushed her hair until it shone like golden silk. She pulled Maud to her feet and, after a final assessment, nodded. "There. You're ready for an audience with the king."

Maud drew in a shaky breath. "Are you certain he's not angry with me?"

"Trust me. You have nothing to worry about. Now, go. You don't want to keep him waiting."

She left, and Alix alternated from pacing the small chamber to sitting on the window seat, listening for her return.

The door handle creaked, and Maud burst into the room.

"Alix! The king is allowing me to marry Jacques." Her eyes glowed and a radiant smile curved her lips. "I never thought it would happen."

Alix hugged her. "I'm sure you two will be very happy."

"We have until after Easter to prepare. There's so much to be done, I don't know where to begin."

"Queen Joanna and I have some experience with planning a wedding."

"I still can't believe this is truly happening. Thank you."

"Whatever are you thanking me for?" Alix laughed. "It was the king's decision."

"If you hadn't asked Queen Eleanor if I could accompany you, I'd still be in Poitiers, working for Melisende. I might never have met Jacques."

Now that Maud's future was settled, a weight had been lifted from Alix's shoulders. She was thrilled Maud had found someone with whom she could spend her life, but a twinge of jealousy gripped her. If only her own future was as optimistic.

*~*~*

Alix and Elisabetta wove their way through crowds of people as they meandered through the market. Soldiers patrolled the streets daily to keep order after Conrad's failed uprising, but the citizens didn't appear to care that they were watched like hawks. They mingled and chatted, different dialects mixing seamlessly. Vendors called out to passersby to come and look at their wares. The rich aromas of fresh baked bread and cooked meats hung heavy in the salty sea air.

They headed away from the central square toward the Genoese section of Acre in search of a seamstress. The tradition of wearing a wedding dress was centuries in the future. Typically, women in this time wore their best dress to get married, but all of Maud's were well-worn from traveling. Joanna had suggested she get a new one.

"I'm glad we have the name of a reputable seamstress, as so many cost a fortune and the results are pitiful," Elisabetta said.

"Joanna has used this woman before and recommends her. Of course, that's only if we can find her shop. This place is a maze."

Small lanes splintered from the main road through town and led deep into the Genoese area. The shops were intermixed with houses, and being poorly advertised, it was hard to tell which was a business and which was a domicile. They finally reached a small, unassuming building which matched Joanna's description. After arranging a time for the dressmaker to come to the palace for Maud's fitting, Alix and Elisabetta retraced their steps back to the square.

A commotion ahead of them halted their progress. Richard and his men appeared in the distance, cutting a path through the crowd. They were swept up in undulating waves of people as they pushed forward to get a closer glimpse of the king.

Alix gazed at him openly, free to do so from her location. His polished hauberk glittered in the sun, but his head was bare, an indication he didn't expect any skirmishes. As usual, he was mounted on Fauvel. The dun steed moved fluidly, his muscles rippling under his coat, which shone like spun gold. The horse shied as the cheers became louder, and Richard tightened the reins to keep him in check.

He grinned at the citizens, but his ever-watchful gaze scanned the crowd for any altercations. Although Conrad had retreated to Tyre, he still had supporters in Acre who were willing to do his bidding. A group of nearby prostitutes whispered to each other as they stared at Richard.

Growls from behind her sent chills down her spine, and she glanced back to see a couple of mangy dogs fighting over a scrap of meat. By the time she turned back, Richard and his men had passed. The crowd's interest waned, and they dispersed. Alix and Elisabetta began the walk back to the palace.

"Those women aren't the only ones who have their eye on the king," Elisabetta teased as she winked at Alix.

"I've no idea what you mean."

"Come now, dearie. I've seen the way you look at him. You still love him. Why you keep denying it to yourself is beyond me."

Alix focused on the ground as her cheeks burned. "Is it that obvious?"

Elisabetta cocked her head. "There's a glow about you when you're around him. I don't presume to speak about the king's feelings, but his mood changes too. He's more carefree and, dare I say . . . happy?"

"It matters not, since nothing can ever come of it."

"Why not?" Elisabetta crossed her arms.

"He's married."

"Everyone knows that's not a marriage. It's an arrangement," the older woman scoffed. "I doubt I've seen two people more miserable. Three, including you. You were happier when we were traveling to Marseille and tried to hide your relationship with the king."

*I do want to be with him, more than anything.* "It's not that simple. What about Queen Berenguela?"

"I understand you don't wish to hurt her, but to be honest, she wouldn't be surprised if he did take other women to bed. Kings are expected to have mistresses."

They reached the palace, and Alix took a deep breath to release the sudden tightness in her chest. That word was one crux of the matter. If she rekindled their relationship, she would be the other woman.

Elisabetta put her hand on Alix's arm. "I told you a long time ago, there's no shame in being with him. Especially since he loves you."

Alix managed a weak smile as she turned and walked to her room. Every moment she spent with Richard, however brief, filled her with happiness and contentment. When they were apart, she always looked forward to the next time they'd cross paths. Being with him felt right. It was only her modern morals that were against it.

Remorse coursed through her concerning the way she'd acted toward her father. He must have wrestled with this conflict before he made his own choice. She knew firsthand what it felt like to have the man you love be unfaithful. Now she was trapped in the same dilemma. What would *her* decision be?

*~*~*

The days crept closer to Easter, and Richard's return to Ascalon. Maud's dress was almost finished, and the seamstress was making last-minute alterations. Joanna was feeling under the weather, so Alix had offered her help to the dressmaker, in case it was needed.

Berenguela stood back and studied the dress as Maud turned in a circle. The long sleeves hung past Maud's hands and were delicately stitched with silver thread, which matched the stitching at the bottom of the floor-length, indigo-blue garment.

"You've done a splendid job," she said to the seamstress, then turned to Alix. "Do you have any suggestions?"

Alix shook her head. "It's beautiful as is."

Berenguela escorted the woman out, and Alix and Beatrice helped Maud undress.

"I can't believe I'm to be married. I'm excited, but nervous as well." Sadness crossed her face. "I always thought I'd have my mother to help guide me through this."

Alix patted Maud's shoulder. "You have us, and we'll do everything we can to make sure you have a beautiful wedding."

"I'm looking forward to the ceremony, but I'm nervous about later that night . . ." Her cheeks flushed and she stared at the floor.

"She's worried about what happens after the putting to bed," Beatrice said. "You can explain it to her."

Alix's eyes widened. How did the discussion turn to this? "Yes, yes, of course. If you have any questions, I'll try to answer them."

Maud glared at Beatrice. "I know what happens between husbands and wives. What if I don't please him?"

"What are you girls talking about?" Berenguela asked as she entered the room.

"Pleasing your husband," Beatrice said.

The queen drew herself up. "Explain that."

"I'm afraid I'll disappoint Jacques on our wedding night." Maud's voice trembled.

Berenguela glanced at Alix and cocked her brow.

"You won't disappoint him. It's clear he's besotted with you," Alix stated.

"What's it like to lie with a man you love?" Beatrice asked.

This wasn't something Alix was comfortable talking about. She tried to think of a safe explanation, but Berenguela took the initiative.

"As a wife, you want to please your husband, but the intimacy of the act also brings you closer together."

"But is it pleasurable for women too?" Maud asked.

"Yes, quite. Now, enough questions. You two get ready for supper."

The girls left the room, giggling. Berenguela looked amused. "That was unexpected, but I understand her fear. I felt the same when I married Richard."

"I think every bride has moments of uncertainty before the wedding, but Jacques loves her. I doubt she could do anything to disappoint him."

"I'm sure they'll be very content . . ." Berenguela's voice faded. She turned and walked to the table, then spun around, her hands clasped together. "My marriage isn't what I expected, Alix. I know it was an arrangement, but I hoped it would be happy, or at least satisfying. These past weeks are the longest we've been together since we married, but it's become painfully clear Richard and I have little to nothing in common. To be honest, both of us are happier when we're apart."

Alix poured two cups of wine and handed one to Berenguela. Her heart twisted at the thought of being trapped in a loveless, empty marriage.

"Marriage is hard enough when you know the person. You and Richard are essentially strangers. It takes time to get to know someone, and this isn't the best situation. Defeating Salah-ad-Din is Richard's priority. Once we return to France, you'll be able to focus on your marriage. With time, it will get better."

"I don't think so." Berenguela frowned. "Being a princess, I knew my parents would look for a suitable royal husband for me, but I had no great desire to even marry. I'd be happy if I could have entered a convent, but that wasn't my choice. I want to do my duty as a wife and give him heirs, and as his queen, support the decisions he makes."

She stared into the depths of her cup. "I can't remember the last time Richard stayed the night. I know many men vowed abstinence when they took the cross, but he finds no pleasure with me, and he hasn't taken a mistress. I'm not sure why he hasn't." Berenguela paused and looked at Alix. "Unless he can't have the woman he desires."

Alix's throat closed and the air rushed out of her lungs. "Do you think there's someone else?"

Berenguela nodded. "I believe so. I think that's the main reason our marriage is troubled." She placed her cup on the table and gave a wry smile. "I feel like I'm always confiding in you, but I couldn't possibly discuss this with Joanna. Thank you for hearing me out."

The door snicked shut behind her, and Alix collapsed into a chair. Berenguela didn't seem to suspect she was the woman Richard had feelings for or she might have ordered Alix to stay away. Alix gulped down her wine, then pulled Berenguela's untouched cup to her.

Richard didn't find pleasure in the marriage bed, but he hadn't sought out other bedmates. A bubble of happiness floated through her, knowing she was the last woman he'd been with before his marriage. Reliving their kiss in the garden sent her thoughts down paths she wasn't prepared to travel. He'd made it clear he wanted her, and she wanted him just as much. But at what cost?

God knows she was just as unhappy as he apparently was. What if they did rekindle their relationship? Elisabetta was correct—it was acceptable for kings to have mistresses, and no one would think less of him.

Could she sacrifice her ethics to be with the only man she'd ever love?

## ~ *Chapter 28* ~

THE STIFF REAR WIND CAPPED the waves with white froth and aided the rowers' efforts as the galley sped south to Ascalon. Richard leaned on the gunwale, his gaze fixed on the sandy expanse of the desolate coast.

"I don't mean to question your decision, but do you think we made the right one in returning to Ascalon?" André asked. "Conrad isn't to be trusted. Who's to say he won't launch another attempt to capture Acre?"

"I could ill afford to stay any longer. The French gave their word they would stay until Easter. I need to return and, hopefully, convince them to change their minds."

"Damn Hugh," André growled. "He and Philippe are too much alike. They want to enjoy the spoils of war, but only if someone else wins it for them."

"Too true, cousin." Richard gripped André's shoulder. "But glory will be ours when we reclaim Jerusalem."

The galley rounded a rocky outcrop, and the walls of Ascalon came into view. They entered the calm harbor and men gathered along the edge. The oarsmen tied the boat and Richard disembarked, raising his hand in acknowledgement to the greetings. Henri pushed through the crowd and grinned at his uncle.

"We expected your return weeks ago. I assume the delay was due to Conrad?"

"Correct, but we'll discuss it later. First, show me what progress has been made."

"Leaving Geoffrey in charge of the repair surprised me, but he's done a remarkable job." Henri paused while men nodded and called out to Richard. "The walls are almost complete and many of the buildings within are inhabitable."

"Excellent, considering the majority of my money has gone to pay for it." Richard chuckled.

Henri and Richard walked along the perimeter. Walls that had been demolished into rubble now stood twenty feet high, providing a vantage point, as well as protection from an attacking army.

They paused to examine a guard tower that was being rebuilt. Several masons were mixing mortar in large buckets but stopped to explain the methods they used to cement the stones together. Richard praised their efforts, then, pleased that his orders were being carried out to his satisfaction, headed back toward the harbor.

"You must be famished after your journey. Join me for supper."

They reached Henri's tent, and he ushered Richard in. After ordering the servants to prepare food, he filled two cups with wine.

"Tell me what happened in Acre," Henri said.

Richard raised his brow. "Even from afar, Philippe casts a wide net."

"What has he done now?"

Henri frowned after Richard recounted the situation. "Damn that man. I hope Conrad was made to pay for his actions."

"I did what I could, but he has too many powerful allies." Richard took a deep drink from his cup, then studied his nephew. "The majority of the French army will leave to join Conrad. I realize that your loyalty is being tested. What's your decision?"

"Must you even ask? I told you before we left Acre, I'll fight under your command. That hasn't changed."

A relieved smile crossed Richard's lips. "I'm glad to hear it. Together, we will reclaim the Holy Land."

*~*~*

The day after Richard returned to Ascalon, the French leaders approached him and requested safe passage to Acre. Per their agreement he allowed them to leave. With a much smaller army at his disposal Richard needed to reassess the best way to attack Salah-ad-Din. He was sitting in his tent with André and Henri, discussing their options when Jacques opened the flap to the tent and motioned for a tall, thin man to enter.

"Your Grace," the man said as he bowed. "I'm Robert, the prior of Hereford. I've been sent on behalf of William of Longchamps."

Henri cocked his brow. "Isn't that your chancellor, Uncle?"

"Yes, it is." Tendrils of dread coiled through Richard. "Tell me what's happened."

"Men that you have appointed to govern England in your absence have been exiled. William, included."

Richard clenched his fist and leaned forward, his eyes glittering. "Who's behind this?"

Robert paled and swallowed convulsively. "Your own brother, Sire—John, Count of Mortain."

"Where is William now?"

"He fled to Normandy. John wasted little time in approaching the earls and nobles and demanding oaths of loyalty and submission to him." Robert's voice hardened. "He's also taken money from the treasury. You must return to France at once to end these injustices against you."

Richard gave a curt nod. "Go with my squire. He'll find you accommodation and food."

The prior left, and Richard stared into the distance as anger washed over him. "Damn John! I'd thought treachery would come from Philippe, not my own brother."

"Can we trust everything that Robert relayed? If John is threatening your kingdom, wouldn't your mother muster forces against him?" Henri asked.

"I'm sure she's trying to keep him in line, but John has always coveted what others have. In my absence, my kingdom is ripe for the taking."

Henri's breath gusted out. "You can't stay. You need to return to France and protect your realm."

"Henri's correct. If John manages to turn even less than half your nobles to his side, I fear Philippe will take advantage of the rebellion and make his own move." André's gaze shifted from Henri to Richard. "The sooner you return, the better. It took weeks for Robert to arrive. What has since happened in the interim?"

"I can't leave without putting an end to this war. If the infidels seize the country, I doubt there will be little chance to recoup it. I'll call a meeting tomorrow with my council and decide on a course of action."

*~*~*

The sweltering heat in the tent exacerbated the pounding in Richard's head.

He'd spent the night trying to come up with implementable solutions and was left with few options. He looked at the men crowded around the table.

"I've received news that my brother is trying to usurp my kingdom."

Questions and curses erupted from all sides. Richard waited until the cacophony subsided. "I have little choice but to return to France as soon as possible."

"Damn John." Baldwin's lips twisted. "I never thought he would have the courage to cross you."

"What will happen to our war?" Geoffrey de Lusignan asked. He glanced at the other men. "If you leave, who will be put in charge?"

The murmuring swelled again until Richard raised his hand. "That is precisely why I called this council. I'll stay until I find a replacement. The only question is who that person will be." He nodded toward Geoffrey. "I'm aware that you desire to return to France. Therefore, the choice is between Conrad and Guy."

Geoffrey gave a sardonic grin. "That's not really a choice, is it? After the fiasco at Hattin, no man will follow my brother. You named him King of Jerusalem, but everyone knows that you are in charge. Once you leave, his position is precarious at best." He glanced at the council. "As much as it pains me to admit it, I must choose Conrad. He has the support of the French and has proven himself to be a worthy commander."

Richard eyed his council. "Is everyone in agreement, then?"

The men nodded and called out their assent.

"It's decided. I name Conrad King of Jerusalem," Richard stated.

"What will happen to my brother?" Geoffrey asked. "Now that he's not king, I doubt he'll take kindly to being deposed."

"There is the matter of Cyprus. I'd sold it to the Templars, but they haven't paid in full. I feel certain that they could be persuaded to sell it to Guy."

Geoffrey chuckled. "I think he would be amenable to that, especially since he has no opposition."

Men began to file out of the tent. But Henri lingered. "Uncle, Conrad will be pleased to know that, at long last, he's to be king. How do you plan to tell him?"

"I thought we could travel together to Tyre and announce it. Afterward, we'll continue to Acre. There's a wedding that I need to be present for, else I'd never hear the end of it." Richard grinned.

"Hold still one moment, Maud," Alix said.

She pinched Maud's cheeks until they pinked, then stood back and studied her. The dark-blue dress complemented Maud's fair coloring and her waist-length hair shone like gilded silk.

"You look beautiful. What do you think, Your Grace?" Alix turned toward Joanna.

Joanna smiled. "I agree. Now, let's not keep the groom waiting."

They left the room, Beatrice and Maud following them, giggling and whispering to each other.

"I'm glad Richard was able to come for the wedding, but he seems preoccupied. He's said nothing to me. Has he spoken to you?" Joanna asked.

Alix shook her head, but she had her suspicions of what was on his mind and who was involved. "I've hardly seen him, but then, I've been quite busy."

A group of people stood outside the palace, and as Maud exited, they cheered loudly. Richard and Jacques turned as they approached. Jacques's eyes widened and a huge smile lit his face. He hurried to Maud, took her hand, and kissed it, much to the amusement of the crowd.

At Richard's nod, Jacques and Maud made their way to the church. André acted as best man and rode behind them, followed by Richard and Berenguela. Richard escorted Maud to where the bishop waited, and André walked with Jacques.

After the bishop asked whether the bride and groom were of marriageable age, were not related by blood, and willingly entered into the marriage, Jacques plighted his troth to Maud. Alix blinked back tears of happiness. Maud, at last, was marrying the young man she loved.

She dabbed her eyes and glanced at Richard. He stood next to Berenguela, but the distance between them was palpable. As if feeling the weight of her gaze, he turned and smiled. Her heart filled with warmth.

The bishop gave a short speech about the sanctity of marriage, blessed the ring, and handed it to Jacques.

He slid it onto Maud's finger. "In the name of the Father, and of the son, and of the Holy Ghost, with this ring I thee wed."

The bishop's words about marriage rang hollow. Words bound a wife and husband together but didn't make a marriage. Alix wanted what Maud and

Jacques had—a true love match. Richard's marriage was cold and empty, but didn't he deserve to be happy too?

The doors to the church opened, and everyone filed in for Mass. After it was over, the bishop gave Jacques the kiss of peace and bestowed the same upon Maud.

"What a lovely wedding," Elisabetta sighed. "I hope they'll be very happy."

Alix nodded. "I'm sure they will be."

They walked the short distance back to the palace and Joanna went to the kitchen to check on the food while Alix and Elisabetta made sure the hall was ready for the festivities. The tables were covered with cream-colored linen table runners that were sprinkled with rose petals. Candles were positioned on the tables so there would be light as the night wore on.

"Did we forget anything?" Alix asked.

"I think it's perfect," Elisabetta said. "Now I need to find the minstrels. I hope they haven't spent the past few hours in a tavern."

Laughter and boisterous voices echoed in the hall. Richard and Berenguela entered, followed by the rest of the group. Fortunately, the minstrels were close behind and didn't look the worst for wear. Alix and Elisabetta took their seats next to Beatrice, but stood with everyone when Maud and Jacques entered. A small table for two had been placed below the royal table. Once the couple was seated, servants brought dishes laden with meats and vegetables and flagons of wine.

"I've never seen Maud so happy." Alix took a sip of spiced wine.

Elisabetta grinned. "That boy was smitten with her before we left France. He'll make her a fine husband."

Servants moved through the hall, lighting candles as the sun set. After the dishes were removed, the minstrels began to play a lively song. A space for dancing was cleared, and Richard led Berenguela down from the dais. He motioned for Maud and Jacques to join them, and once they stood up, some of the guests did too. It wasn't long before a young page asked Beatrice to accompany him. Alix danced several times with Rob then bowed out to allow others to take her place.

Beatrice returned to the table, her cheeks flushed from the exercise. "Soon they will go to their room for the night?"

"I imagine so. It's getting late, and I think the guests have had more than their share of wine," Alix said.

When Richard announced it was time for the couple to retire for the night Jacques grinned and held out his hand to Maud. Alix and Elisabetta stood and followed Joanna, Berenguela, and Richard's men as they made their way to the wedding chamber.

Boisterous voices penetrated the curtains as Alix and Joanna helped Maud get dressed for the night. Once she was in her nightclothes and in bed, she clutched the blanket to her chest with white fingers.

"Is the bride presentable?" Richard called out.

Maud nodded at Joanna's questioning gaze. Berenguela parted the curtains and raucous applause and cheers erupted in the room. Maud's cheeks flamed as the men pushed Jacques forward amidst bawdy jokes.

"I'm going to ask the king to keep it brief so as not to embarrass her," Alix whispered to Elisabetta. She moved toward him, but stopped as he approached.

"From the look on your face, I assume you're going to ask me to keep the banter to a minimum?"

"If you don't mind. She's quite nervous already."

"I'll make sure my men behave." Richard chuckled.

*~*~*

Alix woke the next morning and looked over at Maud's empty bed. It seemed strange to have the small chamber all to herself now. Richard had kept a tight rein on the men last night, and by the time they left the newlyweds to themselves, Maud was laughing at some of the jokes.

The pale early morning sun bathed the room in a soft glow. It was too soon for breakfast, and since sleep was impossible, she decided to get up and take a quick stroll in the garden.

She saw no one as she walked through the halls and headed outside. The leaves rustled as the wind whispered through the trees. Dew coated the grass like small diamonds that twinkled in the light. A branch cracked under her foot.

"Can't a man find some peace and quiet?" A baritone voice growled.

Alix jumped and spun around to find Richard sitting on a bench. "An ordinary man, yes, but a king doesn't have that luxury. I'll leave you to your thoughts."

"Wait. I have some news."

The tone of his voice unnerved her. She walked over and sat beside him. Tension emanated from him in waves.

"I've received word that John is rebelling and trying to gain support from my nobles. My absence provided the perfect opportunity." He leaned forward, his arms on his thighs.

Sympathy welled up inside her. She knew how torn he was. He couldn't lose his kingdom, but he'd made a vow to reclaim the Holy Land. Although it was more for glory than any true religious zeal, abandoning his oath wasn't something he would willingly do.

"I've never trusted your brother, but damn John for his duplicity. When are you leaving?"

Richard gave a short laugh. "Besides André and Henri, you're the only other person who's asked me that. My own council was more concerned with the fate of Jerusalem than with the loss of my realm."

"How do Joanna and Berenguela feel?"

"I haven't told them yet. I didn't want to cast a shadow on the wedding. Joanna will see things my way. I'm not certain about my wife."

"I'm sure Berenguela would want you to return home. She's your queen, and she has a personal stake in your kingdom."

"She'll agree with my decision, but I doubt she'll be pleased about it." His face darkened. "She believes that reclaiming Jerusalem takes priority." His voice rose, startling a bird that was sheltering in a nearby bush.

"If you haven't defeated Salah-ad-Din by the time you depart, who will you leave in charge?"

"The list of men I trust with the task is short. The only one that I and my council agreed upon was Conrad."

Alix's eyes narrowed. "How could you choose him? He attempted to claim Acre, and he's been instrumental in convincing the French to join him."

"Between Conrad and Guy, who do you think will be able to lead the army?" He gave a hollow laugh. "Jesu, even I couldn't defeat Conrad or gain his cooperation. I can't expect Guy to."

"I suppose Conrad's in a better position to rule, and his wife, Isabella, does have a claim to the throne." She brushed strands of hair from her eyes. "I'm glad you told me what happened."

He dragged his hands through his hair. "I'm losing everything—the Holy Land, my kingdom, you . . ."

"You're not losing me."

"Haven't I already?"

The raw pain in his voice sliced through her heart. She ached to hold him in her arms and ease his suffering.

Richard stood and held out his hand. Alix took it and rose to her feet. Her nerves tingled at the contact with his warm skin. Her gaze met his and the urge to lose herself in his kiss and feel his body pressed against hers overwhelmed her. She pulled her hand from his grasp and rubbed it to erase the feeling. How much longer could she deny what she wanted?

They walked in uncomfortable silence until they reached her room. "I appreciate that you kept the jesting in the bedchamber to a minimum. For me, that would be the worst part of the wedding. That is when—I mean—if I were to marry," Alix stammered.

Richard raised a brow. "Forgive me if I don't look forward to that day."

The light laugh died in her throat as she realized that Richard wasn't jesting. Her gaze darted up and down the hall. They were alone. Did she dare act on what she'd been agonizing over for months?

Historically, Richard's marriage was unhappy, regardless of Alix's presence. In this time, infidelity was accepted, even expected, so what was stopping her? One fear was how her friends would treat her, but if Elisabetta's view was any indication, then that wasn't an issue. Berenguela was her friend, and she didn't want to hurt her or cause her any embarrassment, but their marriage wasn't based on love.

Could she go against her twentieth-century morals? Her own overwhelming need and the stark look in his eyes convinced her. Alix reached out her hand, took his, and led him into her room.

*~*~*

Richard's breath caught in his chest as she walked to him and caressed his cheek. For several heartbeats, a glimmer of hope coursed through him, but then he forced it away. He knew her mind. He gripped her wrist and stepped back.

"Stop, Alix." His tone was harsh. "Don't toy with me. I'm at the end of my tether."

"No games," she whispered.

She put her hands on his shoulders and flicked her tongue against his lips, teasing his mouth open. Richard's heart jolted. Desire for her had smoldered like embers for months and now erupted like a wildfire that raced through his blood. Richard knotted his hands in her hair and crushed his mouth against hers. His equilibrium tilted as she met his desperate kisses, her tongue tangling with his. He pulled her hips against his growing arousal. She moaned as she shifted against him. His willpower shattered.

They stumbled backward until he reached the cot. She fell on top of him, her lips never leaving his. A raw, aching need surged through him, but he had enough restraint to ask the question that could change everything between them. He rolled over and gazed down at her.

"Love, do you want this? I need you to be sure. Please be sure," he breathed.

"I've never been more certain."

She gripped the bottom of his shirt and pulled it off, then untied his chausses and shoved his braies down below his hips. His hands trembled as he pushed her skirt up to her waist. All thoughts of taking his time and pleasuring her vanished. He needed her now. He positioned himself between her thighs and slowly entered her. Alix's breath keened in his ear and a whimper escaped her throat. His mind shut down and his body took over as he began to move, thrusting deeper each time.

Her soft moans escalated until she cried out and clenched her legs around him. He slowed down to give her time to recover and to hold his own imminent climax at bay. Under control again, he increased his speed. Her fingers dug into his shoulders as he brought her once again to the brink.

"Richard!" she called out as her body convulsed underneath him.

His own world exploded as he gave in to the pleasure. His body still shaking, he collapsed on top of her, completely sated. She held him as their ragged breaths slowed.

"I love you," she whispered.

"And I you, always."

The rhythm of her pounding heart lulled him into a contented daze. Alix's auburn hair fanned across his chest, and her leg was tucked between his. She shifted in his arms and nestled closer. He'd missed the intimacy and familiarity between them.

He felt no guilt that, after tortuous months, at last he was with the woman he loved. A woman not his wife. But in Alix's eyes, it was wrong. Had the tenuous relationship they were rebuilding been destroyed? Now that his thoughts had coalesced, one question burned in his mind.

"Love, do you regret being with me?" His heart clenched as he awaited her answer. Returning to a platonic relationship would be hell for him, but if it was her wish, he'd respect it.

Alix looked up at him. "No, I don't regret anything we've done." She kissed him, then settled back in the crook of his arm.

His breath gusted out. "You don't know how I needed to hear that. What changed?"

"After my father was unfaithful, I saw the pain my mother went through. I hated him for hurting her and destroying our family. I was convinced what he'd done was wrong, and I couldn't forgive him for that."

She trailed her fingers in random patterns through the sprinkling of golden hair that covered his chest, sending sparks of electricity shooting through his veins.

"Not once did I consider my father's feelings. For too long, my parents were unhappy and fought constantly. But then he met someone, and everything changed. I didn't want to admit to myself that another woman gave him what he needed because it felt like I was betraying my mother."

She paused and glanced up at him. "I never expected to find myself in the same position and having to come to terms with what my heart truly wants. Our lives are as fragile as a candle flame. What if I'd died from my illness? Or you, during battle? I don't want to live a life wishing I'd made different decisions. I've been miserable since I ended our relationship. This morning, being with you made me realize what I've missed."

Richard pulled her close. "Are you saying what I hope you are? Can we return to what we had?"

"Does this answer your question?"

His muscles jumped as Alix skimmed her fingers down to his stomach. Desire rekindled as she replaced her fingers with her lips, her tongue carving trails across his heated skin. She pulled his chausses and braies completely off and tossed them to the floor.

Alix stroked him, and Richard sucked in his breath in anticipation as her lips slid down his length. Her lack of shyness during their lovemaking was as much an aphrodisiac as what she was doing to him. She swirled her tongue and gripped him tighter, sending him careening toward release. He clenched his jaw and tried to maintain control.

In tune with his body's response, Alix stopped before he reached his peak. She shifted position to straddle him. Richard sat up and tugged off her dress.

He traced her collarbone with his fingers, then swept them down her flawless skin until he brushed her breasts. Her lips parted as he rubbed her nipple, then she gasped as he sucked it. He lightly pulled with his teeth until she moaned and swayed into him. Her rocking motion pushed him again to his limit. He placed his hands on her hips and matched her rhythm until she cried out and climaxed in his arms, pulling him over the edge with her.

Richard collapsed onto his back, holding her tight until his body calmed. If he was going to hell for his sins, he couldn't think of a more pleasurable way to go.

Alix pressed a lingering kiss on his lips, then got out of bed and walked to the table. She lifted a flagon and, at his nod, poured some wine into a cup.

"Jesu, you're beautiful."

She smiled a bit shyly at him as she returned to bed. He drew her close, relishing the warmth of her body against his.

"Can you stay longer?" Alix looked at him with heavy-lidded eyes.

"There's nowhere I'd rather be than here with you."

In between sharing wine, soft kisses, and talking, he was able to put aside John's actions and the war that preyed on his mind. For the first time since she'd ended their relationship in Messina, his soul was at peace.

Richard rolled away from the bright afternoon sun streaming through the window and inhaled the scent of sandalwood. Memories of the past several hours flooded through him, and a smile curved his lips as he glanced at Alix, who lay curled up against him. As much as he wanted to stay and forget the outside world for a bit longer, his absence was likely already noted and remarked upon. He slipped out of bed so he wouldn't disturb her, then picked his clothes off the floor and began to dress.

"Leaving already?" Alix murmured as she propped herself up on one elbow.

"Regrettably, yes. I would like nothing more than to spend the entire day with you, but I need to find Henri and tell him to travel to Tyre to give Conrad the news that he'll be named king."

Alix sat up and pulled the blanket to her shoulders. "It's probably best you send your nephew. He can be more diplomatic than you."

He chuckled and crossed the room to place a lingering kiss on her lips. "When it comes to Conrad, you're correct about that."

He sucked in his breath as she let the blanket fall to her waist. She leaned forward to run her fingers down his shirt to his chausses. Heat stirred in his groin.

"Are you certain you can't stay?"

She looked at him, her hazel eyes filled with desire, and all thought of leaving vanished. Alix was the only woman he'd ever been powerless to resist.

"I think Henri can wait."

## ~ *Chapter 29* ~

IN THE DAYS AFTER REIGNITING their relationship, Alix had to be satisfied with brief stolen moments in the garden, exchanging heated kisses, and lingering looks when they were together.

Richard had returned to Ascalon, which made keeping their secret easier to keep, but she felt like a hypocrite. Not because of what they'd done, but because she'd been so adamantly against it. Although she doubted she'd be reviled for committing adultery, she couldn't bear it if her friends' opinion of her lessened.

Alix and Joanna were leaving the dining hall after breakfast when Henri, trailed by Baldwin and Rob, strode to them. Henri took Joanna aside. Alix could only catch urgent whispers.

"What's happened?" Alix asked Rob.

Rob exchanged a quick glance with Baldwin and, at the latter's nod, said in a low tone, "Two days ago, Conrad was murdered. He was to have dinner with his wife, but she took too long over her bath. Instead, he went to dine with the bishop of Beauvais, only to find out he'd already eaten. On his way home, he was ambushed by two assailants and stabbed."

"It was definitely a misfortunate day for him," Baldwin said in a droll tone.

"Who could have done something like that?" Alix asked.

"Conrad's entourage was with him, and they were able to capture the killers. Both are now dead, but one confessed that a man they call 'The Old Man of the Mountain' ordered his death."

"He has assassins who he sends to do his bidding," Henri explained as he and Joanna rejoined them. "Apparently, he had a disagreement with Conrad." He grimaced. "Once the Duke of Burgundy found out, he wasted no time and attempted to seize Tyre. Hugh tried to force his way into the palace where

Conrad's widow, Isabella, retreated. She said no one was allowed in except for the King of England or the King of Jerusalem."

"I wouldn't be surprised if Hugh suggests that Richard ordered Conrad's death to sway Isabella to his side," Alix mused.

Henri cocked his brow. "He *is* putting the blame on Richard, and the rumor is spreading through the French camp."

"What will happen now? Isabella has a claim to the throne. Who's to say that Hugh won't force her to marry him so he can become king?" Joanna asked.

"Messengers have been sent to inform Richard of Conrad's death. I hope to receive word from him soon, but first I'm going to Tyre and try to enact order," Henri said.

Joanna frowned. "If Hugh has convinced the army that my brother is behind this, your alliance with him puts you in danger."

"I'm aware." Henri smiled grimly. "I'll be careful."

Joanna turned to Alix after the men left and pressed her hand to her chest. "I can't imagine what Isabella must be going through. She's pregnant, and her husband has been murdered. What will happen to Jerusalem? Richard doesn't need this additional problem."

"Conrad is dead, and Guy has been named King of Cyprus. Who would Richard trust to rule Jerusalem? I see only one man who encompasses all the qualities that Richard would want in a king."

Joanna pursed her lips, then her eyes widened. "You think he'll name Henri?"

"It makes perfect sense. For the last two years, he's been in Acre, fighting against the Saracens and proving himself in battle. He's nephew to both Richard and Philippe. Both armies respect his leadership. Not to mention, for the first time, Richard would have the full support of both armies."

"A decision needs to be made soon. Richard must return home and fight for his own kingdom."

All of Richard's well-laid plans were crumbling. His ambition of liberating Jerusalem would fail. Instead, Alix could only stand by and watch history play out.

Resoluteness burned in her chest. She couldn't change the course of events, but one thing he wasn't going to lose was her. She'd be there for him as his lover and confidant, even if that meant putting her desire to return to her time aside.

"Queen Isabella arrives today?" Maud asked as she and Alix walked to the market. Their medicinal supplies were running low, and Alix wanted to make sure they had the necessary herbs to make Isabella comfortable during her pregnancy. At Alix's nod, she continued. "Within a week, her husband was murdered, and she remarried."

"I'm sure Henri is still in shock over what happened. But the French respect him, and I think he'll make a good ruler, although he isn't technically the King of Jerusalem. Since Isabella was forced to divorce her first husband to marry Conrad, that marriage was considered to be adulterous, since Humphrey still lives. Richard isn't even sure if *this* marriage is legal."

"I wonder what will happen with the baby. If it's a boy, will he be the heir, even if Henri and Isabella have children of their own?"

Alix knew that, historically, the baby would be a girl. Aloud she said, "Let's hope she has a daughter. Speaking of marriage, I don't think I need to ask how yours is."

When Richard returned to Ascalon, he'd allowed Jacques to stay behind in Acre and spend time with his new wife.

Maud's face brightened. "I'm happier than I could have thought possible. Jacques has been—very attentive. Now I know what you've lost with the king. I wish things were different for you."

Alix gave a small smile. One day, their renewed relationship would be discovered, but for now, she wanted to keep it to herself.

A low rumble of thunder boomed in the distance. "Come, we need to hurry," Alix urged. "I don't wish to get caught in a storm."

The first drops of rain fell as they left the apothecary's shop. After a quick jog the last quarter mile, they made it to the palace before the sky unleashed a downpour. Maud went to find her husband, leaving Alix with several hours to herself before supper.

After putting the herbs in the small coffer in her room, she gathered her toiletries and headed to the baths. Elisabetta and a couple of Berenguela's ladies were finishing their ablutions when she arrived. She nodded to them and took her time unpacking her supplies in the hope they'd soon leave. Bathing with others still made her uncomfortable. The duennas left, but Elisabetta crossed her arms and leveled a glance at Alix.

"This is the first opportunity I've had to ask what's going on between you and the king?"

Alix's mouth dropped open, and her muscles stiffened. "I don't know what you mean."

"The last few days he was here, it was clear that you were—more friendly, shall we say? Are you two sharing a bed again? Tell me the truth." A grin spread across her face.

Alix nodded, a bit relieved to not have to keep lying. "Do you think less of me?" she asked in a low voice.

"Jesu, no. There's nothing for you to be ashamed about." Elisabetta took Alix's hands in hers. "For the first time in months, both of you look happy."

"I am happy, but you must keep it a secret. No one can know, especially Queen Berenguela. I couldn't bear for her to find out."

"I won't say a word. I'm just glad you changed your mind. You belong with him." Elisabetta sighed. "I wager every woman wishes she had a man who looked at her the way he looks at you."

Alix smiled. "He makes me feel like I'm the only woman he cares for."

"Because he does. Take your bath and I'll see you at supper."

Elisabetta's reaction eased Alix's mind, but she still needed to be careful. Although Berenguela had told her that her marriage was unhappy, finding out that someone she considered a friend was involved with her husband would only add to her misery.

*~*~*

Aware that Isabella's life had just been turned upside down, Joanna wanted her to feel welcome and had the cooks prepare an exquisite meal. Nobles from the French army who'd escorted Henri and his new bride from Tyre to Acre began to file into the hall. At last, the newlyweds arrived.

Alix gasped. "She's much younger than I thought she'd be, considering she's been married twice before," she murmured to Joanna.

Isabella was beautiful, with waist-length, chestnut-colored hair, amber eyes, and a creamy porcelain complexion. It was impossible to ignore the gentle swell of her stomach. Henri held his wife's arm protectively and guided her through the maze of people. His future had been rewritten since Conrad's death. He was essentially the ruler of Jerusalem, a new husband, and soon to be a stepfather.

When they reached the royal table, it was clear from the way Henri looked at his wife that he was already besotted with her, and she with him. Berenguela made the introductions, naming Alix as Joanna's kinswoman.

"I hope you found your chambers satisfactory," Berenguela said after everyone had been seated. She'd made certain that Isabella had one of the most lavish rooms, although that meant her moving into a smaller one.

"They're very comfortable, thank you," Isabella replied. "I appreciate your hospitality. The last week has been overwhelming."

"I understand," Joanna said with an empathetic smile. "I, too, lost my husband unexpectedly, but without an heir, it turned out quite differently for me. You couldn't have married a better man than Henri, and I'm not saying that only because he's my nephew."

"He's been very understanding, considering the circumstances of the marriage." Isabella placed her hand on her stomach. "Most men don't marry with the plan to raise another man's child."

"When is your due date?" Alix asked.

So many women in the Middle Ages died in childbirth from complications that could be resolved with medications and procedures that existed in the future. Alix had some knowledge of pregnancy, but finding a good midwife or doctor was a priority.

"In three months' time."

"I'm familiar with medicinal herbs and techniques that could help ease any uncomfortable symptoms you might have."

"I appreciate that. I've had an easy pregnancy so far, but it's my first, and I'm still learning what to expect."

If Isabella had any misgivings about how she would be treated based on her last husband, they were put to rest. Soon she was laughing and chatting easily with the women until darkness fell. Henri interrupted and suggested they retire for the night since they'd arrived that day and he didn't want her to exhaust herself.

Isabella gave him a look that suggested very little sleep would occur. After they said their goodbyes and left, Joanna smiled.

"I'm glad to see that they both look very content."

"Marrying Henri to Isabella was a shrewd move on Richard's part. Leaving Henri to rule Jerusalem will give Richard peace of mind when he returns to France," Alix said.

Berenguela sighed. "I pray that Richard claims Jerusalem soon. I miss home. When we return, I hope we'll be able to spend more time together. I feel like I'm saying goodbye to him as soon as he arrives."

Joanna laughed. "Richard has never been one to stay in a location for very long. Be prepared to travel often."

"Marriage to your brother has already proved to be quite an adventure."

Alix's stomach tightened. After she'd agreed to travel to Outremer, she'd been focused on experiencing the crusades. Lately, with her renewed relationship with Richard, she hadn't given any thought to returning to France, let alone Austin and her own time. The brooch hadn't allowed her to go home after his wedding. Was its agenda making sure they reunited? Would it work now, and more importantly, did she want it to?

*~*~*

Richard lifted his hand to shade his eyes as he assessed the walls that surrounded Ascalon. The city was almost rebuilt. He had a base of operations where he could receive goods from Acre by sea, and he'd cut off Salah-ad-Din's supply chain from Egypt. Now he needed to reinforce his stronghold in the south.

He'd sent word to Henri that he planned to capture Darum and wished for him and the Duke of Burgundy to join his army. His dislike for Hugh had increased in the days following Conrad's death, but he needed the French army.

Waiting had never been his forte. Once again, he turned to stare at the empty expanse of cobalt-blue water, willing himself to see galleys in the distance.

"Not to disparage your nephew, but Henri just got married. I'm sure he'd like to spend some time with his wife before he returns to Ascalon," André called out as he approached.

"I don't begrudge him taking his pleasure in the marriage bed." A smile crossed Richard's lips as he remembered his time spent with Alix, relearning the curves and the feel of her body. If he didn't have other obligations, he gladly would have stayed in Acre. He motioned for André to join him as he walked back to camp.

"We travel to Darum tomorrow. I can't afford to wait any longer. Once we take the city, the Turks' supply chain will be further diminished."

"Do you think we can capture it with only our men?"

"My scouts have returned and estimate there are about three hundred Turks within." He grinned at his cousin. "I say that's a fight we can easily win."

*~*~*

Richard glanced at André and Rob as a multitude of distant voices and the clanging of armor filtered in through the open tent door. "I take it the French have finally arrived."

They went outside and waited for Henri to appear. He cantered to them, Hugh on his heels, and reined in his horse.

"Is it true, Uncle? Darum has been captured?"

Richard nodded toward the nobles' colorful banners mounted on the city's walls. "Yesterday, as a matter of fact." He laughed at the chagrined look on Henri's face. "I don't hold it against you, lad. In fact, Darum is yours. Consider it a belated wedding gift."

Henri smiled. "I appreciate it, but you could have at least waited for my arrival. Tell me about the battle. Did the Saracens put up a fight at all?"

He motioned for Henri and Hugh to enter his tent and join him at the table. "The stone throwers were manned day and night. The main tower was surrounded by a ditch with paving on one side. I ordered sappers to dig and break through the paving to undermine the wall. We destroyed one of the enemy's mangonels and continued to bombard the towers until several collapsed. At that point, the Turks realized it was a losing battle."

Hugh frowned. "It doesn't sound like the fighting was very intense."

"I must disagree. We took Darum in four days with a small number of men," Richard stated as he leveled his gaze at him and tried to keep his hatred for the man from boiling over. The fact that Hugh had abandoned the English army still rankled, but the lie he'd spread about Richard ordering Conrad's death had been the final straw.

"When the Turks realized they were losing, did they not negotiate for surrender?" Henri asked.

"They tried. If the garrison had surrendered the castle upon our arrival, I would've let them go. However, they decided to fight. Many of my men were killed or wounded. At that point, I wasn't in a negotiating mood."

Richard gave a thin smile. "After the main tower collapsed, the garrison had nowhere to retreat and surrendered. We claimed the castle and rescued about forty Christians who were being held captive. In return, we captured three hundred Turks."

Hugh nodded grudgingly. "When you put your mind to something, the other side usually regrets it." He drained his cup and stood. "I'll see to the army." He nodded and left.

Henri grimaced as he refilled his cup. "I'm surprised you managed to be civil toward Hugh. It galls me that he suggested you had anything to do with Conrad's death. I've made it known that it was assassins behind the murder, and most of the men take that as truth."

"If I'd killed Conrad, I'd admit it. Speaking of the man, how are you enjoying marriage?"

A smile flashed across Henri's face. "Considering over a week ago I was unmarried and not looking for a wife, it's been surprisingly good. Isabella is unlike any woman I've met. She's intelligent and strong-willed, not to mention beautiful." He paused to take a sip of wine. "My only concern is the child she's carrying by Conrad. What if she has a son?" He leaned back in his chair and crossed his arms. "The nobles and citizens have promised me that my children will inherit the kingdom, but I fear they only said that to convince me to marry her."

"You're a well-respected commander and, since you're my nephew and Philippe's, you can unite the French and English armies and our interests. As for the matter of the child, we must wait."

## ~ *Chapter 30* ~

RICHARD SPLASHED COLD WATER ON his face, pulled on a shirt, then motioned to Jacques to allow the visitor in. Cold fingers crept down Richard's spine as the French messenger's words cut like knives.

Richard dismissed the man, despair filling his heart. Philippe had seen an opportunity to worm his way into the English court and he'd taken it. John and Philippe were in an alliance, and he was thousands of miles away, powerless to do anything. Would he have a kingdom to return to?

The tent flap rustled and he glanced up.

"I saw the courier leave. What news did he bring?" André asked.

"John continues to try and sway my nobles to his side, but now he has an ally—Philippe."

André sucked in his breath. "This changes things."

"It took over eight weeks to deliver the message. What has happened since then? Can I afford to stay here any longer?"

Richard shoved his chair back and paced the breadth of the tent. "If I leave now, would I return in time to save my kingdom? What about Jerusalem? It's within striking distance. We could launch an attack to retake it, but there's no guarantee we'll succeed." He glanced at his cousin. "I vowed to do everything in my power to reclaim the Holy Land. I can't turn my back on that, but you know what my realm means to me."

"Richard, I came to Outremer to stand by your side as my king and my friend. No matter what your decision, I'll continue to do so."

"I've never doubted your loyalty or friendship. Salah-ad-Din's army is much larger than ours. I refuse to enter into a battle we have little hope of winning."

"I understand your reasoning, but the men came to Outremer to defeat the infidels. They're set upon marching to Jerusalem. I don't know if you'll be able to change their minds." André clapped his hand on Richard's shoulder and left.

Richard's jaw worked. His cousin had voiced the truth he'd tried to ignore. Time was slipping away. In order to regain Jerusalem, he needed to negotiate. If he planned an attack upon the Saracen's ally, Egypt, he might be able to bring Salah-ad-Din back to the bargaining table. Richard also wanted to trade prisoners. If there was a chance that Will de Préaux was alive, he'd do everything in his power to bring him home.

But he'd been thwarted every time he mentioned it. His ability to maintain control was crumbling. For the first time since arriving in the Holy Land, the conviction that he would return home victorious dimmed. He wanted the glory that would come with defeating the infidels, but the loss of his empire would destroy him.

*~*~*

Three days later, news that Hugh had met with his army council and decided to retake Jerusalem with or without Richard's involvement infiltrated the camp. The cheers and revelry lasted well into the night, but Richard was unable to celebrate, torn between saving his kingdom or Jerusalem.

If, by some miracle, they managed to defeat the Saracens and claim the Holy City, their chances of keeping it were slim.

He deliberated for a couple of days, then announced to the army he would remain in Outremer until the following Easter. He then gave the order to march upon Jerusalem. Henri returned to Acre to gather reinforcements and Richard's army assembled twelve miles from the gates of Jerusalem to await their arrival.

Salah-ad-Din's men harassed Richard's supply carts from Jaffa daily, but other than small skirmishes, there was no major attack on the camp. Instead, Salah-ad-Din reinforced his army at the foot of the city and waited for his own caravans to arrive from Egypt with much needed food and supplies.

Richard's spies had alerted him to the arrival of the caravans. He tracked them for days, then launched a vicious attack. Most of the enemy escaped but left behind spices, gold, food supplies, weapons and armor, and medicine. More importantly, the English army captured thousands of camels, horses, and mules. In retaliation, Salah-ad-Din poisoned the drinking water around Jerusalem and destroyed the cisterns.

Richard called a council meeting and put forth his argument to conquer Egypt instead of Jerusalem. Unsurprisingly, the French army, led by Hugh, refused. An impasse was reached. The French attempted to initiate an attack, but without Richard's help, it failed. Once again, within miles of the Holy City, the army was forced to retreat.

*~*~*

Alix bolted upright, her surroundings sharpening as the blanket of sleep wore off. The banging on the door began again, and she stumbled out of bed to open it. Richard pushed past her. He and his household knights had arrived earlier that day with the crushing news that they'd turned back from Jerusalem. Supper that evening had been a solemn affair. Richard and Berenguela were notably absent, and whispers of arguments between them became the topic of conversation.

She peered into the hall, her gaze darting to both ends to see if his entrance had been witnessed. The hall was empty. She breathed a sigh of relief as she shut the door.

"Richard, you shouldn't be here. What if you'd been seen or heard?"

"I needed to see you."

She walked to him, wrapped her arms around his waist, and lay her cheek against his chest.

He held her tight. "I've failed everyone," he whispered.

Alix looked up. The stark desolation in his eyes tore at her soul. "You haven't failed. This was never going to end the way you envisioned."

"Why do you say that? Did you never believe in me?"

"I've always believed in you, in your convictions, but time is running out. You have far more to lose than any of these men. Your realm is in danger of being overthrown."

Richard pulled away and stalked to the window, staring into the inky night. "We were so close to the Holy City, but I gave the order to turn back. I can only imagine what the men must think of me. The English King who turned away from Jerusalem not once but twice." Bitterness filled his voice.

"If you had taken it, what then? How long would you be able to claim it as yours? Richard, you have a limited number of men in your army. Salah-ad-Din has an endless horde he can summon to his aid. Most of the men in your army wish to return home. Once they left these shores, the Saracens would simply attack and retake the city."

She walked to him and took his hands in hers. Although she'd always known the outcome, her heart ached for what he had to accept. He was a brilliant strategist and commander, but so was Salah-ad-Din. Richard had never lost a battle or retreated, but this war was different. He was fighting on foreign soil with men who planned to walk away once their goal was met.

Richard wanted the glory that came with reclaiming the Holy Land. In his mind, it would cement his status as the savior of Christianity and a great king, but his hopes were melting away like morning mist burned off by the sun.

"I know you don't want to hear this, but this might be for the best. If you'd defeated Salah-ad-Din, we both know you would stay and ensure that it was kept in Christian hands, but what of your kingdom? The longer you remain here, the more time John and Philippe have to sow the seeds of dissension amongst your nobles. You know what Philippe is capable of. He won't stop until he defeats you."

Richard's eyes hardened. "I should have known that French snake would break his promise to me, but I didn't expect John to."

"Your kingdom is more important. You need to return home and defend it."

He gave her a bleak smile. "My only option is to meet with Salah-ad-Din and arrange a truce. We've been at war for too many years, and I hope both sides are ready to come to an agreement."

"I think you'll find Salah-ad-Din will concur." She stifled a yawn behind her hand. "I'm sorry, but I was asleep when you pounded on my door."

"I apologize for waking you, Love, but as always, you've put my mind at ease."

"Now that you're here, will you stay the rest of the night, or are you expected elsewhere?"

He gave a wry laugh. "After hearing the news that we turned away from Jerusalem, I doubt my wife cares where I stay the night. Besides, I don't wish to be anywhere else."

Alix returned to bed, and Richard joined her after pulling off his shirt and removing his boots. He kissed her, then drew her close. She nestled into his muscular arms and inhaled his comforting and familiar scent—soap and spiced wine mixed with something intangible that was all him.

*~*~*

Alix burrowed under the blankets and tried to prolong sleep.

The mattress dipped as Richard shifted position. He pulled Alix close to kiss her. "Good morning, Love."

Alix smiled at him. "For a moment, I thought I was dreaming. I've missed waking up beside you."

"I've missed you as well. Last night was the first time in weeks that I slept through the night."

He got out of bed and stretched. Her pulse raced as she watched the play of his muscles highlighted by the rays of the sun. Once again, she was amazed that this legendary man had chosen her.

"I take it you must leave soon?" Alix asked as she padded to her trunk and pulled out a dress.

Richard nodded. "I need to meet with my council and decide on the best course of action. If you manage to dress in a timely fashion, I'll escort you to the dining hall."

Alix playfully swatted his shoulder and walked to the small, cordoned off section which she used for her daily ablutions. She'd just finished splashing cool water on her face when a rap at the door echoed in the room. Alix's heart stopped. No one could know Richard was here. She scrubbed her face dry and pushed the curtain aside.

"Who is it?" she called out.

"It's Joanna. May I come in?'

"One moment, please? I'm not presentable yet." Alix stared at Richard. "What are you doing?" she hissed as he walked to the door.

"I'm tired of having to skulk." Richard grinned, then opened it. From where she stood frozen, Alix heard Joanna's gasp.

"Good morning. Come in, Alix has just finished dressing." He winked at Alix. "I'll see you later."

The door shut behind him, and she took a shaky breath. This was not how she wanted to disclose her renewed relationship with Richard. She'd given her word that she wouldn't do anything to jeopardize their marriage. What would Joanna's reaction be?

Joanna raised her brow. "How long has this been going on?"

Alix's cheeks burned and she focused on a spot on the floor. "Since Maud's wedding. I thought my feelings would fade over time, but they didn't." She raised her chin. "I gave you my word that I wouldn't come between them, but things changed."

"It's no secret there are problems in my brother's marriage. I'd hoped things would improve with time, but that hasn't been the case. I feel that even if you'd stayed in France, the outcome would be the same." Joanna walked to her and laid her hand on her shoulder. "I'm glad you're with Richard again. He'll need your support, considering the unsettling news he's received from home."

Relief washed over Alix. She valued their friendship and Joanna's opinion of her was important, but she still wanted to hide the relationship from Berenguela.

"Philippe knows this is the opportune time to try and manipulate John," Alix said to change the subject.

"I can't believe Mother hasn't stopped John's treachery. What if Richard is overthrown? I can't stomach the thought of John in control. It would only be a matter of time before Philippe turned on him and claimed the kingdom."

Heaviness filled Alix's heart. If what she knew of history stayed true, Joanna's fears would come to pass, but the events leading up to it would be quite different and much more painful.

Joanna frowned and chewed on her lower lip. "Even if Richard left within the week, it would take a couple of months to sail home. Who knows what destruction John could cause in that time?"

"Your mother won't allow Richard to lose his kingdom."

"I know she'll do everything in her power to keep John in line, but the sooner Richard returns home, the better."

Alix mustered a smile, unable to tell her the truth. Richard wouldn't set foot in his kingdom again for almost two years.

*~*~*

Richard paced the galley's deck, his nerves taut. He'd been in the midst of finalizing his plans to leave Acre and return home when messengers from Jaffa had arrived. Salah-ad-Din had attacked the city, and the survivors were besieged in the citadel. His ships had already been equipped for the journey to France and he'd immediately set sail for Jaffa. Henri traveled by land with the Templars and Hospitallers.

The expected day's travel had turned into three since the galleys had been becalmed south of Haifa. Richard chafed at the forced idleness, aware that, with each passing hour, the plight in Jaffa grew more dire. At last, the winds turned favorable.

The blood-red sun peeked over the horizon as the galleys approached Jaffa. Richard's heart sank as he took in the bleak scene. Hundreds of Turks swarmed the beach and the hill below the city. Were they too late?

"What are your orders, Sire? Four days have passed since Jaffa was attacked. There's no way of knowing how many are alive." André narrowed his eyes.

"I have no doubt we can defeat the enemy, but I don't wish to lead an army into battle for naught." Richard glanced at his men. "What are your thoughts?"

Baldwin gestured toward the shore. "I'm willing to fight. I refuse to allow the enemy to win."

"We're outnumbered and our men might already be dead, but if you give the order, I'll join you," Rob stated.

Georges lightly bounced his sword in his hand. "If I should die today, I'd rather die by your side, Sire."

Richard cocked his brow. "Let's hope it doesn't come to that. I prefer to live and see another day."

He scrutinized the shore and the hill leading to the city, searching for any sign that the men still lived. His knights would follow him to the ends of the earth, should he ask, but he wouldn't lead them into certain death needlessly. A movement near the water's edge stilled his gaze. A priest had jumped from the citadel onto the sand, then dove into the sea and was swimming toward the galley.

"Throw him a rope!" Richard yelled to the rowers.

The man was hauled on board, dripping and shivering.

"What news is there?" Richard demanded. "Are the men dead?"

"No, Your Grace," the priest gasped. "What's left of our people are awaiting your arrival."

"Thank God, they still live. Where are they?"

"They're in the citadel, lined up and prepared to die."

Richard clenched his jaw and faced his men. "There's no time to waste. We came here to endure and suffer death. If we must die, may shame fall on the men who don't join us."

He ordered the galleys to approach the shore. The air was thick with the enemy's arrows, but most fell harmlessly short. The crossbowmen aboard the ships returned fire. Their arrows hit their marks. Richard jumped into the sea, clad only in his hauberk. He gripped his crossbow and shot at any Turk within distance.

His comrades followed without hesitation, attacking the enemy. Faltering under the onslaught, the Turks fled, pursued by the knights, until they'd claimed the beach for themselves. Afterward, they gathered driftwood, wooden planks, logs, and barrels from the remnants of old battered ships and galleys on the shore to construct a fortification against the enemy.

"I don't have to tell you how lucky you are, do I?" André asked. "You could have been injured, or worse."

Richard glanced down at his unprotected legs. "Time was of the essence. Fortuitously, the water wasn't too deep," he chuckled.

After leaving soldiers, servants, and crossbowmen in charge of protecting the beach, Richard approached the city wall. He tightened his grip on his sword as yells and jeers from the Turks filtered down the hill, but none confronted him. He crept forward until he reached a small opening in the wall and climbed a spiral staircase that led to the Templar's house.

There he found Saracens looting and ransacking the castle. He unfurled his banner on the wall in the hope that the men in the citadel would see it. Relief washed over him as muffled cheers from the Christians filled the air. All was not lost.

Richard fell upon the Turks, who barely put up a fight from this unexpected assault. He brandished his sword, dispatching several quickly, then chased them out into the city square. They fled toward the men who'd escaped from the citadel and exacted their own revenge. When it was finished, the streets were filled with bodies.

"Sire! Are there still infidels within the city?" Baldwin called out as he ran to meet Richard.

"Not anymore. Where is Salah-ad-Din's camp?"

Baldwin pointed toward a grove of trees. "The Turks escaped in that direction."

"Then let's not tarry. Gather the men and follow me."

Richard found only three horses in the city, and after mounting the sturdiest, he gave the other two to André and Baldwin. The Turks shot arrows and darts at them but fled when Richard and his knights approached. They pursued the enemy until their horses tired, and the enemy pulled further away. Frustration gripped Richard as he reined in his lathered horse.

"If only I'd had Fauvel, this would have ended differently."

"If you were on Fauvel, you would have had to fight the enemy alone. These horses are worse than pack mules," Baldwin jested.

They returned to the city, and Richard ordered his pavilions to be set up outside the walls, in case the enemy decided to launch a surprise attack.

*~*~*

Richard wiped sweat from his brow and took a deep draught of warm wine. The tent was sweltering, but provided a little relief from the stench of death that permeated the air in the heat of the summer sun.

He glanced across the table at Henri. "Once again, you managed to avoid the battle."

Henri ducked his head. "It wasn't for lack of trying. We were nearing Caesarea when we got word the Turks had set up an ambush along the road. We waited for a couple of days but were unable to verify this. To avoid a potential slaughter, we decided to travel by sea."

Richard grinned. "I don't fault you for your caution, and you're here now. Salah-ad-Din likely won't admit it, but high-ranking officials in his camp can see that this war is coming to an end. I've sent letters to his brother, Safadin, with negotiations for a truce, but we can't agree on the terms. I want Ascalon to remain in Christian hands, but they want it destroyed."

"I see that the walls of Jaffa have been repaired. We have protection in case we engage them once again in battle."

"I expect one," Richard said. "Salah-ad-Din's army is camped five miles from here. He obviously has no intention of peace."

"Then let this be the last battle. We'll defeat the enemy once and for all. You need to return to your kingdom. Now that I'm King of Jerusalem, with a wife and a child on the way, returning home for me isn't possible."

Henri left, and Richard lifted his cup to his lips with an unsteady hand. He'd gotten little sleep while they were becalmed as he'd prowled the deck and tried to keep his men's spirits from flagging. For the last couple of days, he'd stayed awake until the early morning hours, supervising the rebuilding of the walls.

He drained his cup, removed his boots, and collapsed onto his cot. He prayed his nephew was correct and they would defeat the infidels. With Philippe and John in an alliance, he couldn't afford to stay much longer.

Exhausted, he succumbed to Morpheus.

Yells and shouts slowly penetrated the fog of sleep that enveloped him.

"Arm yourself! Arm yourself!"

Richard leapt out of bed. Jacques sat up from his mat on the floor and stared around, dazed. Richard pulled on his hauberk and gripped his sword. "Stay here, lad."

He emerged from his tent into utter chaos. The men had been asleep, and, at the alarm, had hurriedly taken up arms in preparation to attack. Most were half-dressed, wearing only what they'd worn to bed. He looked toward the ridge, where the enemy streamed down like a swarm of ants.

André cantered to Richard, leading a horse. Richard and ten mounted knights, including Henri, Baldwin, and Robert, Earl of Leicester, readied for the advance. Battalions were immediately drawn up, arranged in ranks and troops, and commanders assigned to each.

Richard turned toward his own battalion and assessed the line. The men knelt on their right knees, their toes dug into the soil for more purchase. They gripped their shields in their left hands while the blunt end of their lances were fixed into the ground, the sharp iron ends pointing toward the enemy. Behind the soldiers, crossbowmen worked in pairs. One man discharged his bolt while the other reloaded.

Richard held his steed in check, as the rising sun illuminated the plain and the enemy. Muttering and prayers broke out behind him as thousands of Turks advanced.

"Men, hold fast to your position!" he called out as he rode up and down the line, trying to encourage the soldiers. "Let courage grow and oppose the enemy. If we flee, we will face almost certain death. Either we triumph courageously or die gloriously."

Cheers burst from the men's lips, but were silenced as drums pounded in the distance. The enemy swept across the plain.

"Stand firm!" Richard yelled as the first wave of Turks approached.

He prayed his men stayed in position. If one section broke, the entire line would falter. His heart thundered in time to the drums as the enemy bore down on them. Then, at the last minute, they veered away.

Richard stared in surprise for several seconds, then quickly gave the order for the crossbowmen to fire. A dense volley of bolts and arrows found their marks. A second line of Turks approached but, like the first, turned away without engaging. Urgency spiked through Richard's veins. The enemy was unwilling to attack the unmovable Frankish line.

"Rob!" Richard called out as he galloped nearer. "I'm tiring of these delay tactics. We need to attack now while we have the advantage. Stay here and keep the men in position."

Richard rode down the entire line, gathering every knight who had a horse. Gripping their lances, they galloped toward the enemy and smashed into them, unhorsing and impaling the unlucky ones. Their momentum carried them through to the last line. Richard wheeled his mount around. Robert of Leicester had been thrown from his horse and was surrounded by Turks, barely able to keep them at bay. Richard raced toward him, scattering the enemy as he approached.

Robert looked up, breathing heavily. "Once again, you have impeccable timing, Sire."

"I'd rather not lose good men for want of a horse," Richard said. "Is that yours?" He nodded at the blood that dripped down Robert's hauberk.

"No, I can fight."

A horse wandered riderless a few yards away, and Richard retrieved it. Robert had just mounted when distant yells and clanging of metal erupted. They charged toward the melee. The enemy had regrouped, broken through the battalions, and was storming the city. Richard entered Jaffa with Robert and some crossbowmen, where they were attacked by three heavily armed Turks. After dispatching them, they chased the rest of the infidels out of town.

Richard ordered the gates by which the enemy had gained entrance to be blocked and guarded. He then returned to his army, who were desperately fighting to keep from being overwhelmed. The mass of Turks pressing toward him was constant. Sweat slicked his palms, and he tightened his grip on the hilt. He searched for his men, but the fighting had drawn him further away from the safety of the city. Icy fingers trickled down his spine. He was on his own.

For what seemed like hours, Richard was surrounded by an endless influx of Turks. He urged himself to keep moving and slashing at the enemy, knowing he couldn't hesitate or miss his mark. If the enemy discovered who he was, his death would be swift and brutal. Richard's crusade would be over. Will de Préaux's sacrifice would have been for naught.

The Turks parted to allow a massive emir to enter the fray. The adrenaline that had sustained Richard was fading. He had to make a stand, if not to save his life, then to show the enemy he wouldn't cave before them.

The emir galloped toward him. He gripped his sword, waited until the last moment, then swung the weapon, his muscles screaming from the exertion. Steel flashed in the sun as it arced toward its target. The man slumped in his saddle, then fell to the ground. The Turks lost heart with the death of their champion and gave Richard a wide berth as he withdrew toward the safety of the city.

Cheers from his men filled the air as he joined them.

"We thought for sure you were dead, Sire. We tried to reach you, but we had our own battles to contend with," Baldwin said.

"Jesu, lad, when you became separated from us . . ." André's voice faded.

"God was on my side, for certes." Richard mustered a grin, but his gut tightened at their words. In the midst of battle, his only thoughts were of survival. Now that he was relatively safe, the enormity of what he could have lost shook him to his core—his kingdom, reclaiming Jerusalem, and those closest to him, especially Alix.

Richard turned his steed toward the plain where the battle continued to be fought, although the Turks were retreating into the hills. The sun was dipping toward the horizon when cheers rose from the exhausted, but victorious, men. Any surviving Turks had fled, and the dead covered the field.

André studied Richard and frowned. "You're looking quite the worst for wear. I'll send the physician in case you have need of him."

Numerous arrows and darts were embedded in Richard's blood-spattered hauberk. It was on the tip of his tongue to disagree. The thought of appearing weak in front of his men galled him, but his body ached, and his lungs burned with each labored breath. The skin on his palms had split from gripping his sword for hours, and now he could hardly open his hands. "I won't argue with you."

He reached his tent, and Jacques ran out to grab his horse's reins.

"Is it over? Have we won?"

"This battle is ours." He grinned at Jacques and pushed aside the tent flap. His head swam, and he staggered to a chair and collapsed into it.

"Your Grace? Should I send for the doctor?" Jacques asked as he entered the tent.

"No need to," Ralph said as he strode past. "Let's see what we have, shall we?"

With Jacques's help, Ralph plucked arrows from Richard's hauberk. The ones buried too deeply were broken at the hilt to be removed later. Jacques tugged the hauberk off, and Ralph carefully pulled the padded jerkin away from Richard's skin. He clenched his jaw as the material was ripped from lacerations. Bluish-purple bruises covered his chest from the impact of the arrows. Richard sucked in his breath as Ralph pressed his hands on his ribs.

"You'll be in pain for quite a few days, but I don't think you have any cracked bones." He dug through his bag and put a jar of salve on the table, along with a selection of herbs. "I wish I had stronger medicine, but this will do for now. If the pain worsens or you have trouble breathing, send for me at once."

The doctor left, and Richard handed the jar of ointment to Jacques, who carefully applied it to the cuts and bruises. Although he tried to be gentle, Richard still winced.

"That's all I can take, lad. I'll do the rest myself." He steeled himself as he scooped out some salve, knowing this would be the most painful. "God's bones," he muttered as he smeared the ointment into his ravaged hands.

"Is there anything else I can do, Your Grace?"

"Keep guard and wake me if anyone comes."

Jacques nodded. "I will, Sire."

*~*~*

Richard tossed and turned as he tried to kick the sweat-soaked threadbare blanket off. His body was on fire, and every inch of skin hurt to the touch. Low voices conversed not far away, and he forced his eyes open and blearily looked at André and Henri.

"What are you doing here?" he choked out.

André glanced at Henri. "Jacques told us you were ill. We've called the doctor."

"How long has it been this time?"

"Two days have passed since the battle. We hoped you'd recover, but your fever spiked."

Richard swallowed, but his throat was as parched as the dusty plains they'd battled on. "Can I have some water?"

Jacques rushed to fill a cup, then held it steady for Richard to drink from. His stomach rebelled and he rolled over, retching onto the ground.

The tent door opened, and Richard closed his eyes against the piercing light. His head spun, and once again, he was violently ill, dry heaving until his stomach cramped.

Ralph lifted Richard's wrist to feel his pulse, then looked at the red, swollen wounds on his hands. He pulled the damp sheet down to Richard's waist. "Tell me if you have any pain."

He gently pressed on different areas around his torso and abdomen. Richard shook his head.

"The lacerations are healing, and I don't think you have internal injuries. The cuts on your hands are infected and breathing in the noxious stench of the dead isn't healthy for anyone. I'll leave some herbs for your fever and more salve, Your Grace." He gave the medicine to Jacques, then gathered his bag and left.

"Has Salah-ad-Din attempted to attack since I've been ill?"

André shook his head. "They lost many men, and I'm sure this is a bitter defeat. They expected to take Jaffa easily, but our men held out until our arrival."

"Hopefully, we can reconvene and then launch an attack."

The look that André exchanged with Henri sent Richard's heart plummeting. His most trusted men were losing faith in their belief that they could defeat the Saracens. Or they were losing faith in him.

A sudden coughing fit wracked his body. His lungs ached with the exertion, and he fought to draw in shallow breaths until the paroxysm subsided. Exhausted, he slumped against his pillow.

"Cousin," André said, "you're not going anywhere until you recover. Rest now. We'll return this evening."

"Can I get you anything, Your Grace?" Jacques asked as he hovered by the bed.

"No, just leave me."

The tent flap rustled, and he was alone. Despair filled his soul. Once again, his body had betrayed him. His crusade was on the verge of failure, and he was powerless to stop it.

For a couple of days, Richard felt stronger, but that morning, he relapsed. He refused to hold a meeting lying in bed and forced himself to get up to sit at the table. He nodded to Jacques to allow Henri and the leaders of the Templars and Hospitallers to enter his tent.

"As you know, I've been ill, and I plan to travel to Acre to recover fully," Richard announced. "I wish for you to go to Ascalon and defend it against any potential attacks. I'll leave men here as well. After I've recuperated, I'll return to Jaffa, and we will defeat Salah-ad-Din once and for all."

"Your Grace, we have no wish to guard Ascalon in your absence, or any city for that matter," a Templar leader burst out.

The rest of the men nodded in agreement.

"Is that so?" Richard asked, his words falling like stones.

Henri stepped forward. "Uncle, in light of your illness, we didn't tell you that after the enemy was defeated, the French army marched to Caesarea. I sent messengers to entreat them to return, even telling them you were sick and needed their help." His gaze slipped and he looked at the far corner of the tent. "They refused. We don't have enough soldiers to fight, and of those we have, few wish to try."

Richard took a shaky breath. "Is there nothing I can say or do to change your minds?"

The men glanced at each other, unable to meet his gaze, and shook their heads. Heaviness filled Richard's heart as he saw determination in their eyes. Angrily, he dismissed them.

"Henri, stay," Richard said as the men filed out. "Is there no one who will follow me?"

"You know I will always fight by your side, but this is madness. The men want to return to their homes, not stay and fight a losing battle day after day."

"Are you willing to give up everything that we've fought so hard for? We captured Acre after a two-year siege. We've rebuilt towns that we can use as fortifications and for storage supplies. We can still defeat Salah-ad-Din."

"At what cost? Countless men have died and the ones left are unwilling to stay. I have a responsibility to remain and protect the Kingdom of Jerusalem. I'll do everything to keep the Saracens from reclaiming what they've lost, but I see only one real solution." Henri walked toward the tent door.

Richard clenched his jaw. If he negotiated a truce with Salah-ad-Din, it would be temporary. Once the term limits expired, fighting for the Holy Land would begin again.

"Wait. Send out an edict that I will pay any man to aid me in my fight."

Henri paused long enough to nod. Richard rubbed his temples, his head pounding anew. How many men would join him, and would he even be able to lead them? He felt wretched. This illness was unlike any other he'd encountered. A new fear crept through him. What if he never recovered?

With less than half the army remaining in Jaffa, it took only a couple of hours for news of Richard's offer to circulate through the camp. But the number of men who flocked to his side was far fewer than he expected.

"Is it true that only two hundred infantry and fifty knights, most from my own household, have agreed to join me?" Richard asked.

"Yes, Sire. As we speak, soldiers are returning to Acre. We can't mount an offensive with any hope of winning with those numbers," André responded.

Numbness crept through his body. His campaign was spiraling out of his control.

"Then I have little choice," he muttered, his spirit low. "Summon Humphrey de Toron."

Once André had left, Richard slumped back on his cot, shaking with chills. The herbs weren't working, and the telltale signs of Quartan fever were manifesting. He needed more potent medicine if he hoped to ever recover.

Jacques boiled the last of the feverfew and, when it was cool enough to drink, helped Richard sit up and sip it.

Voices outside grew louder, and Richard motioned for Jacques to move away so he could sit up by himself. Humphrey, André, and Rob entered the tent.

"Your Grace," Humphrey said, as he bowed. "I heard you have need of me."

"I would like to negotiate a truce with Salah-ad-Din for the Kingdom of Jerusalem. The terms I insist upon are that we'll exchange prisoners and Christians will continue to hold Ascalon."

"Very well. I'll return as soon as I can."

André broke the heavy silence that lingered after Humphrey's departure. "Do you think Salah-ad-Din will agree to a treaty?"

Richard raised his brow. "I don't know, but I pray he does."

"I, for one, am looking forward to sailing home," Rob said. "It's been too long since I've seen my family."

André nodded in agreement. "I miss my wife too. Hopefully, she still misses me."

Guilt washed over Richard. His men had given up so much to join him in this cruel, inhospitable land. He, on the other hand, had been able to be with the most important person in his life—Alix.

"We'll return home soon, I promise."

*~*~*

The next day was one of the longest that Richard could remember. Sleep hadn't come easily, and time seemed to creep backward as he waited for Humphrey to return. Darkness was inching across the land when Baldwin barged into the tent. Richard bit back his retort when he saw Georges and Humphrey hurrying in after him.

Humphrey unrolled a parchment. "Your Grace, I have Salah-ad-Din's offer."

Richard stilled and waited for him to continue.

"Jaffa will be restored to the Christians. They can inhabit it freely, as well as the coast and mountains surrounding it. Salah-ad-Din sanctioned peace between the Saracens and Christians, allowing them to have safe passage everywhere. The Christians also will have access to the Church of the Holy Sepulchre. There will be an exchange of prisoners as you'd wished." Humphrey paused, then continued, "Ascalon is to be destroyed. For a period of three years, beginning from next Easter, no one will be allowed to repair it. After that time, it will be ceded to whomever is occupying it."

Richard was silent. If the Christians could keep control of Ascalon he'd feel more confident that the Saracens would keep their word.

"Those are more generous terms than we could have hoped for," Baldwin stated.

Richard shook his head. "I can't leave Ascalon in enemy hands. Salah-ad-Din will simply reestablish his trade route. I accept the other conditions, but on the subject of Ascalon, I must stand firm."

"Sire, I argued that point for hours, but he resisted."

"If the city is destroyed, then it limits the amount of goods transported from Egypt. Salah-ad-Din can't wage a war easily," André said. "I urge you to accept the treaty. I realize this isn't the outcome you wanted, but it benefits both sides."

Richard's stomach tightened as he glanced at his friends and most trusted men. He'd led his army halfway across the world to fight the infidels and reclaim the Holy Land. His health was failing him, and his kingdom was in danger of being usurped by his own brother. If he didn't agree to the truce, he could lose everything. Not trusting his voice, he raised his hand and signaled his acceptance.

Instead of returning victorious, he'd negotiated peace for three years. A strange sense of calm replaced the turmoil that had churned within him. On September 2, 1192, almost one year and three months since he'd arrived in Acre, his war was over.

## ~ *Chapter 31* ~

ALIX BRUSHED RICHARD'S HAIR FROM his brow, relieved his skin was still cool to the touch. It had been three days since he'd arrived, feverish and suffering from infected wounds. She hadn't left his side even when Berenguela visited.

The door to the sickroom slowly creaked open. "How is Richard this morning?" Joanna asked in a low voice.

Alix turned. "The fever has broken, and he finally was able to sleep through the night."

Joanna walked to the bed. "I hope we can leave this country soon. I knew Richard would face potential injuries during battle, but he's been ill so often. I fear for his health."

"I believe he's on the mend, but I can send Ralph in to see him if that would ease your mind."

"No. I trust your medical knowledge, and I think my brother would rather you tend to him."

Alix smiled and turned back. From what Ralph had told her, Richard had relapsed on the journey from Jaffa to Acre. When he arrived, he was burning with fever and could hardly draw a full breath without coughing. Her heart had constricted when she pulled his shirt off to cool his flushed skin with a damp cloth. Yellowish bruises and healing cuts from numerous arrows still marred his skin.

Hours had morphed into days as she stayed by his side, wiping his brow and helping him sip the bitter brew of herbs and medicines that Ralph brought. Finally, his fever broke. Tears of relief had trickled down her cheeks when he opened his eyes and whispered her name.

Joanna sat down in the chair by the bed. "Why don't you go and get some rest? I'm sure you've gotten less sleep than he has. It won't help if you become ill again."

"I appreciate that."

Alix shut the heavy wooden door behind her and went to her room. Waves of exhaustion crashed over her, but when she curled up on her bed, her thoughts spun, and any hope of sleep vanished.

Richard's crusade was over. Although nothing had been said yet, historically, Joanna and Berenguela returned to France at the month's end. Richard would depart later, but instead of arriving home, he would be captured and imprisoned.

Alix would give anything to spare him the hardships he would endure, but she couldn't change the future. She needed to return to Austin, but she couldn't be certain that Richard's history would remain the same. What if events changed?

Her heart raced as another thought gripped her. Seven years had passed since she returned to France to correct history. How long did that account for in her time? How would she explain her absence to her friends and family?

A knock on the door provided a welcome break from her thoughts. She called out for the person to enter. Maud walked in with Elisabetta.

"How is the king? Is he recovering?" Maud asked.

Alix nodded. "He should be back to full health in a week or so."

"Has he mentioned when we will return to France? Coming here has been an incredible experience, but I'm ready to go home. I'm looking forward to seeing Sybilla and Melisende. Imagine their surprise when they learn I'm married."

Alix laughed. "I think they'll be more than surprised, but I have no idea when we're leaving."

"Queen Joanna has requested that I continue to serve her. To think, I traveled from France a laundress and will return a queen's maid. What will you do, dearie, after we return?" Elisabetta asked.

Alix shrugged. "I'm not quite sure. I've been away from my own family for several years, so perhaps it's time I went home."

Elisabetta pursed her lips. "I hope you're not planning to stay away too long, now that your situation has changed."

Alix shook her head in warning, but Maud was too perceptive.

"You and the king found your way back to each other!" She clasped her hands together. "That's so romantic."

Elisabetta grinned. "It's obvious the lass is still in the flush of marriage, but she's right."

"I hope this doesn't become common knowledge. I'd like to keep it secret for as long as possible."

"We won't breathe a word," Elisabetta said. "However, once we return home, it will be harder to hide."

She wished Elisabetta's words were true, but with Richard absent for several years, it would be easier than she thought.

*~*~*

Alix returned to Richard's room to relieve Joanna and to check on him, but found him seated alone at the table.

"Should you be out of bed? Where did Joanna go?"

"I was tiring of her fretting like a mother hen over me, so I told her to leave." He gave her a tight smile. "Earlier, I heard a commotion in the distance. I assume the party has returned from Jerusalem."

In accordance with the treaty, the men had started their pilgrimages. André had led the first group and had returned that afternoon.

"Richard, are you certain you won't reconsider?" Alix took a seat across from him. "This is your chance to visit Jerusalem."

"I don't regret negotiating since I was able to secure Will's release, but . . ." Richard's jaw clenched. "As long as the Saracens claim Jerusalem as theirs, I refuse to set foot in the city. The only way I will enter it will be as a conqueror."

Alix glanced out the window to hide her disappointment. Richard would never return and fulfill his dream. She reached out and held his hand. "I wish you'd change your mind. The best-laid plans often go awry."

A pageboy opened the door. Alix tried to pull her hand away before the visitor walked in, but Richard tightened his grip. She shifted in her chair as André's eyes widened.

"I never thought I'd see the day, but this explains why Richard is much easier to be around now, all things considered." He grinned as he pulled out a chair and poured a cup of wine. "It's about time."

Richard chuckled. "How did you find Jerusalem?"

"It was magnificent." André leaned forward, his eyes glowing. "Seeing the Holy Sepulchre was an experience I'll never forget. It wasn't without its difficulties, however. The envoys who carried your letter asking for safe passage fell asleep waiting for a messenger from Safadin, who offered to provide an escort." He took a sip of wine. "We passed them while they slept. Fortunately for us, they managed to catch up, and we sent them ahead to provide the charter. Even with the treaty, it felt like we were walking into the lion's den. But I'd do it again."

"When does the next party depart?" Alix asked.

"In three days. Cousin, if you're feeling stronger, you should join them. I know this isn't how you envisioned reclaiming Jerusalem, but because of you, Christians are now free to pray at the most holy sites. You deserve to enjoy your victory."

Richard glared at him and shook his head. "Not until Jerusalem is liberated from the infidels will I look upon the city."

"There's still time to change your mind." André stood. He nodded to Richard and winked at Alix before taking his leave.

Richard shoved his chair back, the legs scraping on the floor, and stalked to the window. As if the sky were a painter's canvas, the setting sun washed the horizon in hues of orange and red that reflected on the buildings of Acre, setting them ablaze. Moments later, the colors deepened into purple and blue.

"I vow that I'll return once I make sure my kingdom is protected." Richard dragged his hand through his hair. "God's bones . . . what if I'm too late?"

Alix walked to him, put her arms around his waist, and lay her cheek against his back. "Your mother would never allow you to lose your realm. You'll have a kingdom to return to."

He exhaled and turned to look down at her. "We'll leave for France at the end of the month. It's been years since you've seen your family. I understand if you have things to attend to at home."

Home. The simple word conjured so many emotions—security, contentment, warmth, and love. But her parents and friends weren't the only ones who embodied all those qualities. Richard did too.

She'd tried to use the brooch and return to Austin, but maybe her time here wasn't over yet. Perhaps he was her reason to stay. All she was certain of was that no matter where in time she was, Richard *was* home.

Alix reached up and caressed his cheek. "I do miss my family, and I'll see them someday. For now, I choose to stay with you."

"You don't know how much that means to me. I admit I was selfish in asking you to come to Outremer, but I wanted you by my side. I lost you once.

I couldn't lose you again." He cupped her face in his hands. "You captured my interest the first moment I saw you, and my heart soon after. You're the only woman I want to be with. I wish things were different. I know being with me isn't easy."

"It would be simpler if you were a commoner," Alix teased. "I never expected to fall in love with the King of England, but I wouldn't change anything. I love you, always and forever."

"And I, you," Richard murmured, then kissed her deeply until her head spun.

When he finally broke the kiss, his breath was as uneven as hers. She gazed at him, silhouetted against the velvety darkness pinpricked with countless stars. Love filled her heart. Their lives had become so entwined, she didn't want to imagine her life or future without him. She couldn't spare him the adversities he'd face on his return to France, but she wouldn't leave without making sure that Richard came home.

He smiled and pulled her close. "I'm ready to return to my kingdom and reclaim it. Let's go home, Love."